European Developments in Human Resource Management

Ariane Hegewisch and
Chris Brewster

Cranfield
UNIVERSITY
School of Management

**KOGAN
PAGE**

First published in 1993

Apart from any fair dealing for the purposes of research or private study, or criticism or review, as permitted under the Copyright, Designs and Patents Act, 1988, this publication may only be reproduced, stored or transmitted, in any form or by any means, with the prior permission in writing of the publishers, or in the case of reprographic reproduction in accordance with the terms of licences issued by the Copyright Licensing Agency. Enquiries concerning reproduction outside those terms should be sent to the publishers at the undermentioned address:

Kogan Page Limited
120 Pentonville Road
London N1 9JN

© Ariane Hegewisch and Chris Brewster, 1993

British Library Cataloguing in Publication Data

A CIP record for this book is available from the British Library.

ISBN 0 7494 1128 7

Typeset by Books Unlimited (Nottm), Sutton-in-Ashfield, NG17 1AL

Printed and bound in Great Britain by Biddles Ltd, Guildford and Kings Lynn

European Developments in Human Resources Man

CONTENTS

LIST OF FIGURES

LIST OF TABLES

THE CRANFIELD MANAGEMENT RESEARCH SERIES

The Cranfield Management Research Series represents an exciting joint initiative between the Cranfield School of Management and Kogan Page.

As one of Europe's leading post-graduate business schools, Cranfield is renowned for its applied research activities, which cover a wide range of issues relating to the practice of management.

Each title in the Series is based on current research and authored by Cranfield faculty or their associates. Many of the research projects have been undertaken with the sponsorship and active assistance of organisations from the industrial, commercial or public sectors. The aim of the Series is to make the findings of direct relevance to managers through texts which are academically sound, accessible and practical.

For managers and academics alike, the Cranfield Management Research Series will provide access to up-to-date management thinking from some of Europe's leading academics and practitioners. The series represents both Cranfield's and Kogan Page's commitment to furthering the improvement of management practice in all types of organisations.

THE SERIES EDITORS

Frank Fishwick
Reader in Managerial Economics
Director of Admissions at Cranfield School of Management

Frank joined Cranfield from Aston University in 1966, having previously worked in textiles, electronics and local government (town and country planning). Recent research and consultancy interests have been focused on business concentration, competition policy and the book publishing industry. He has been directing a series of research studies for the Commission of the European Communities, working in collaboration with business economists in France and Germany. Frank is permanent economic adviser to the Publishers Association in the UK and is a regular consultant to other public and private sector organisations in the UK, continental Europe and the US.

Gerry Johnson
Professor of Strategic Management
Director of the Centre for Strategic Management and Organisational Change
Director of Research at Cranfield School of Management

After graduating from University College London, Gerry worked for several years in management positions in Unilever and Reed International before becoming a Management Consultant. Since 1976, he has taught at Aston University Management Centre, Manchester Business School, and from 1988 at Cranfield School of Management. His research work is primarily concerned with processes of strategic decision making and strategic change in organisations. He also works as a consultant on issues of strategy formulation change at a senior level with a number of UK and international firms.

Shaun Tyson
Professor of Human Resource Management
Director of the Human Resource Research Centre
Dean of the Faculty of Management and Administration at Cranfield School of Management

Shaun studied at London University and spent eleven years in senior positions in industry within engineering and electronic companies.

For four years he was a lecturer in personnel management at the Civil Service College, and joined Cranfield in 1979. He has acted as a consultant and researched widely into human resource strategies, policies and the evaluation of the function. He has published ten books.

ACKNOWLEDGEMENTS

With one exception, all the authors in this book have an association with Cranfield School of Management. Ariane Hegewisch and Chris Brewster work there now; Len Holden was a research officer there. The other authors are based at our partner Schools in the Price Waterhouse Cranfield Project. The exception is Professor David Guest, who has been a valuable, and much appreciated, critic of our work. These associations and the common data bases that we utilise, give, we believe, a coherence and consistency to this text, without detracting from the variety and difference of perception which a text on such a diverse area as Europe should reflect.

Some of the chapters in this volume draw on previously published work and this is acknowledged in detail, where appropriate. As editors, we are grateful to the publishers and editors of the following journals for permission to use this material:

Employee Relations
International Journal of Human Resource Management
Personnel
Personnel Review.

Three people whose names do not otherwise appear deserve a special mention. We are indebted to Lesley Mayne, who has played a crucial and ever expanding role at the heart of the Price Waterhouse Cranfield research project; to Sarah Atterbury, without whose organisational, and many other, skills this book would not have been produced within the deadline, or perhaps at all; and to Christian Sirnes, who has also helped in the preparation of the book. As editors we are grateful to them, to the authors, and to the series editors, for the chance to present a book on a subject critical for Europe in the 1990s.

1

DEVELOPMENTS IN HUMAN RESOURCE MANAGEMENT IN EUROPE — AN INTRODUCTION

Ariane Hegewisch and Chris Brewster,

Cranfield School of Management

In this book the following standard abbreviations are used in referring to countries: Switzerland (CH), Germany (D), Denmark (DK), Spain (E), France (F), Italy (I), Norway (N), Netherlands (NL), Sweden (S), United Kingdom (UK). Results from the third year of the PWCP survey are being processed at present and are due to appear later in 1994 (Brewster and Hegewisch 1994).

Management literature in the 1980s highlighted the importance of human resource management in order to maximise competitive advantage. The technological and economic changes of the last decade require managers to develop new competencies to manage their working futures (Morgan 1988). Increasingly, these require an international perspective in order to manage people in different cultures and with different customs. Comparative international research for several decades now has examined production systems and management strategies in different cultural and national circumstances; increasingly, attention is also focused on people management and differences in management techniques and strategies in this area (Pieper 1990; Brewster and Tyson, 1991; Poole 1990; Hendry and Pettigrew 1990; Thurley and Wirdenius 1991; Guest 1990).

The focus on aspects of people management is all the more apposite in the light of the significant changes in Europe over the last few years that bear directly upon this topic. In this brief introductory chapter we do not intend to analyse them in any detail, but it is worth reminding readers of a few of the more dramatic changes that have taken place.

The 1980s was a time of unprecedented technological change. This has led to many, often quite fundamental, changes in employment working practices and industrial relations. While the speed of technological change is likely to stay with us, attention has started to focus on another significant change, the demographics which lie behind the European labour market. All the major economies in Europe have had a declining birth-rate. The effect has been that recently, and increasingly in the next few years, the number of young people coming into the labour market has and will decrease, both numerically and proportionately. Together, the demographic availability of workers and the technological innovations have substantial implications for HRM in Europe. In this book we are concerned with the issues that this demographic change poses for employing organisations, rather than with the problems for European governments in supporting increasing numbers of elderly people through taxes on a declining number of work-age citizens. Recruitment, for most employers, has focused on school-leavers. A declining availability of such potential employees will create pressures, not just on recruitment policies themselves but also on labour cost structures, on training programmes and for human resource planning.

A second change in Europe has occurred in the very definition of 'Europe' itself. The boundaries of the European Community are under debate with the creation of a 'European Space' which includes the countries (Sweden, Norway, Finland, Austria, Iceland and Liechtenstein) which many hope will soon join the EC. A more fundamental challenge to management practices is presented by the developments to the East. The distinction between East and West Europe becomes less valid as the changes in what were Communist East Europe work through. That these changes have been much lengthier to work through (certainly in the case of East Germany they are/were much more complicated than assumed) — and that they have implications for HRM — is indisputable (see, for example, Brewster 1992; Pieper 1992; Hegewisch *et al.* 1993).

The third area of significant change that we would point up lies with the EC. The implementation of the Single European Market has involved a lengthy series of changes which have occurred over a number of years. It is propitious that this book appears in the year which sees the full implementation of the Single European Market, but we recognise that the changes involved, particularly in the area of social policy, have been under way for some time (Brewster and Teague 1989) and will continue in the future.

The fourth and fifth areas are the European aspects of world-wide change; in particular, the general increase in cost pressures and the specific results of the recession. Europe has been, at least as much as any other part of the world, an area where managements have faced ever greater requirements for cost-effectiveness. In the private sector this has come about partly because of the rapid development of international competition. The EC was, in part, formed to provide Europeans with the ability to compete in world terms. On a local scale the advent of the EC has an explicit aim: the fostering of international competition. At the same time, throughout Europe there have been increasing public sector spending constraints which have put very similar requirements for cost-effectiveness on managers there. For the vast majority of private and public sector organisations, human resources constitute, by a considerable margin, their major operating cost. For all organisations human resources are their only means of effective use of all other resources. Thus over the past few years HRM has become an even more critical issue in management.

This has been exacerbated by the economic recession of the early 1990s. Whilst this has affected many areas of the world it has had a major impact in Europe, and particularly in the UK, Ireland and the Nordic countries. Even if it has not been felt so severely elsewhere, it is arguable that no European state has escaped its impact. The effect has been redundancies — since human resources are such a key element of costs — and rising unemployment levels. The impact on European labour markets and HRM has been substantial.

This book consists of a series of papers: some written specifically for this volume and published here for the first time and some taken or adapted from previously published material. All bear directly on the key issues of HRM in Europe and, where comparative, draw on the same database.

This is done in a number of the chapters by analysing developments in the overall concept of HRM in Europe; in some chapters these issues are addressed by comparative analysis of developments in particular aspects of HRM; and some highlight HRM practices in individual countries, providing illustrations of the cultural diversity which is such a feature of this continent.

HRM IN EUROPE: CHAPTER OUTLINES

It is against this background of research into HRM in Europe that the chapters in the HRM section of the book are presented. In the first section the authors focus specifically on different issues in HRM rather than just outlining country comparisons.

2. **A European perspective on human resource management**
   Chris Brewster, Cranfield School of Management, UK and Frank Bournois, Université Jean Moulin, France

This chapter examines the concept of HRM, noting particularly its origin in the USA and critiques of the concept in Europe. Data from the Price Waterhouse Cranfield Project is presented in order to identify differences between various European countries in their approaches to HRM. It is argued that there is a need for the development of a model which relates more closely to European HRM; and some tentative thoughts about such a model are proposed.

3. **Is there a Latin model in the management of human resources?**
   Jaime Filella, ESADE, Spain

It has been argued that within Europe different models of management are discernible: the Latin, the Central and the Scandinavian. Focusing on the Latin model, Professor Filella analyses the concept of such a model through an examination of the data and by comparison with the other areas of Europe. His chapter concludes that whilst there is no definite answer to the question of whether there is a 'Latin model', there is evidence for the existence of such a model.

4. **Human resource aspects of decentralisation and devolution**
   Jacob Hoogendoorn, Erasmus University, Rotterdam, The Netherlands and Chris Brewster, Cranfield School of Management, UK

Responsibility for human resource management is being spread around organisations in two ways — by decentralisation, the allocation of personnel tasks formerly undertaken centrally to more local parts of the organisation; and by devolution, the allocation of roles formerly undertaken by personnel specialists to line managers. Evidence from the Netherlands presented in this chapter indicates that both processes are working there, but with a considerable degree of doubt as to whether line managers can handle devolved personnel tasks. Comparative data from across Europe shows that the Netherlands is in the top half of countries devolving these functions. The authors argue that such decentralisation and devolvement may mean a new role for personnel specialists.

5. The decentralisation of pay bargaining: European comparisons
Ariane Hegewisch, Cranfield School of Management, UK

This chapter considers the decentralisation of pay bargaining currently widely discussed in the UK. Other countries in Europe have not gone so far, but a clear trend towards decentralisation is perceptible, although national or industry-wide bargaining is still widely used. There is also an accompanying increase in the devolvement of responsibility for pay issues from personnel specialists to line management and these trends have been accompanied by a steady rise in variable pay across Europe.

6. Does strategic training policy exist? Some evidence from ten European countries
Len Holden, De Montfort University, UK and Yves Livian, ESC Lyon, France

Organisations across Europe see training and development as a major personnel function objective. They use it as a recruitment mechanism. Employers are increasing their spending on training, although at present spending above 4 per cent of the wage bill on training is rare. Holden and Livian attempt to assess the strategic nature of this investment showing, for example, that evaluation of training needs is widespread, but the mechanisms for it are rather blunt. The compulsory requirement to spend proportions of the wage bill on training, which operates in France, seems to be successful.

7. The challenge of management development in Western Europe in the 1990s
Martin Hilb, University of St Gallen, Switzerland

In this chapter Professor Hilb summarises the state of human resource development in Western Europe and abstracts a series of general trends likely to become increasingly important during the decade.

8. Human resource management in Europe: evidence from ten countries
Chris Brewster, Cranfield School of Management, UK and Henrik Holt Larsen, Copenhagen Business School, Denmark

The subject of human resource management (HRM) and its development has been much contested in the literature. In particular, there is no distinctly 'European' approach to HRM and, indeed, our knowledge of comparative HRM practices in different European states is limited. This chapter draws on the PWCP research data to argue that practices in these countries can be categorised *inter alia* by the degree of integration of HRM into business strategy and the degree of devolvement to line managers. Using these two dimensions gives a quite distinct picture of differences in HRM practices in the ten European countries. These differences are analyzed and the validity of the model is discussed. The authors believe that the data presented raises the need to consider different conceptual approaches to HRM.

The final chapters of the book take us to the national level, providing more specific examples of aspects of human resource management as illustrations of the range and diversity of employment regulation and sophistication across the Continent.

9. HR management: an international comparison
Eduard Gaugler, Mannheim University, Germany

Professor Gaugler, one of the most distinguished authorities on personnel management in Germany, provides our overview chapter. This chapter sets the scene by attempting to identify common themes of personnel management which are universal across cultures in order to identify those issues where national cultures predominate.

10. Human resource management in Greece
Nancy Papalaxendris, Athens University of Economics and Business, Greece

The first of these country chapters argues that Greek personnel management has only recently become more sophisticated, largely under the influence of multinational companies which, in spite of operating with a relatively small number of employees, bring with them more systematic approaches which have given greater status to the personnel function.

11. Changing management approaches to employee relations in Ireland
Patrick Gunnigle, University of Limerick, Eire

This chapter also examines a country with high levels of unemployment, agriculture and multinational investment. It provides an overview of the debates on the changing role of personnel management in a country half-way between the more regulatory European approach of central wage determination and collective bargaining and the more deregulated US/UK approaches.

12. Recruitment, reform and the Italian labour market
Stefano Folletti, Giampiero Giacomello and Jonathan Cooper, SAIS, Johns Hopkins University, Bologna, Italy

Arguably one of the most centralised and regulated labour law regimes in Europe is found in Italy, even if much actual practice is improvised. The chapter by Folletti, Giacomello and Cooper illustrates this by taking one particular aspect of HRM — recruitment and selection.

13. **Current perspectives on human resource management in the United Kingdom**
    David Guest, Birkbeck College, University of London, UK

The final chapter, by Professor Guest, draws on the situation in the UK to examine the extent of progress in the adoption of HRM policies and practices. After examining some of the available literature, he focuses on the issues of selection, training and performance-related pay to argue that despite much activity by personnel departments, there is little evidence of a more strategic approach by the function, and little evidence of a link to performance.

ASSESSING EUROPEAN DEVELOPMENTS IN HRM

Overall, the conclusions to be drawn from these analyses are many. They depend, to a certain extent, on the perspective that is employed. From within Europe we can examine both issues and processes. The issues include those where there are common trends and those where no single direction can be observed. Amongst the common trends, we would include movements towards:

- a higher profile for the human resource management function;
- a greater sharing of HRM responsibilities with line managers;
- a focus on training and development;
- increasing variability in pay;
- a slow but clear decentralisation of pay determination (and other aspects of HRM);
- a lesser focus on trade unions;
- more and wider communication with employees through a range of channels;
- greater flexibility in employment practices.

Amongst the issues where no unidirectional trends are discernible are:

- the recognition of, and dealings with, trade unions;
- participation and employee involvement;
- the focus on equality and discrimination in the workforce;
- the level of state regulation and involvement in the employment relationship.

There may be some common trends discernible in HRM issues; but not in HRM processes. It is clear that the way HRM is handled remains quite different in each of the different European countries. It is particularly interesting to note that our data shows *country* to be a more significant indicator of difference than organisational *size* or *sector*. This is, in one way, only a surprise because national level analyses have given so much emphasis to the differences which size or sector make to HRM. That is reflected in our findings, but they also show that country is the more important variable. Given the influence of different national cultures, traditions, politics, economics, legislation and trade unions, this is readily understandable. It needs to be given a higher profile in the literature.

Pulling back to a slightly larger perspective, it is clear that despite the similarities and differences in various trends and the differences in HRM processes, there are national groupings within Europe. The country studies point up the differences between the British/Irish approach to human resource issues and that found in other countries. Filella makes a strong case for the Latin countries and the Scandinavian countries to be assessed as two more cohesive groups, each having within them, at least in broad terms, similar approaches to HRM.

Finally, from a global perspective it is clear that European HRM is different, and distinct, from the approaches developed in, for example, the USA and Japan. Europe needs a model of HRM that re-emphasises the influence of such factors as culture, ownership structures, the role of the state and trade union organisation (Brewster 1994). The evidence presented here suggests that managements in Europe are well aware of the influence of Governments, and trade unions, within their enterprises; that they do not necessarily see them as negative; and that they are nonetheless, in many cases, very successful organisations.

Models which include these areas within a concept of HRM take us back towards the industrial relations system approach first outlined by Dunlop (1958). In his model, the state and its agencies, employers and their associations, and employees and their representative bodies formed the constituent elements.

This call to re-establish the primacy of the wider industrial relations concept is not a nostalgic attempt to cling to an established older theory or to deny its replacement by a new one. The publication of the work by Kochan *et al.* (1986), examining the transformation of industrial relations in the USA, has breathed new life into this theory. An otherwise very important book is limited in its analysis by its lack of a comparative, international framework. The evidence presented here is that the argument that governmental, market and labour-management relations are interwoven would have been all the stronger if they had drawn international comparisons. We believe that the evidence from Europe suggests that HRM theory needs to adopt the wider perspective of the model proposed by Kochan *et al.*, and a more comprehensive view of the actors in the system, if it is to become a theory that stands the test of international application (Brewster 1994).

METHODOLOGICAL NOTE:* RESEARCHING HUMAN RESOURCE MANAGEMENT IN EUROPE

Because most of the chapters in this book draw on a unifying data source, details of that research are outlined here in order to enable readers to understand the methodology and representativeness of the data, and to prevent unnecessary repetition in the subsequent chapters. Whilst data on European labour markets is far from comprehensive and is open to considerable criticism, it is, in general, available to researchers. When we turn to human resource management policies and practices within employing organisations however, the picture changes. Little data exists which allows a systematic analysis of European trends in this area.

Available comparable labour market statistics, such as the EC Labour Force Survey, are broad in their approach to employment, concentrating more directly on the type and size of employment than on aspects of human resource management or personnel policy within organisations. The study of personnel policies, on the other hand, is usually limited to case studies, and while the importance of case studies to an accurate understanding of human resource management is clear, it was felt that these needed to be complemented with a wider survey approach which could establish how generalisable or specific findings from case studies were. This is especially so given that case studies tend to concentrate on larger, more 'advanced' companies; generalisation from their practice might give a false impression of the general state of the art in the field.

Human resource management in most European countries is strongly influenced by the national legal and institutional framework, even if, as some observers stress, organisations across Europe are faced with common economic and structural changes which appear to elicit similar responses in personnel management strategies (Grahl and Teague 1991;

* Sections of this note draw on Brewster C, Hegewisch A and Lockhart T (1991) 'Researching Human Resource Management: the methodology of the Price Waterhouse Cranfield Project on European Trends', *Personnel Review*, vol 20, 6, pp 36–40 and permission for this is gratefully acknowledged.

Gaugler, Chapter 9 in this book). It was felt to be important that a primary frame of reference for analysis should be organisational level data collected on a national basis.

Methodology for researching HRM in Europe

The Price Waterhouse Cranfield Project was established in 1989 as a direct response to the absence of comparable European data. The next few pages of this chapter detail the methodology of the Project so that it does not need to be repeated in each of the subsequent chapters which draw on that data.

In order to obtain an accurate picture of policies and trends, it was decided to carry out an annual survey of employing organisations, repeating it at least three times. In the first year of the project, 1990, the survey covered five countries: France, Germany, and the UK, as the largest European economies; Sweden, as the largest Scandinavian EFTA member; and Spain, as a less industrialised economy within the European context. The second year extended the group of participating countries by a further five: Denmark, Italy, and the Netherlands, as further EC members, and Norway and Switzerland, as additional EFTA member states. Most of the chapters in this book utilise data from this group and this year (ie 1991).

The Project had two particular objectives: the first was to monitor over time the impact of the Single European Market (SEM) on human resource management practices in Europe, including such issues as whether the SEM is leading to a harmonisation of personnel policies, and whether there are significant differences in trends in EC and EFTA member states. Given the recent application of many of the EFTA countries to join the EC, this last point has, of course, become more marginal.

The second objective was to establish how far there had been a shift in personnel policies towards 'strategic human resource management'. The definition of human resource management, particularly strategic human resource management, has been the subject of some debate in the literature. In Britain, in particular, one can distinguish a more 'functional' approach, which distinguishes between 'personnel management' and 'human resource management' by identifying particular policies (see, for example, Guest 1989, 1991). The alternative interpretation of HRM, as typified by Hendry and Pettigrew (1990), highlights to a greater extent the issue of strategic integration between human resource management policies and corporate objectives, stressing that the outcome of such integration is contextual and cannot be linked to any particular set of policies.

To some extent, the definitions are overlapping in so far as both stress the need for strategic integration. The PWCP survey reflected this and sought to establish the involvement of personnel departments in corporate strategy formulation. Deeper investigations of the strategic integration of HR policy need to take account of more organisational and environmental variables than is feasible in a broad survey approach. We therefore chose a more functional definition of human resource management. In other words, the survey was designed to establish how far personnel policies are planned, coherent and interactive with corporate strategies; how far there has been a shift towards greater flexibility and individualisation of the employment relationship; and what developments are taking place in areas such as recruitment, training and remuneration. This methodology allows movement away from any narrow conception of HRM and is thus able to make at least a broadly comparative contribution to some of the concerns of the 'alternative', non-functional literature.

The survey was based on a postal questionnaire. This concentrated on hard data: factual information about policies and practices rather than attitudes. The questionnaire covered the following subject areas:

- HR departments and HR strategy;
- recruitment policies;
- pay and benefits policies;
- training policies and evaluation;
- contract and working hours flexibility;
- industrial relations and employee communication;
- responses and attitudes to the approaching Single European Market.

In designing research tools for international comparisons, researchers are faced with a dilemma: should one insist on the gathering of identical information, at the risk of losing or misunderstanding data, or should the design be adapted to take account of national differences — and put at risk the comparability of the study? (Brewster and Tyson 1991)

It was decided that, in the interest of long-term comparability of trends, if at all possible an identical questionnaire would be used in all countries. In some areas national differences had to be incorporated; one major area here is that of staff categories. In France, for example, it is common to use three staff categories: Cadre, referring to management and some professional employees; ETAM, who are administrative, technical and supervisory staff; and operatives. These are not only customary definitions, but are also defined in law. There is little point therefore in trying to force French personnel managers into the customary British four-fold division of 'management', 'professional/technical', 'clerical', and 'manual'. On the other hand, in Germany most companies have different policies for dealing with skilled manual workers (*Facharbeiter*) and semi- and unskilled manual workers.

Other differences arose from the different levels of regulation through employment legislation. 'Job sharing', for example, is more narrowly defined in several European countries than in the UK and under that more narrow definition is illegal. Similarly, some countries prohibit private recruitment agencies, or provide an automatic right to trade union recognition, and therefore questions asking whether private recruitment agencies are utilised or whether trade unions are recognised would simply make little sense to respondents in those countries. Another problem presented itself in the design of questions on equal opportunities policies. In Britain and the Netherlands, such discussions generally refer to the reversal of discrimination against women, ethnic minorities and people with disabilities. In France, on the other hand, even though the proportion of black and ethnic minority people in the workforce is very similar, a reference to ethnic minority people was not included because the French partners of the Project feel that such a question would raise concerns over civil liberties.

However, in the majority of questions there were few such difficulties. A potentially more serious problem is the selection and interpretation of

Table 1.1   European partner schools of the Price Waterhouse Cranfield Project

Switzerland:	Hochschule St. Gallen
Germany:	Universität Mannheim
Denmark:	Handelshojskolen, Kopenhagen
Spain:	ESADE, Barcelona
France:	Groupe ESC Lyon
Italy:	SAIS, Johns Hopkins University, Bologna
Norway:	Handelshoyskolen BI, Oslo
The Netherlands:	Rotterdam Business School, Erasmus University
Sweden:	IPF, University of Uppsala
UK:	Cranfield School of Management

topic areas. In order to overcome a potential British bias in the design of the questionnaire, Cranfield School of Management worked closely with academic partners in each of the participating countries (see Table 1.1).

The drawing up of the questionnaire was preceded by several bilateral international discussions in order to identify major issues of interest and priority. The draft questionnaire was then tested with personnel managers in the participating countries. This process highlighted interesting differences in national priorities and concerns. Take the issue of health and safety, for example. In Britain this still tends to be seen as a rather narrow, manufacturing-related, issue and thus at the moment is not at the forefront of HR development. In Sweden, on the other hand, health and safety, understood as a general reference to the working environment, is seen as one of the major challenges to personnel management in the next decade, particularly with regards to a workforce which will be older as well as more demanding in terms of what it expects from its working life. Another good example is flexible working. In Britain and Germany its discussion lately has been closely linked to demographic change and the re-integration of women into the labour market. In France, on the other hand, where demographic discussions are much less prevalent, flexible working is seen as a response to general changes in life-style, not particularly linked to female labour force participation.

Thus, even if the questions are identical, respondents will interpret them within their given cultural and legal context. The primary frame of reference for the interpretation of results has to be the national context. In each country, therefore, a panel of personnel experts was been set up to discuss their national results in the light of their own organisational practice and to provide qualitative analysis; only after this process had taken place were general conclusions drawn.

Translation

One issue in standardising the questionnaire was to ensure the correct translation into each relevant language. The draft questionnaire was developed in English. In order to ensure uniformity, the questionnaire for each country was first translated and adapted into the other languages and then re-translated into English to test whether the translation gave a correct interpretation of the English term. At the same time the translation was tested with personnel directors to ensure that the terms and questions were comprehensible. The translation process, however, is not merely a technical process, but again highlights cultural differences. For example, the fact that it is difficult to find a term in German or French for 'mission statement' is a good indication of the prevalence of that concept in those cultures.

Responses

Altogether almost 35,000 questionnaires were mailed in 1991. The sample size varied between countries for obvious reasons; in general, at least 50 per cent of private sector organisations of the required size were approached, evenly distributed across industrial sectors. The only major exception was Italy, where the public availability of appropriate address lists was relatively poor.

Overall, 6300 organisations responded in the second year of the survey. Of these 5449 responses were usable and were included in the evaluation. The non-usable returns were in general excluded mainly because, in the event, they employed less than 200 people, the minimum size for inclusion in the survey. The detailed response rates for each country are set out in Table 1.2. The numbers of responses for all countries are sufficiently large to allow reasonable statistical confidence in national results.

Table 1.2   Response rates and number of responses by country

	Percentage	Number
CH	16	230
D	15	933
DK	19	478
E	14	297
F	15	988
I	10	199
N	28	303
NL	19	223
S	42	295
UK	19	1503

Table 1.3 shows the distribution of responses according to industrial sector; each national sample is broadly representative of the underlying sectoral distribution of the economy of the participating country. All figures in this book represent unweighted averages; no attempt has been made to weight the sample according to the underlying national distribution by sector.

Sample distribution by size

As can be seen from Table 1.4, the size distributions of the national

Table 1.3 Distribution of responses by sector (per cent; rounded to nearest whole figure)

Country	CH	D	DK	E	F	I	N	NL	S	UK
Agriculture, hunting, forestry, fishing	0	0	1	1	2	0	1	1	1	1
Energy and water	4	4	2	5	2	2	6	4	3	3
Chemical products, extraction and processing/non-energy	7	9	4	13	5	9	7	7	2	5
Metal manufacturing, engineering, data processing	23	33	12	21	24	29	11	14	21	20
Other manufacturing	10	17	15	20	14	20	8	12	15	18
Building and civil engineering	3	4	6	3	4	1	3	3	2	3
Retail and distribution, hotels, catering, repairs	14	7	11	8	7	11	5	8	6	10
Transport and communications	4	2	5	4	4	9	3	7	6	5
Banking, finance, insurance, business services	15	11	9	14	8	6	5	14	8	12
Personal, domestic, recreational services	5	0	2	1	1	0	0	1	1	1
Health services	4	2	6	4	8	2	8	8	5	6
Other services	0	4	3	1	0	3	2	2	6	2
Education, inc. universities, further education	0	2	1	1	0	0	2	0	4	3
Local government	6	1	19	3	6	1	26	14	13	9
Central government	2	0	5	0	0	1	3	3	5	1
Other	2	4	1	2	13	7	8	3	2	1

responses are also broadly representative of the underlying national distribution.

The survey is aimed at establishing trends in the development of personnel policies. It therefore was felt sensible to limit the sample to those organisations more likely to have some formalised approach to personnel management.

Table 1.4 Distribution of responses by number of employees per organisation (% rounded to nearest whole figure)

Country	CH	D	DK	E	F	I	N	NL	S	UK
200–499	31	37	39	40	36	35	43	51	31	22
500–999	24	27	26	27	28	23	29	27	20	24
1000–1999	21	18	18	15	17	12	15	13	21	16
2000–4999	14	11	11	11	11	18	9	6	17	17
Over 5000	10	7	6	8	9	12	4	4	12	18

Research suggests that the threshold to a specialist personnel function lies with a couple of hundred employees (Semlinger and Mendius 1989); thus only organisations employing at least 200 people were included. In some countries, such as Denmark, the Netherlands or Spain, this definition excludes at least half of the working population; in others, such as Sweden or the UK, the small firm sector is much less significant. However, the study of smaller employers requires a different questionnaire design which is outside of the scope of this Project.

As the concentration of ownership and the average size of organisations vary substantially between countries, large organisations are more heavily represented, for example, in the national sample of Britain where 35 per cent of responding organisations employ 2000 and more people, than in the Netherlands where only 10 per cent of respondents are of that size. As a general observation, in all countries the likelihood of formalised personnel policies increases with numbers of employees and this has to be taken into account when results are compared across countries.

Respondents

In general, organisations were approached by means of publicly available mailing lists, ideally personalised to the head of the personnel function. In countries such as Denmark, Italy, Norway and Sweden, the national personnel management organisation participated in the survey and provided access to its membership lists. In Germany, on the other hand, experience shows that a higher response rate can be achieved by going straight to the top of an organisation, the chief executive, who will then ensure that the questionnaire is filled in. Overall, in a large majority of cases the questionnaire was filled in by the most senior personnel manager in the organisation (Table 1.5). The next most frequent respondents were other specialist personnel functions such as training officers.

Table 1.5 Respondents: Percentage of organisations where the most senior personnel manager/director completed the questionnaire

CH	D	DK	E	F	I	N	NL	S	UK
79	55	59	63	74	66	73	72	79	60

Public sector

Public sector employment in the ten countries in our sample accounts for 15–40 per cent of total employment and care was therefore taken to ensure that public administration was properly represented in the survey. In this book 'public sector' is generally used in the sense of public administration, covering central and local government, health and higher education. In countries such as Denmark, Norway, the Netherlands and Sweden, public and private sector personnel management are fairly integrated; there is only one professional body for personnel management and there is an overlap in training courses and educational routes. This integration is also reflected in the composition of mailing lists and generally it was not necessary to supplement the general lists in order to obtain a satisfactory sample of public sector respondents. This has not, however, been the case in countries such as Germany, France, Italy or Spain. For example, in Germany individual local authorities will only participate in surveys if these have been approved by relevant local authority federations. Moreover, a special German public sector translation had to be prepared in order to take account of public sector terminology. This was mailed to a selected sample of organisations provided by the local authorities' federation*. Similar procedures were followed in France. However, in Italy and Spain this has proved more difficult and consequently public sector response has been low.

REFERENCES

Brewster, C and Teague, P (1989) *European Community Social Policy: the impact on the UK*, Institute of Personnel Management, London

Brewster, C and Tyson, S (eds) (1991) *International Comparisons in Human Resource Management*, Pitman Publishing, London

---

* The federation, the Deutscher Städtetag, did not support the annual repetition of the survey. In the second round of the survey the respondents of the first year were approached again, this time with the general questionnaire. Response rates fell from 95 to 20 organisations.

31

Brewster, C (1992) 'Starting again: industrial relations in Czechoslovakia', in *International Journal of Human Resource Management*, vol 3.3, pp 555–74

Brewster, C (1994 forthcoming) 'European Human Resource Management: Reflection of, or Challenge to, the American Concept' in Kirkbride, P (ed), *Human Resource Management in the New Europe of the 1990s*, Routledge, London

Brewster, C and Hegewisch, A (eds) (1994 forthcoming) *Policy and Practice in European Human Resource Management: Evidence and Analysis*, Routledge, London

Dunlop, J T (1958) *Industrial Relations Systems*, Henry Holt & Co, New York

Grahl, J and Teague, P (1991) 'Industrial Relations Trajectories and European Human Resource Management', in Brewster, C and Tyson, S (eds), *International Comparisons in Human Resource Management*, Pitman, London

Guest, D (1989) 'Personnel and HRM: can you tell the difference?' *Personnel Management*, January, pp 48–51

Guest, D (1990) 'Human Resource Management and the American Dream', *Journal of Management Studies*, vol 27–4, pp 377–97

Guest, D (1991) 'Personnel Management: the end of orthodoxy?' *British Journal of Industrial Relations*, vol 29, 2, pp 149–76

Hegewisch, A, Hanel, U and Brewster, C (1993) 'An Initial Examination of HRM Change in the Eastern Länder of Germany', Interim Report for AngloGerman Foundation, Cranfield School of Management, UK

Hendry, C and Pettigrew, A (1990) 'HRM: an agenda for the 1990s', *International Journal of Human Resource Management*, vol 1.1, pp 17–25

Kochan, T A, Katz, H C and McKersie, R B (1986) *The Transformation of American Industrial Relations*, Basic Books, New York

Morgan, G (1988) Riding the Waves of Change, Jossey-Bass, San Francisco

Pieper, R (ed) (1990) *Human Resource Management: An International Comparison*, Walter de Gruyter, Berlin

Pieper, R (1992) 'Socialist HRM: An analysis of HRM theory and practice in the former socialist countries in Eastern Europe', *International Executive*, vol 34, 6, pp 499–516

Poole, M (1990) 'Human Resource Management in an International Perspective', *International Journal of Human Resource Management*, vol 1.1, pp 1–15

Semlinger, K and Mendius, H G (1989) Personalplanung und Personalentwicklung in der gewerblichen Wirtschaft, RKW, unpublished

Storey, J (ed) (1989) *New Perspectives on Human Resource Management*, Routledge, London

Thurley, K and Wirdenius, H (1991) 'Will Management Become European? Strategic choices for organisations', *European Management Journal*, vol 9.2, pp 127–34

2

A EUROPEAN PERSPECTIVE ON HUMAN RESOURCE MANAGEMENT*

*Chris Brewster, Cranfield School of Management, UK
and Frank Bournois, Université Jean Moulin, France*

INTRODUCTION

The concept of human resource management (HRM), and the associated concept of strategic human resource management, are being debated increasingly in the literature and used increasingly within employing organisations. The history of the concept of HRM has been summarised elsewhere (Hendry and Pettigrew 1990, Beaumont 1991). It developed initially from work in the United States of America in the 1960s and 1970s and emerged as two distinct, though perhaps not fully formed, strands in the mid-1980s. Since then the concept has been an ever more visible feature of the academic literature, of consultancy services and of organisational terminology, particularly in the USA and Great Britain.

The concept of HRM was taken up most enthusiastically in the related cultures of first, Great Britain, and then Australasia. The terminology has begun to spread into Scandinavia and, far less, into continental Europe. In France, for example, the first book to address the topic of strategic HRM specifically was not published until 1988 (Besseyre des Horts). This article examines the concept from a European viewpoint. Implicit in our discussion is the European experience of cultural diversity, which makes us conscious of the need to be aware of national differences in the collection of data and the development of theory. In particular, we wish to explore the notions of difference and similarity. What differences are there between European countries in the way they manage human resources? And to what extent is there sufficient similarity in Europe to

---

* This chapter first appeared in *Personnel Review*, Vol.20,6, 1991. Permission for its reproduction here is acknowledged with gratitude.

require us to question whether there may not be significant differences between HRM in Europe as a whole and the United States of America? Furthermore, we address the issue raised by the possibility of such differences: can American models of HRM be applied to Europe?

In outline, therefore, this chapter takes a brief look at the concept of HRM and some of the recent writings about it; examines some significant new data on what is, in practice, happening in employing organisations across Europe; suggests some differences in approaches to HRM in different European countries; and proposes a re-evaluation of the models of HRM currently in use.

HRM is, strictly speaking, more a bundle of overlapping notions than a concept in its own right. In particular two distinct approaches ('hard' and 'soft') have been identified regularly in the literature (Legge 1989, Beaumont 1991, Hendry and Pettigrew 1990). These 'hard' and 'soft' views were emphasised most clearly in the mid-1980s by two competing texts: the first, edited by Fombrun *et al.*, published in 1984; the second, by Beer *et al.* was published in the following year, and stands, in essence, as a manifesto for the then newly developed HRM element of Harvard's MBA. It is only necessary in the context of this article to point out the key distinctive features of each approach.

The 'hard' approach focuses on the 'resource' side of the phrase 'human resource management'. It argues that people are organisational resources and should be managed like any other resource: obtained as cheaply and used as sparingly as is consistent with other requirements, such as those for quality and efficiency; and that they should be developed and exploited as fully and profitably as possible. The words 'human' or 'people' are used rather than 'employees' because techniques such as outsourcing, subcontracting and franchising would in certain circumstances be seen as entirely appropriate to a hard view of HRM. The approach tends to have a much closer relationship to corporate strategy — with HRM often seen to follow such strategies. It is most typically linked to contingent analyses of corporate strategy, or product life cycle theories or organisational growth theories. Fombrun *et al.* express this view as follows:

> Just as firms will be faced with inefficiencies when they try to implement new strategies with outmoded structures, so they will also face problems of implementation when they attempt to effect new strategies with inappropriate HR systems.
>
> Frombrun, Tichy and Devanna 1984

British consultants Cook and Armstrong (1990) sum this up very clearly, using data from a British electrical firm:

In Thorn EMI, as elsewhere, corporate strategy sets the agenda for HR strategy . . . it should not in itself be over-influenced by HR factors (HR strategies are about making business strategies work).

By contrast, the 'soft' approach to HRM concentrates upon the 'human' side of 'human resource management'. It argues by contrast that people are a resource unlike any other — for most organisations far more costly than other resources, but for all organisations the one factor which can create value from the other resources. This is the resource whose creativity, commitment and skill can generate real competitive advantage. This most precious resource therefore requires careful selection, extensive nurturing and development, proper rewards and integration into the organisation. As such this approach will tend to concentrate on 'employees' and stands clearly in the long tradition of human relations and developmental studies. In this approach human resource management is more symbiotically related to corporate strategy: the presence or absence of certain skills may push the organisation into or out of certain markets or products, for example.

The 'soft' view of HRM typically refers to a (unitary) view of the organisation in terms of a team, competing against other organisations, and with the development and growth of the team players inevitably contributing to the success of the whole. This viewpoint was captured in an American text on human resource planning and development (HRPD):

> In an ideal HRPD system, one would seek to match the organisation's needs for human resources with the individual's needs for personal career growth and development. One can then depict the basic system as involving both individual and organisational planning, and a series of matching activities designed to satisfy mutual needs . . . growth and development must be organised to meet both the needs of the organisation and the needs of the individuals within it.
>
> Schein 1987

Thus, although Schein admits that there will sometimes be a need to have components 'that reflect the need for either a new growth direction or a process of disengagement of the person from his or her job', key objectives will include such things as the need to reduce costly turnover.

These American views of HRM have come under increasing criticism in Europe. The concept has been criticised (Hendry and Pettigrew 1986; Guest 1987; Legge 1989; Guest 1990; Conrad and Pieper 1990, Staehle 1988, Weiss 1988; Albert 1989), for being imprecise, prescriptive, and lacking evidence as to its acceptance by employers. It has been attacked for being just 'personnel management' in another guise; and for being inappropriate to, for example, British industrial relations practice.

In order to examine the concept in detail, however, it is necessary to identify, from the range of approaches available, key features of HRM acknowledged or implied by most authors — and to test these features against actual practice.

The impact of national culture on business and business theories has been widely explored (see, for example, Hofstede 1980; Laurent 1981; Trompenaars 1985; and for an attempted brief summary Brewster 1991). One conclusion is that the US, the source of much internationally accepted management theory (we would include HRM theories) 'is quite untypical of the world as a whole' (Trompenaars 1985). The United States is unique in many ways, not only culturally but in the economic structure of the country. Guest (1990) has stated that 'HRM can be seen as a contemporary manifestation' of the American Dream. Although he draws his view of the American Dream without reference to the national culture literature, his analysis will be used here as a way into the cultural limitations of current concepts of HRM.

THE ELEMENTS OF HUMAN RESOURCE MANAGEMENT

Many of the specific areas or actions have been examined by Guest (1990) who summarises evidence about the 'use of innovative techniques of the sort typically associated with HRM'. Two other texts also attempt to pull together some of these approaches to identify a limited number of core elements of HRM. Mahoney and Deckop (1986) examined what they saw as the differences between 'personnel' and 'HRM'. They argue that, overall, HRM involves a wider and broader view in six specific areas:

1. employment planning: from a narrow technical focus to closer links with business strategy;
2. communication with employees: from a collective, negotiating focus to a more general approach to more direct communication with employees;
3. employee feelings: from job satisfaction to concern with the total organisational culture;
4. employment terms: from selection, training, compensation policies focused on individuals to a concern with group working and group effectiveness;
5. employment cost-benefits: from a concern with cost-reduction through such strategies as reducing turnover, controlling absenteeism to a focus on organisational effectiveness and the 'bottom line'.
6. employee development: from individual skills to longer-term employment capabilities.

In a similar, but slightly different way, Beaumont (1991) identifies five 'major items typically mentioned' in the US literature as part of HRM:

1. relatively well-developed internal labour market arrangements in such areas, for example, as promotion, training, individual career planning;
2. flexible work organisation systems;
3. contingent compensation practices and/or skills or knowledge based pay structure;
4. high levels of individual participation in task-related decisions;
5. extensive internal communications arrangements.

Together, these two attempts to synthesise the elements of HRM show some areas of consistency (wider communication, for example); some areas of greater or less detail (for example, presumably flexible work organisation is intended to be a contribution to the bottom line; training for the longer term is an aspect of developing an internal labour market); and some areas of uncertainty (not only are the elements of compensation which are seen to be evidence of HRM different, but even within Beaumont's synopsis he finds two different elements).

The problems of determining the main elements of what constitutes HRM from the many, often conflicting, models available are obvious from the preceding outline. This is complicated by the fact that all organisations have to handle the subjects covered by HRM — recruitment, promotion, skills, remuneration etc, whether or not they subscribe to theories of HRM *per se*. Analysis of both the prescriptive and the more academic writings on the topic indicates that three major elements are implied in most texts, even if not specifically mentioned. These are as follows:

- **a close involvement of HRM and corporate strategy**
- **an employing organisation with a considerable degree of independence to take personnel decisions**, including *inter alia*, an independence of remuneration policy, allowing for a 'bottom line' focused contingent pay policy; and an absence, or at least a minimal influence from, trade unions;
- **a preference for a carefully controlled, or in some conceptions internal, labour market**. This would include, *inter alia*, freedom to recruit as the organisation deems appropriate; an absence or limitation of restrictions on employment contracts; and a substantial degree of training and skill development.

THE PRICE WATERHOUSE CRANFIELD DATA: FINDINGS

Each of these elements is potentially testable. We examine them through the data provided by a major survey of HRM practices in Europe.

HRM and business strategy

One of the most widely discussed distinctions between HRM and old-fashioned personnel management is the closer linking of the former to business strategy (cf Schreyögg 1987, Wohlgemuth 1988, Butler 1988). This is largely a feature of the more prescriptive writing; there is little compelling evidence that such linking is taking place in reality, even in the United States (Guest 1990).

The most obvious way for such linkage to exist is if the head of the personnel or human resources function has a place on the main Board of Directors of the organisation and gets involved in the formulation of corporate strategy from the outset.

Table 2.1 Head of Human Resources function on main Board of Directors or equivalent (% of organisations)

CH	D	DK	E	F	I	N	NL	S	UK
58	*	53	80	83	18	67	44	87	47

The data shows that such representation varies considerably across Europe (Table 2.1). Sweden, France and Spain all have more than eight out of ten organisations reporting to the head of the personnel or HR function on the main Board of Directors or equivalent. Several countries (UK, Netherlands, Italy) show less than half of their employing organisations with such representation. The position in Germany needs explaining. Not only does Germany have a complicated, two-tier, Board structure, but a change in translation meant that the figures from that country are non-comparable. When the same translation was used in the first year of the survey (1989–90), Germany reported 18 per cent of organisations having representation at Board level.

The role of the function is far from completely clarified by knowing whether its head is represented in the top decision-making structure of the organisation. Many such departments are not involved in corporate strategy formulation, for example (see Table 2.2). In broad terms around half of the organisations in these ten countries involve HR specialists from the outset in strategy formulation (raising intriguing questions about the activities of some Board members who, apparently, are not so involved).

Table 2.2 HR involvement in development of corporate strategy (% of organisations)

	CH	D	DK	E	F	I	N	NL	S	UK
From the outset	48	55	42	46	50	32	54	48	59	43
Consultative	20	19	30	21	22	23	24	31	28	27
Implementation	6	6	9	8	12	17	6	8	4	8
Not consulted	14	8	4	2	2	3	4	3	5	7
Don't know/missing	12	13	15	23	13	25	11	12	6	15

On the face of it, this provides limited encouragement for those who look for a close link between HR and business strategy; unless (see, for example, Ackermann 1986, Lengnick-Hall and Lengnick-Hall 1988, Cook and Armstrong 1990, or Miller 1989) it is accepted that the only way this link can work is from corporate strategy down to HRM practices. We have already made clear our view that this is a narrow view: there are innumerable examples of cases where corporate strategy decisions taken for logical business reasons — but in ignorance of human resource factors — have failed because of that ignorance.

The figures show that in most countries between a third and a half of the organisations involve the senior human resource specialist in strategy formulation. In the other cases their role begins at a later stage in the process. A significant number of the senior personnel specialists responding were not involved at all or only involved at the implementation stage. Again, there are variations between countries: more than half the organisations in Sweden, Norway and Germany have their senior HR specialist involved from the earliest stages of strategy formulation: less than a third of the Italian organisations do so.

We have made an attempt to map these differences in the input of HRM to the formulation of corporate strategy in Figure 2.1. This utilises the data presented above, plus other material which we do not have the space to cover here. For details of the construction of this figure and the relevant measures, see Bournois 1991; 1991a. Figure 2.1 ranks the ten countries on two axes: the formalisation of strategies and the involvement of HRM in strategic processes. For the purposes of this article, the figure is most valuable in clarifying the relationships between HRM and corporate

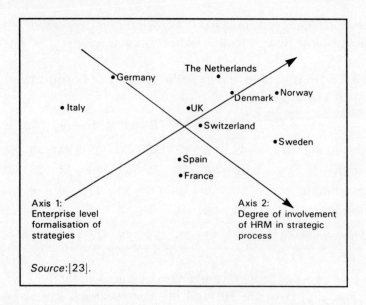

Figure 2.1 Position of the ten countries in relation to strategy formalisation and HRM input to strategy.

strategies and the different tendencies visible in the different countries. It is noticeable that the categories identified by others (see Filella's Chapter 3 in this book) are identifiable here too.

Organisational autonomy

Central to the concept of HRM as currently propounded is the notion of organisational independence and autonomy. However, the European system tends to have considerably less independence than, for example, the North American model. This applies both at the level of corporate ownership and structure and at the level of HRM. In Europe public ownership, whilst it has decreased to some degree in some countries, remains widespread. Furthermore, a US-style pattern of shareholding among private sector companies is limited in Europe. In some countries, Germany being the most obvious example, banks own a substantial share of most major businesses in a complex, interlocked manner (Randlesome 1991).

At the level of HRM, many European countries are more centralised and coordinated. The point is clear if the pay determination system is examined. For organisations of more than 200 employees, basic pay for

Table 2.3 Level of determination of basic pay (% of organisations)

Country	CH	D	DK	E	F	I	N	NL	S	UK
National/industry-wide collective bargaining	n/a	n/a*	62	41	31	59	77	78	68	37
Regional collective bargaining	n/a	n/a	17	18	10	2	22	n/a	8	8
Company/division	38	n/a	13	22	46	45	16	22	32	31
Establishment/site	n/a	n/a	9	15	24	12	13	6	11	32
Individual	50	n/a	10	8	14	9	13	8	13	6

*Question not asked as nearly all pay bargaining in Germany is centralised
Note: numbers may not add up to 100 as respondents could choose more than one level

manual employees is often set outside the organisation. This is the case for nearly all German organisations (see, for example, Randlesome 1991). For more on HRM in Germany, see Hinterhuber and Holleis 1988.

Even in the UK, where there has been a concerted effort by Government, employers' associations and many employers to drive pay determination down to the company level, our data shows that there are still 37 per cent of organisations where basic pay for manual workers is still established in national industry bargaining (see Chapter 5 by Hegewisch in this book; also Milward and Stevens 1986 and Marginson *et al.* 1988).

The work by Marginson *et al.* also shows that, in a typically informal way, many multi-site UK businesses maintain a considerable involvement from head office in HR decision-making. These conclusions are not uncontroversial; in a summary of these surveys, and his own research on the topic, Kinnie concludes that, although there is some evidence of a move towards the decentralisation of management and of bargaining structures in the UK, 'these changes do not necessarily lead to an increase in decision-making discretion for establishment managers' (Kinnie 1989, p 33). Morris and Wood (1991), however, have argued that this may underestimate the extent of change. There is little controversy about the fact that the European organisations continue to accept, to a substantial degree, the establishment of pay levels outside the organisation.

Trade union influence

Europe is, in general, a highly unionised continent. Trade union membership and influence varies considerably by country, of course, but is always significant. The OECD reports that Sweden has union membership of 85 per cent of the working population, the UK around 40 per cent, and France has 12 per cent. Only 3 per cent of Swedish organisations in our survey reported union membership to be less than 50 per cent and only 16 per cent of UK ones had no union representation. In many European countries trade union recognition for collective bargaining purposes is required by law wherever there are trade unions and, even in the UK, where there is no legal mechanism for enforcing recognition, 72 per cent of organisations with more than 200 employees still recognise trade unions.

Table 2.4   Trade union recognition (% of organisations)

CH	D	DK	E	F	I	N	NL	S	UK
*	*	91	73	*	91	96	43	*	72

* Question not asked: position determined by legislation, not managerial decision

For a majority of organisations the union influence has changed little over the last three years but there are some differences between the countries. Union influence at the workplace has fallen sharply in the UK, Italy and France, stabilised in Sweden, Switzerland and Denmark (where roughly equal numbers of organisations report increasing compared to decreasing influence), and actually increased elsewhere.

Table 2.5   Change in union influence over previous three years

Country	CH	D	DK	E	F	I	N	NL	S	UK
Increase	18	25	18	44	7	8	38	34	20	4
Decrease	13	10	12	12	46	38	6	9	21	52
Same	69	65	70	44	47	54	56	57	59	44

Overall the data shows that trade unionism remains widespread and important in Europe; an importance that current EC approaches will certainly not diminish, and may enhance. At the same time, the use of communications channels which focus on the individual is increasing in many organisations, particularly in Sweden and the UK.

Employee communication

The subject of employee communication is not only a central strand in certain concepts of HRM, it is also a live issue for trade unions, for many employers and commentators and for the European Community. There is a clear drive to increase the extent of such communication at a variety of levels.

The latest proposals from the European Commission on the subject of employee involvement — a hardy perennial which has been the subject of extensive debate over the last 30 years — offer a series of options for the member states. These are, in effect, an attempt to draw on the best practice available in all the Community countries rather than to impose the system which exists in one state on the others.

The survey results confirm the fact that consultation in Europe is not only widespread, but is increasing. In France, for example, the law *(Code du Travail)* requires consultation with employee representatives on relevant issues in all private sector organisations employing more than 50 people. For a given topic, such as an annual pay increase, the works council *(comité d'enterprise)* has to be consulted formally before the final award can be implemented. By contrast the UK has no legal requirements for consultation except in very particular (and mostly EC-inspired) cases, such as when there is a collective redundancy. In general the British system has relied on the voluntary system of collective bargaining to ensure that the workforce is made aware of managerial decisions and company performance.

The considerable moves that have been made by many employers to expand the degree of information given to the workforce, irrespective of legal requirements, is clear from our data (Table 2.6).

Table 2.6 Information on financial performance to employees (% organisations)

Country	CH	D	DK	E	F	I	N	NL	S	UK
Management	91	94	95	88	90	88	95	97	95	91
Prof/Technical	63	72	75	46	63	55	71	73	53	70
Technical (S/CH) D*	58	45							65	
Clerical	39	52	69	14	51	32	62	45	60	53
Manual	38	41	56	9	14	24	61	41	51	47

*Skilled Craft Workers

This general increase in all channels of communication reflects the requirement to generate significant commitment amongst the workforce with the aim of improving organisational performance; a central theme of HRM.

These examples indicate areas in which organisational managements operating in Europe have much less autonomy and freedom of action than those in the United States of America, for example. These instances could be multiplied: in most of Europe legal constraints on the employment contract are substantial. There are considerable variations in how an organisation may recruit, what salaries may be paid, what hours may be worked and in what pattern, how many holidays must be given and how employment contracts can be terminated (for details see Brewster *et al.* 1992). Overall, however, across Europe HRM is supported, or constrained, by numerous factors of ownership, trade union and employee involvement and legal requirements, which mean that managerial autonomy is far from complete.

The controlled labour market

Internal and external labour markets are used to some extent by all organisations. The balance between the two is the critical determinant and on this issue different views of HRM provide different results. The 'hard' approach will in many circumstances imply an organisational version of the core-peripheral labour market model introduced by Atkinson (1984; 1984a), with the organisation trying to limit its legal and moral commitment to employees and ensure that the workforce is fully occupied by employing workers on a range of atypical contracts. Thus there would be seen in many sectors to be substantial advantages in the widespread use of part-time and temporary work contracts, 'labour only' subcontracting and similar practices.

'External' labour market

Table 2.7 shows that many organisations in these ten countries have more than one-tenth of their workforce on part-time contracts and on temporary or fixed term contracts. Furthermore, this is a developing trend in most countries. The table shows that a considerable percentage of organisations have increased their use of these contractual arrangements over the last three years. Subcontracting is increasing by similar proportions. Grahl and Teague (1991) have argued that the UK is following a strategy of competitive flexibility which would be defined as following many of the tenets of HRM. Indeed they state that 'probably the single most important factor here is the upsurge in human resource management' (p 80).

Table 2.7   Use of atypical contracts (% organisations with more than 10% of employees on following terms)

	CH	D	DK	E	F	I	N	NL	S	UK
Part-time	37	20	37	3	13	6	41	35	44	24
Temporary	4	1	4	23	9	3	8	18	14	7
Fixed term	10	12	8	26	15	10	11	3	1	5

Other widely touted new employment relationships (annual hours, contracts, homeworking, teleworking) are shown by our survey to be restricted to a small percentage of organisations.

This is a subject that is causing increasing concern within the Commission of the European Community. The Social Charter includes a provision to extend workers' rights to individuals on atypical contracts and the European Court of Justice has been making judgements under the Equal Opportunities legislation which are restricting the cost advantages of employing workers on these contracts. Currently, however, there are indications here that support the view that European organisations are looking to create a more controlled external labour market for themselves.

Internal labour markets

The internal labour market, by contrast, is typically stressed in the 'soft' version of HRM. In its simplest conception, an internal labour market exists where organisations tend to recruit at the bottom, with people expected to remain with one organisation for their whole working lives, rather than the organisation recruiting widely with people expecting to have to move employment between organisations.

There is some evidence from the survey that Germany approximates more to the internal labour market model and Britain to the external, as 63 per cent of German organisations recruit less than 30 per cent of their managers externally, compared with 59 per cent of British organisations.. At the other end of the hierarchy, though job centres are used by approximately two-thirds of the organisations as a means of recruiting manual and clerical workers, private recruitment agencies are used by 48 per cent of UK employers for clerical vacancies and by 14 per cent of UK employers for manual vacancies. Such agencies are not used by German employers for these groups.

There are some significant differences in other areas. For example 81 per cent of UK organisations advertised externally for clerical workers in 1990–91 (87 per cent in 1989—90) compared to 66 per cent in Sweden and Germany (73 per cent and 68 per cent respectively in 1989–90).* Sixty-three per cent of German organisations used apprenticeships to fill vacant clerical positions, whereas hardly any UK employers did so. For manual worker vacancies, UK employers were significantly more likely to advertise externally, the Germans much more likely to rely on apprenticeships. Sixty-seven per cent of British employers advertised manual vacancies externally, and 41 per cent of German organisations.

Employee development

A concentration on developing the skills of employees through training is a central theme of many texts on HRM. Many organisations in Europe are spending considerable amounts of money on training (Table 2.8). They are devoting substantial amounts of time to this purpose as well. Table 2.9 uses manual workers, the group that receives least training, as an example. Even here, more than one in ten organisations in the UK devotes five or more days, out of a presumed working year of around 200 days, to training. In themselves, however, these figures may be misleading: they take no account of significant differences in the educational system and state-supported vocational training systems in operation in these countries. In Britain the inadequacy of the educational system for many people, particularly those who go into manual work, and the paucity of nationally provided training, have been the subject of considerable debate and formed a central plank in the Labour Party's attack on the Conservative government at the beginning of the 1990s.

Table 2.8 Proportion of annual salaries and wages currently spent on training (valid %)

	CH	D	DK	E	F	I	N	NL	S	UK
2.01–4.00%	26	24	20	14	43	15	17	20	19	21
4.01 % and above	11	16	13	10	32	9	19	16	25	18

* The decline in external advertising reflecting the recession and rising unemployment in the UK and Sweden in 1990–91; but was not affecting the greater propensity of British organisations to advertise externally.

Table 2.9 Days' training per annum per manual employee, average (valid %)

	CH	D	DK	E	F	I	N	NL	S	UK
Less than one	36	38	25	14	13	22	20	14	73	21
One to three	36	35	31	20	37	41	28	32	20	37
Three to five	17	15	27	25	25	19	28	29	5	24
Five to ten	5	9	12	22	20	14	17	17	2	13
Ten days and above	2	4	5	19	6	5	8	8	0	6

Here again, the implication is that the overall similarity of the figures amongst employing organisations in these European countries is significant, but just as important are the differences in the support which employers enjoy from their Governments.

Discussion: need for a 'European Model'

Our evidence here suggests that two paradoxical trends run through HRM in Europe. First, there are clear country differences which can only be understood and explained in the context of each national culture and its manifestations in history, law, institutions and trade union and employing organisation structures. Second, there is an identifiable difference between the way in which HRM is conducted in Europe and the situation in the United States of America; a difference which allows us to speak of a European form of HRM and to question the appropriateness of the HRM concept as defined by some US commentators in this other continent (Cox and Cooper 1985). (We would add that intuitively we believe that there may also be questions about the relevance of the US form of the concept in other continents.)

It is frequently argued that there is a direct correlation between strategic HRM and economic success. Porter (1985) believed that HRM can help a firm obtain competitive advantage. Schuler and Macmillan (1984, p 242) make a similar point, that 'effectively managing human resources' gives benefits which 'include greater profitability'.

Other authors make the point explicitly: 'Firms that engage in a strategy formulation process that systematically and reciprocally considers human resources and competitive strategy will perform better . . . over the long term' (Lengnick-Hall and Lengnick-Hall, 1988, p 468). One author has even elevated HRM to the position of 'the only truly important determinant of success' (Beyer 1991, p 1); Salaman (1991) comments 'this is an obvious but important point'.

The results indicated in this paper challenge this 'obvious' point. National differences in human resource management (and in certain practices linked to a strategic view of HRM) have no obvious correlation with national differences in economic performance. This leads us to argue that simple assumptions about strategic HRM being linked to economic success are inadequate: and re-emphasises our view that the US-based concept of HRM is culturally limited and too narrow.

With respect to the three elements of HRM that seem to be common to most views of the subject — correlation of people management with corporate strategy, organisational autonomy and controlled labour markets — our findings show that in Europe there is a greater degree of influence from the social partners and from government than exists in the United States. This may go some way towards explaining the lack of correlation of particular *organisational* strategies with economic success: there are other factors to take into account.

The focus in some US writings on HRM, and in their European followers, has been on (presumed autonomous) management or (as in Lengnick-Hall and Lengnick-Hall 1988, Schuler and Macmillan 1984, Schuler *et al.* 1992, Ackerman 1986, Besseyre des Horts 1987, 1988), on a strategic determinism in which management's task is essentially to establish the 'fit' of HRM to a given scenario. Valuable as these texts have been, we argue that the uncritical import of such concepts of HRM is inadequate in the European situation (cf Hofstede 1983, Cox and Cooper 1985). For Europe more account needs to be taken of other inputs into HRM strategies. After all 'we are in culturally different contexts' (Weiss 1988, p 206).

> Rather than copy solutions which result from other cultural traditions, we should consider the state of mind that presided in the search for responses adapted to the culture
>
> Albert 1989, p 75, our translation

We need a model of HRM that re-emphasises the influence of culture, or of ownership structures or trade union organisation. Clearly, the European evidence suggests that managements can see the unions, for example, as social partners with a positive role to play in human resource management: and the manifest success of many European firms which adopt that approach shows the explicit or implicit anti-unionism of many American views to be culture-bound.

Interestingly, this takes us back to the original propositions on HRM theory, or even back to 'industrial relations' models. Beer *et al.* (1984) originally suggested that the 'map of the HRM territory' should cover the factors governing the context in which policies at the organisational level will be developed. This point has been reiterated by Poole (1990). The factors include 'stake-holders' interests', including government, owners, employees and trade unions, and 'situational factors', such as management philosophy, labour markets, technology and societal values. Poole wants to include concepts of multinationalism, power and strategic choice. It is a matter of semantics as to whether these are contextual issues or issues which should be an intrinsic aspect of the HRM concept. It is noteworthy that it is the American authors who have seen it as contextual and the European authors (such as Poole 1990, but also including Hendry and Pettigrew 1990, in the UK; and Gaugler 1988 and Pieper 1990 in Germany) who have wanted to include these areas within the concept. Attempting to encompass these areas within a concept of HRM takes it back towards the industrial relations system approach first outlined by Dunlop (1958) in which the state and its agencies, employers and their associations and employees and their representative bodies formed the constituent elements.

Until recently a call to re-establish the primacy of the wider industrial relations concept may have been seen as a nostalgic attempt to deny the replacement of an older theory by a new one. However, the recent publication by Kochan *et al.* (1986) has breathed new life into the older theory. A major weakness of an otherwise very important book is its lack of a comparative, international framework. The evidence presented here is that one element of the Kochan *et al.* argument — that governmental, market and labour-management relations are interwoven — would have been all the stronger if they had drawn international comparisons.

It is our contention that HRM theory needs to adopt the wider perspective of the multi-level model proposed by Kochan *et al*; and a more comprehensive view of the actors in the system, if it is to become a theory that stands the test of international application.*

Tentatively, we propose the outline in Figure 2.2 as a first step towards the development of a European model of HRM. This places the process

---

* It is interesting to note that many of the leading modern writers on corporate strategy (Bartlett and Ghoshal 1989; Hedlund and Rolander 1990) suggest that organisations in the future will need to be involving for their workforce, flexible and tolerant of ambiguity. These are all characteristics in which Europe could be said to have a lead. See also Porter 1990.

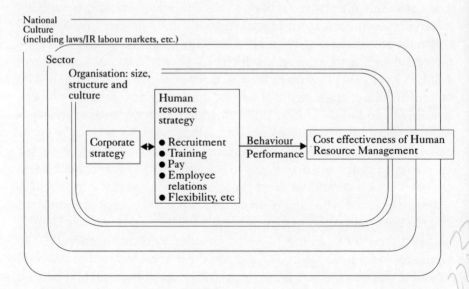

Figure 2.2 A model for investigating human resource strategies: the European environment

of human resource management firmly at the centre of concentric circles of influence or constraint. Immediately influencing it is the organisation itself, within which the HR strategy will be defined and implemented and within which are most of the outcomes of such strategies in terms of the cost-effective deployment of human resources. These influences in turn, however, are not uni-dimensional. Had technology permitted, we could have developed a three-dimensional model showing the related influences of organisation size, structure and culture. We could have included external influences from, for example, education, power systems and employee representation on the organisation level. The model does, however, locate organisational issues clearly within sectoral influences and national influences. The outcomes of the HR strategies of individual organisation, of course, have a lesser, but still real impact at the sectoral and even national levels.

We propose this outline with some diffidence: no doubt it can be improved and refined. We believe, however, that by focusing on organisational strategies within sectoral and national cultures, the model allows for an identification of the important differences which exist between European nations, as well as taking us one step beyond the 'frontiersman' image of the autonomous corporation implicit in much of the earlier American writing on HRM. This more complex model allows those of us researching into European HRM to recognise and assess more readily the differences and similarities in HRM in this varied and rapidly changing continent.

REFERENCES

Ackermann, KF (1986) 'A Contingency Model of HRM-Strategy. Empirical Research Findings Reconsidered', *Management Forum*, Band 6, pp. 65-83

Albert, FJ (1989) *Les ressources humaines, atout stratégique*, Editions L'harmattan, p 75

Atkinson J (1984) 'Flexible Manning: the Way Ahead', *IMS Report*, no 88

Atkinson, J (1984) 'Manpower Strategies for Flexible Organisations', *Personnel Management*, August, pp 32–35

Bartlett, CA and Ghoshal, S (1989) *Managing Across Borders: The Transnational Solution*, Harvard Business School Press, Cambridge, Massachusetts

Beaumont, PB (1991) 'The US Human Resource Management Literature: A Review', paper prepared for Course B884 Human Resource Strategies, Open University Business School

Beer, M, Lawrence, PR, Mills, QN and Walton, RE (1985) *Human Resource Management*, Free Press, New York

Besseyre des Horts, CH (1987) 'Typologies des pratiques de gestion des ressources humaines', *Revue franaise de Gestion*, pp 149–155

Besseyre des Horts, CH (1988) *Vers une gestion stratégique des ressources humaines*, Editions d'Organisation, pp 69–84

Beyer, HT (1991) *Personalarbiet als integrieter Bestandteil der Unternehmensstrategie*, paper to the 1991 DGFP Annual Congress

Bournois, F (1991) 'Gestion des RH en Europe: donnes comparées', *Revue française de gestion*, mars-avril-mai pp 68–83

Bournois, F (1991) 'Gestion stratégique des ressources humaines: comparaisons internationales', Actes du collogue de l'Association Française de gestion des ressources humaines, CERGY

Brewster, C (1991) 'The impact of national cultures', paper prepared for course B884 Human Resource Strategies, Open University

Brewster, C Hegewisch, A Holden, L and Lockhart, T (1992) *The European Human Resource Management Guide*, Academic Press, London

Butler, JE (1988) 'Human resource management as a driving force in business strategy', *Journal of General Management*, vol 13, no 4, pp 88–102

Conrad, P and Pieper, R (1990) 'HRM in the Federal Republic of Germany' in Pieper, R (ed), *HRM: An International Comparison*, Walter de Gruyter, Berlin

Cook, R and Armstrong, M (1990) 'The search for strategic HRM', *Personnel Management*, December, pp 30–33

Cox, J and Cooper, L (1985) 'The irrelevance of American organisational sciences to the UK and Europe', *Journal of General Management*, vol 11, no 2, pp 27–34

Dunlop, JT (1958) *Industrial Relations Systems*, Henry Holt & Co., New York

Frombrun, CJ, Tichy, NM and Devanna, MA (1984) *Strategic Human Resource Management*, John Wiley, New York

Gaugler, E (1988) 'HR Management: An International Comparison', *Personnel*, August, pp 24–30.

Grahl, J and Teague, P (1991) 'Industrial Relations Trajectories and European Human Resource Management', in Brewster, C and Tyson, S (eds), *International Comparisons in Human Resource Management*, Pitman, London

Guest, D (1987) 'Human Resource Management and Industrial Relations', *Journal of Management Studies*, vol 24, no 5, pp 503–22

Guest, D (1990) 'Human Resource Management and the American Dream', *Journal of Management Studies*, vol 27:4, pp 377–97

Hedlund, G and Rolander, D (1900) 'Action in Heterarchies — New Approaches to Managing the MNC', in Bartlett, CA Doz, Y and Hedlund, G (eds), *Managing the Global Firm*, Routledge, London, pp 15–46

Hendry, C and Pettigrew, A (1986) 'The Practice of Strategic Human Resource Management', *Personnel Review*, Vol 15, 5, pp 3–8.

Hendry, C and Pettigrew, A (1990) 'HRM: an agenda for the 1990s', *International Journal of Human Resource Management*, vol 1.1, pp 17–25

Hinterhuber, HH and Holleis, W (1988) 'Gewinner im Verdrängungswettbewerb — Wie man durch Verbindung von Unternehmensstrategie und Unternehmenskultur zu einem führenden Wettbewerber werden kann', *Journal für Betriebswirtschaft*, vol 38.1, pp 2–18

Hofstede, G (1980) *Cultures Consequences*, Sage, Berkely CA

Hofstede, G (1983) 'The cultural relativity of organisational practices and theories', *Journal of International Business Studies*, vol 13:3, pp 75–89

Kinnie, N (1989) 'The Decentralisation of Industrial Relations? — Recent Research Considered', *Personnel Review*, vol 19, no 3, pp 28–34

Kochan, TA, Katz, HC and McKersie, RB (1986) *The Transformation of American Industrial Relations*, Basic Books, New York

Laurent, A (1983) 'The Cultural Diversity of Western Conceptions of Management', *International Studies of Management and Organisations*, vol .XIII, no 1–2, pp 75–96

Legge, K (1989) 'Human Resource Management: A Critical Review' in Storey J (ed), *New Developments in Human Resource Management*, Routledge and Kegan Paul, London

Lengnick-Hall, C and M (1986) 'Strategic human resources management: a review of the literature and a proposed typology', *Academy of Management Review*, vol 13, no 3, p 468.

Mahoney, TA and Deckop, JR (1986) 'Evolution of concept and practice in personnel administration/human resource management' *Journal of Management*, vol 12, 2, pp 223–41

Marginson, P, Edwards, PK, Martin, R, Purcell, J and Sisson, K. (1988) *Beyond the Workplace: Managing Industrial Relations in the Multi-establishment Enterprise*, Blackwell, Oxford

Miller, P (1989) 'Strategic HRM: what it is and what it isn't', *Personnel Management*, February, pp 46–51

Millward, N and Stevens, M (1986) *British Workplace Industrial Relations 1980 to 1984*. The DE/ESRC/PSI/ACAS Surveys, Gower, Aldershot

Morris, T and Wood, S (1991) 'Testing the Survey Method: Continuity and Change in British I.R.', *Work, Employment and Society*, vol 5, pp 259–82

Schein, E (1987) 'Increasing Organisational Effectiveness Through Better Human Resource Planning and Development' in Schein, E (ed) *The Art of Managing Human Resources*, Oxford University Press, New York, pp 25–45

Schreyögg, G (1987) 'Verschlüsselte Botschaften. Neue Perspektiven einer strategischen Personalführung', *Zeischrift Führung und Organisation*, vol 56.3, pp 151–58

Schuler, RS (1991) 'Strategic HRM: Linking People with the Strategic Needs of the Business', unpublished paper, New York University

Schuler, R and Macmillan, S (1984) 'Gaining Competitive Advantage Through Human Resource Management Practices', *Human Resource Management*, vol 23, 3, pp 241–55

Staehle, WH (1988) 'Human Resource Management', *Zeitschrift für Betriebswirtschaft*, vol 5/6, pp 26–37

Trompenaars, A (1985) 'Organisation of Meaning and the Meaning of Organisation: A Comparative Study on the Conception of Organisational Structure in Different Cultures', unpublished PhD thesis, University of Pennsylvania (DA 8515460)

Weiss, D (1988) *La fonction ressources humaines*, Editions d'organisation, Paris

Wohlgemuth, AC (1988) 'Human resources management und die wirkungsvolle Vermaschung mit der Unternehmungspolitik', *Management-Zeitschrift Industrielle Organisation*, vol 56.2, pp 115–18

3

IS THERE A LATIN MODEL IN THE MANAGEMENT OF HUMAN RESOURCES?*

Jaime Filella,† ESADE, Spain

The project of building up the European Community implies that all members states enjoy similar political, social and economic conditions. It is clear, however, that although politically they are all democratic, there are obvious socioeconomic differences. The industrial belt going from England to Austria through the Benelux countries, northern France, Germany and Switzerland, is one of the most prosperous regions of the world. Latin countries within the European Community are at a clear disadvantage. Perhaps they have not yet undergone the social transformations that a fully fledged industrialisation process entails. In this context, therefore, it is relevant to pose the question of how Latin European countries are trying to catch up with their northern neighbours. More specifically, this chapter will focus on human resources issues and on whether or not there is a common pattern in the way they are approached and managed, so as to justify speaking of a 'Latin Model'.

We are assuming that countries within the European Community belong to various geographical clusters, and that such clusters reflect different levels of socioeconomical development. Intuitively, there is a cluster of nations that are Latin. All the European regions surrounding the western Mediterranean basin formed by the eastern coast of Spain, southern France, Corsica and Sardinia, and the whole of Italy, seem to be distinctly *Latin*. By extension, the whole of Portugal and the rest of Spain should also be included as part of the Latin region. Two independent studies seem to confirm the view that there is a Latin European cluster of nations, with some doubt about France. Hofstede's data on national

* This chapter first appeared in *Personnel Review*, vol 20, 6, 1991. Permission for its reproduction here is acknowledged with gratitude
† Professor Jaime Filella is on the staff of the Personnel Department of ESADE, Barcelona, Spain. At the time of writing this article in 1990, he was ESADE's Director General (1988–1992)

cultures in organisations and The World Competitiveness Report has identified a set of Latin Mediterranean nations distinctly different from other European clusters such as the Anglo-Saxon, the Northern European with the Scandinavian countries as a possible distinct group. There seems to be, therefore, a set of countries which can be identified as 'Latin' and, because of their socioeconomic deficiencies relative to the more developed countries in the European Community, there is some justification for such countries to be studied as a unit.

The data bank generated by the Price Waterhouse Cranfield Research Project seems to be a privileged source of information for studying the various practices of managing human resources in Europe and, consequently, to answer the question about the existence of a Latin Model.[*]

The statistical data available up to the end of 1990 will be presented with reference to three clusters: a Latin cluster made up of Spain, Italy and France; a Central European cluster including the UK, the Netherlands, Germany (only the FRG) and Switzerland; and a Nordic cluster with Denmark, Norway, and Sweden as its components. A three-column format will be followed throughout this section except in a couple of cases. The first column will contain the data on the Latin cluster; the second, on Central Europe; and the third, on Nordic countries. In the discussion of the results, our observations will be directed to those trends found to be typical of Latin European nations and different from other European clusters. Finally, by way of conclusion, we shall attempt to define the main features of a 'Latin Model', if there is one, in the management of human resources.

It is but fair to add a note of caution regarding the statistical treatment of the data. Due to the substantial differences in the amount of data available for the various countries and the difficulties of acceding to the data bank through the SPSS or other statistical computer packages, rigorous statistical analysis was not made. The danger, therefore, that conclusions may be impressionistic cannot be discounted. However, the observed differences among nation clusters were sufficiently clear and consistent to lend support to the features mentioned in the discussion of the results and to conclusions drawn therefrom.

---

[*] Of the ten countries included in the Price Waterhouse Cranfield Project, at least two can be clearly defined as Latin: Italy and Spain. France was also counted as part of the Latin cluster, but with some reservations about its northern regions because of their proximity to the European industrial belt.

STATISTICAL RESULTS

We will deal with some of the issues thought to be crucial for HR management in the next decade in Europe. With some minor changes, we have followed the order in which they appear in the Price Waterhouse Cranfield original questionnaire, from the place of the HR Department in the firm to the way the HR policies are framed in view of the *Single European Act* which came into force in January 1993.

The place of the HR department in the firm

The importance accorded to the HR department can be gauged from the number of people working in it, especially qualified personnel, and, most decidedly, from the influence it exerts on the firm's strategic policies. Table 3.1 reports on the strength of the HR department, with a special reference to the number of qualified professionals. The data available does not permit us to specify what kind of qualifications are considered valid in European countries. We assume that a university degree equivalent to a Master's or a Licentiate is normally accepted as an appropriate professional qualification.

Table 3.1 The HR department staff

	Latin	Central	Nordic
More than ten people in HR department	41	42	30
More than five professionals in HR department	24	29	21

Note: Values are percentages of firms in the cluster.

There seem to be no clear differences regarding the number of people working in the HR department. A country by country analysis shows that Spain is a special case. The Spanish HR departments (with only 15 per cent of the firms having more than five properly qualified people in it) compare poorly with other European countries, even within the Latin cluster. Actually, 30 per cent of the French and 27 per cent of the Italian firms have more than five qualified people, which is very similar to firms in Central European countries.

Furthermore, and perhaps more appropriately, the actual place of the HR department within the firm should be inferred from the influence of the department in formulating company policy. Table 3.2 gives three important pieces of information: the percentage of firms that have the HR director on their Board of Directors, and the degree of involvement of the HR director in the formulation of company policies, along with an 'influence ratio'. This ratio purports to assess the effectiveness of the HR director's presence on the Board in framing company policy. It has been calculated by dividing the percentage of firms in which the HR director is involved in framing company policy by the percentage of firms in which the HR director is on the Board of Directors. Ratios of less than 1.00 may indicate that the HR director's presence on the Board does not always guarantee an active involvement in setting policy, while ratios above 1.00 suggest that the HR director is involved in framing company policy even if he is not present on the Board.

Because of the importance of this information we shall depart from the

Table 3.2   HR director's presence and influence

Countries	Presence on Board of Directors[a]	Involvement in Policy Making[b]	Influence Ratio[c]
Latin:			
France	83	57	0.69
Spain	80	60	0.75
Italy	18	43	2.33
Mean	60	53	0.88
Central European:			
UK	47	51	1.08
Germany	19	62	3.26
The Netherlands	44	54	1.23
Switzerland	58	55	0.95
Mean	42	56	1.33
Nordic:			
Denmark	53	49	0.92
Norway	67	61	0.91
Sweden	87	62	0.71
Mean	69	58	0.84

Note:
[a] Percentage of firms in which HR directors are reported to be members of the board of directors.
[b] Percentage of firms in which HR directors are involved in framing policy right from the outset.
[c] Estimated amount of influence exerted by the HR director in a firm.

announced procedure of giving data in terms of the Latin, Central European and Nordic clusters. Instead, we shall give country by country data in order to study the country trends in greater depth.

At least three conclusions may be derived from this data:

1. The degree of the HR director's involvement in framing company policy is almost constant across all countries, regardless of whether the HR director is on the Board of Directors or not.
2. The presence of HR directors on the Board does not automatically imply an equivalent amount of participation in framing policy. Actually, firms in countries with the highest degree of presence (like Sweden, France and Spain) proportionally exert the lowest influence, with ratios around 0.70.
3. The influence ratios are fairly homogeneous among the three Scandinavian countries, with atypical ratios for Italian and German firms within their respective country clusters.

With the focus on the Latin countries, it is important to underline that the data for France and Spain follows a different pattern from that for Italy. While Italy reports only 18 per cent of firms with the HR director on the Board of Directors, 83 per cent of French firms and 80 per cent of the Spanish say that the HR directors are members of the Board of Directors. This is in sharp contrast with their low degree of participation in framing company policy.

Some questions may be raised with regard to this incongruity. What does it mean to have the HR director present at the Board without involving him/her in framing company policy from the outset? Or conversely, does it do any harm to have the HR director on the Board of Directors, even if he/she does not exert any influence?

Before closing this issue, it is interesting to note that it is precisely Spain and France which report a higher number of firms using the Human Resources title to name the department. While most European nations prefer the traditional name of 'Personnel Department' (with percentages preferring the Human Resources title ranging from 0 in Norway to 15 in the UK), Spain and France are very different: 35 per cent of the Spanish firms and 49 per cent of the French report the use of Human Resources in preference to 'Personnel'. Although, by itself, terminology is a minor issue, in the context of the other information given about Spain and France, it may be more than just a semantic problem. It may uncover a hidden wish to give a greater importance to the Personnel Department than it actually enjoys.

In conclusion, the preference for Human Resources as the department title, the inadequate staffing in the HR departments, and the ambiguity in the degree of influence exerted by the HR director in framing company policy point to all some ambivalence about the role of the HR department in Latin countries, at least in France and Spain.

The HR policies: where are decisions made? How are they implemented?

The locus of control is an important indicator of the importance of the HR department within a firm. The data of the Price Waterhouse Cranfield survey throws some light on whether HR policy decisions were made at Headquarters (National or International) or below that level, and whether the responsibility for their implementation lay with the line managers or with the HR director. Tables 3.3 and 3.4 report on these two points regarding six different types of decisions to be made: expansion/ retrenchment of personnel; recruitment/selection; rewards/benefits; health/safety; industrial relations; and training/development.

Table 3.3 HR policy decisions at headquarters

HR Issues	Latin	Central	Nordic
Expansion/Reduction	54	45	41
Recruitment/Selection	57	36	32
Pay/Benefits	79	68	66
Health/Safety	47	44	43
Industrial Relations	61	50	52
Training/Development	60	46	37

Note: Values are percentage of firms whose HR policies are decided at headquarters.

It is clear from Table 3.3 that:

- the issues most easily delegated are Health and Safety;
- decisions regarding Pay and Benefits are most often made by Headquarters;
- more of such decisions in Latin countries are made at Headquarters than in Central or Nordic European countries.

It should be added that the data for French firms is more similar to other European countries than to Spain and Italy. While between 60 and 70 per cent of HR policy decisions in Italy and Spain are made at Headquarters, the French percentages oscillate between 30 and 60.

Table 3.4　Responsibility for HR policy implementation

HR Issues	Latin	Central	Nordic
Expansion/Reduction			
Line Management	13	17	22
HR Department	13	8	8
Shared Responsibility	71	74	67
Recruitment/Selection			
Line Management	7	8	17
HR Department	12	7	3
Shared Responsibility	79	85	78
Pay/Benefits			
Line Management	14	8	12
HR Department	11	17	11
Shared Responsibility	71	72	75
Health/Safety			
Line Management	15	27	25
HR Department	26	19	15
Shared Responsibility	55	52	58
Industrial Relations			
Line Management	8	10	12
HR Department	40	31	29
Shared Responsibility	47	56	57
Training/Development			
Line Management	6	9	16
HR Department	13	14	5
Shared Responsibility	79	80	77

Note: Values are the percentage of firms in which HR Policy implementation lies with line management, or HR department, or some degree of shared responsibility.

Table 3.4 reports data on the same HR policy issues in relation to the locus where responsibility lies. The item in the questionnaire is quite complex. The data obtained has been recast with reference to whether the responsibility lies with line managers or with the HR department, or both.

The results of Table 3.4 indicate that shared responsibility stands out as the most distinctive common feature in the implementation of HR policy decisions in all European nations. Apart from this finding, the results of Table 3.4 are complex and difficult to interpret. Two feeble trends can be detected:

• Scandinavian countries are more consistent in relying on line management for the implementation of HR policies.

- A slightly greater responsibility is noted in Latin countries for the HR department to implement policy decisions regarding Health and Safety and Industrial Relations.

Country data confirms the wide variety of combinations in the way responsibility is shared by line management and the HR department. No clear pattern seems to exist as typical of a country or of a cluster of countries.

Recruitment and retention: the problem of rewards

This is a tricky issue because several aspects have to be taken into account jointly as if they were one single problem. The basic issue is the extent to which a firm can retain suitable people after a careful selection process. In the context of the EC today, the problem of selection and retention of personnel is closely linked with the power of appropriate rewards to retain deserving people. Tables 3.5 and 3.6 summarise the relevant data from the Price Waterhouse Cranfield Project.

Table 3.5 reports how recruitment is conducted in the various countries covered by the survey. For the sake of simplicity, the data has been recast

Table 3.5   Recruitment by categories and methods

Recruitment of:	Latin	Central	Nordic
Managers			
From Own Employees	60	63	54
By Word of Mouth	37	20	21
From Publicity	52	78	83
From Agencies	38	35	18
Technical/Professional			
From Own Employees	64	48	39
By Word of Mouth	42	34	21
From Publicity	76	90	84
From Agencies	24	39	4
Clerical/Manual			
From Own Employees	52	39	41
By Word of Mouth	31	47	22
From Publicity	42	70	66
From Agencies	17	24	13

Note: Values are percentage of firms in a country or cluster of countries using the method indicated to recruit people for the category mentioned in the stem.

in three employee categories (managerial, technical/professional and administrative/manual) with regard to four different selection methods (internally from among the company's own employees, by word of mouth among colleagues and friends, publicity in the newspapers and professional journals, and professional employment agencies or employment bureaux).

Some interesting trends are worth noting in the data reported in Table 3.5. It is clear that:

- In all countries recruitment from among their own employees is used most consistently across all categories, this trend being more clear for Latin countries.
- Countries in Central and Northern Europe rely much more on publicity in newspapers and professional magazines than in Latin countries.
- Latin countries rely more on personal contacts (by word of mouth) to recruit managers and technical/professional people than do Central and Northern European countries.
- Publicity in newspapers and professional journals is the most popular method to recruit technical and professional people across all country clusters.

Table 3.6 takes up the issue of rewards. The data therein can hardly do justice to the HR directors' ingenuity to devise ways of retaining talented

Table 3.6   Methods for payment agreements

Categories	Latin	Central	Nordic	Mean
Managers				
Collective Bargaining	37	24	51	35
Internal Negotiations	40	43	38	38
Individual Agreement	53	54	49	52
Technical/Professional				
Collective Bargaining	41	28	60	42
Internal Negotiations	55	48	39	48
Individual Agreement	38	42	33	38
Clerical/Manual				
Collective Bargaining	56	58	78	65
Internal Negotiations	54	44	33	45
Individual Agreement	16	26	20	19

Note: Values are percentage of firms in a country or cluster of countries using each method.

and committed people. Sometimes collective bargaining, at other times the country's labour legislation, and at all times the danger of odious comparisons stand in the way of rewarding merit beyond the fixed salary levels.

The data of Table 3.6 is cast in a 3 × 3 matrix, namely, by three employment categories (managerial, technical/professional, and clerical/manual) and by the three most common methods of fixing payment levels: by collective bargaining (ie industry-wide negotiations or for the whole nation or region); by internal negotiations (ie negotiations conducted by companies in the same locality or within one single company, or even division of a large company); and by individual agreements.

Some suggestive trends are worth noting in the data of Table 3.6. It appears that:

- Across all country clusters, the most common methods for fixing pay and other benefits are: individual agreements with people in managerial positions, and national and industry-wide bargaining with clerical and manual workers, with only a slight preference for internal negotiations for technical and professional people.
- National, regional and industry-wide bargaining is most common in the Nordic countries across all employment levels.
- Internal negotiations and individual agreements are fairly common in Central European countries for managers and technical/professional people.
- All three methods are used in Latin countries for fixing payment for managers and technical/professional people, with a clear preference for individual agreements in the case of managers and for internal negotiations with technical/professional personnel.

Here again, we find that among the Latin countries France differs from Italy and Spain. Country by country results indicate that 65 per cent of Italian and Spanish firms prefer individual agreements for people in managerial positions, whereas only 31 per cent of the French firms use this method; and the same difference is observed for the technical and professional personnel. While only 19 per cent of the French firms use individual agreement to reward technical/professional employees, as many as 44 per cent of the Spanish and 52 per cent of the Italian firms use this method for people in the same category.

Training and development

Training and Development is another area of great importance to assess company policies with reference to human resource issues. Here we shall confine our remarks to the training budget and to the number of days per employee devoted to training programmes. Tables 3.7 and 3.8 report on these two issues.

Table 3.7 summarises data on the percentage of annual salaries and wages currently spent on training. The format of the table has been changed to take care of France's unique position in this regard. French legislation prescribes firms to devote at least 1.2 per cent of its salary and wage budget to formation. In order to highlight the effects of this legislation, we have put the French results in a separate column at the far right of Table 3.7.

Table 3.7 Proportion of income spent on training

	Latin	Central	Nordic	France
Less than 1 per cent	50	34	32	3
Between 1 and 2 per cent	26	29	26	22
More than 2 per cent	24	38	38	75

Note: In this case 'Latin' refers only to Spain and Italy.
Values are percentage of firms spending the specified proportion of salary and wages on formation.

The results of Table 3.7 suggest that

*   Legislation does make a difference, as can be seen from the French data.
*   Central and Nordic European countries spend considerably more on training than Latin countries (ie Spain and Italy), even when no specific legislation exists fixing how much should be spent.

Country by country data reveals surprisingly identical results for Italy and Spain. Even if the identity in percentages is a coincidence, there seems to be great similarity between these two Latin countries with regard to their conservative policies in the matter of training.

Table 3.8 explores the differences in the mean number of days devoted each year to training. There are some unexpected divergences between the amount of money spent on training and the annual number of days devoted to it. The results by hierarchical levels are as follows.

Table 3.8 Average number of days devoted to training

Categories	Latin	Central	Nordic	France
Managers				
Less than 3 days	23	25	20	22
Between 3 and 5 days	21	37	32	37
More than 5 days	57	38	48	42
Technical/Professional				
Less than 3 days	23	37	22	29
Between 3 and 5 days	19	32	31	35
More than 5 days	58	31	45	37
Clerical/Manual				
Less than 3 days	42	62	62	50
Between 3 and 5 days	25	24	24	25
More than 5 days	31	14	12	26

Note: 'Latin' again stands for only Spain and Italy.
Values are percentage of firms conducting training programmes of different periods of time.

The results show some interesting trends:

- Although France by law has to spend a fairly large amount of money on training, the annual average number of days devoted to training does not differ from other countries.
- Spanish and Italian firms consistently report more days per employee devoted annually to training across all three hierarchical levels.

The Spanish results, and to some extent the Italian, show a puzzling inconsistency. On the one hand, Spanish and Italian firms reported *less* money budgeted for training (see Table 3.7), and on the other, the average number of days devoted to training is considerably *greater*. In the case of Spain this disparity is substantial. The percentage of Spanish firms reporting more than five days per year for training is 69 per cent for managers, 71 per cent for professional/technical people and 43 per cent for clerical and manual workers. Yet as many as 50 per cent of the Spanish firms spent less than 1 per cent of the salaries on training.

An easy explanation is to think that training is cheaper in Spain than in other European countries. However, honoraria for training are not appreciably lower in Spain than elsewhere in Europe. A more plausible answer is that a number of training programmes use instructors from the company itself. After all, due to the acknowledged gap between industry's needs and the educational system, training at the time of induction of new personnel is absolutely necessary. It stands to reason that most of such training would be conducted as 'in-house' programmes by internal people.

Influence of the trade unions

One important point, albeit often very elusive in practice, is the strength of the union gauged by the number of its members. It is difficult to get reliable statistics. Table 3.9 gives the estimates made by the HR directors, based on partial data and well-informed guesses.

Table 3.9 Trade union membership

Percentage of Affiliates	Latin	Central	Nordic
0	3	10	1
1–25	53	34	3
26–75	33	35	22
75	4	9	74
Not known	5	12	—

Note: Values are percentage of firms reporting the estimated percentage of employee membership in recognised unions.

The results of Table 3.9 show that the levels of affiliation are different in the three European country clusters. There is the Scandinavian profile with a very high union affiliation; Latin countries show a much lower degree of affiliation; and Central European countries stand somewhere in between.

To the question of whether, in the opinion of the HR directors, union influence had increased in the last three years, the ratios of Yes to No for the various countries were: Spain: 4:1, France and Italy: 1:6, Central: 1:1, and Nordic: 2:1.

Substantial differences appear quite clearly across country clusters, and more specifically among Latin countries. France and Italy report a waning influence of the union; for every company that reports an increase in influence there are six which say that the influence is less. At the other end, there is another Latin country, Spain, in which for every company reporting a decrease in union influence there are four which say that the influence has increased. Nordic and Central European countries reveal a fairly stable situation during the last three years. Furthermore, comments by Spanish HR directors on these results pointed to a paradox in their companies. They all shared the impression that unions had lost credibility in the eyes of the employees, and yet there was no gainsaying the fact that at the bargaining table (and in the political arena, too) unions had a lot of clout. It is probable that this paradox may be due to the government policy of making unnecessary concessions to the unions, and in its zest to keep unions happy, the government may have overdone it, going beyond the people's expectations.

DISCUSSION OF THE RESULTS

It is time to pull together all the strands present in the reported data. In my opinion, four features stand out: the thrust towards professionalisation; the personal approach to people in managerial positions; the power of the spoken word; and the democratisation role of the HR function.

The ambivalent road towards professionalisation

Managers are aware of the need to have a well-planned and strong HR department. Managing human beings is a complex science and a refined art. It is not enough to have engineers and lawyers with a good record in handling human problems on the shopfloor. With better economic conditions and more qualified personnel, the human factor begins to weigh heavily in the way organisations are to be managed. It becomes an integral part of strategic planning and policy making.

At present, the HR function finds itself in a predicament: the challenge is clear, but the resources to respond are scarce. The HR department has to work under pressure and against many odds. This is true of most countries in Europe. Our contention has been that it is especially true of Latin countries in Europe today. Let us summarise their situation, as revealed by the data reported above:

- strong representation on the Board of Directors with little influence on company policy (Table 3.2);
- tendency towards centralisation of important HR policies (Table 3.3);
- responsibility for policy implementation more with line managers than HR department (Table 3.4);
- appropriate choice of recruitment techniques for the different hierarchical levels (Table 3.5);
- adaptation of payment and reward systems to the various expectations of people at the different hierarchical levels (Table 3.6);
- emphasis on training with inadequate budget provisions (Tables 3.7 and 3.8);

- attention to the union's influence even beyond their membership strength (Table 3.9).

The complexity of the situation is clear. The issues to be faced by the HR department are quite different from simply settling labour conflicts or keeping people happy with better salaries. Incomplete communications, rumours, misunderstandings, group tensions, objective recognition of merit, flexible working hours, promotion policies according to individual expectations, and the like, are all thorny issues in themselves, let alone the problems of solving them in the context of the company's policy and its strategic plans.

Presumably, many of these problems are settled piecemeal by top management. Understandably enough, however, top managers turn to the HR director for assistance, expecting clear-cut answers and ready-made solutions rather than points for reflection and sound advice. The HR directors' predicament is not that much is expected of them, but that people have the wrong type of expectations about what they can and should do or not do.

The sources of the obstacles that adversely affect the HR directors' capacity to respond adequately to the challenges of their job are to be found both in the firms themselves and, remote in origin, deriving from an archaic educational system. There is no gainsaying the importance of recruiting properly qualified people, of placing them in recognised positions within the firm's hierarchy, of having generous budgets and adequate training facilities, and the like. All these factors go a long way towards making the HR directors' task easy; but they are not enough. An atmosphere of trust within the firm, the capacity to appreciate the efforts of others, be they high or low in the organisational hierarchy, and an open culture, are necessary if the HR directors are to respond to what is expected of them.

In addition, they must be properly grounded in the social sciences. The educational system in Latin countries falls woefully short in the provision of the foundations for, and pathways towards, development of good HR professionals. One thing is clear: a degree in engineering or in law is not enough. The HR function requires a more flexible approach to problems. Psychology and sociology, economics and political science must be present to some degree. To manage human beings, one must be knowledgeable as well as sensitive to personal and social issues.

In short, then, managers in Latin countries begin to recognise the importance of the HR department within their respective companies. In view of the results obtained, there is some ambivalence about the role of the HR function among managers in Latin countries. It is suggested that this ambivalence reflects the coexistence of the wish to promote the HR department with some deep-seated, lingering but serious doubts about its capacity to contribute to the company's growth on a par with the departments of finance, marketing or production. The solution is to be found in the full professionalisation of the HR department. The thrust towards this is encouraging; but it is only a thrust, and not a consolidated achievement.

A personal approach to people in managerial positions

Tables 3.5 and 3.6 indicated that the most common method of recruitment in Latin countries, for practically all vacancies in a firm, was to look for persons within the company and, for managerial positions, to contact friends and colleagues in order to spot suitable candidates. Similarly, Table 3.6 showed that in Latin countries impersonal methods of fixing payment and rewarding people were preferred for the manual, clerical and administrative personnel, with a more personalised approach to individuals in the managerial cadre. In other words, what was most distinctive of Latin countries, especially Spain and Italy, was the readiness of top management to deal directly and in a personalised way with their immediate subordinates in senior and middle management positions.

This approach is understandable and it is not exclusive to Latin countries. What is typical is its significance and frequency. The hidden message in all these transactions seems to be: 'It is not the company as such that needs you or rewards you, but the chief executive who, in his benevolence, has personally studied your case and has chosen you or wants to show his approval and personal regard for you'. Such transactions must be short, without hesitation, and always with a touch of trust and confidentiality. It is important, too, that the impression be conveyed that objective criteria are used, but have been adjusted to the 'special' case in hand. Such messages are impressive. At times, however, this approach to people runs the risk of being too overwhelming and even secretive. At other times, it may lead to unnecessary disappointments later on, when a person realises that he or she is no longer useful to the 'Big Boss' and all his personal interest comes to naught.

Two consequences accrue from this way of dealing with people in managerial positions:

- the perpetuation of a sort of 'class mentality' in organisations;
- strong personal dependence on those who wield power and are in positions of authority.

A feature not to be missed is that these transactions are always *oral* and are seldom committed to paper. It is a sort of gentleman's agreement, with the implicit warning that what is graciously given may be unceremoniously taken away. It is plausible that these trends reflect the political and cultural features of the various countries. Those with a well-established socialist tradition, like Sweden, Norway, and Denmark, tend to depend more on collective negotiations to settle differences of interest or of opinion than countries with a more rigid social structure; and thereby appear more professional. By contrast, class-conscious societies like Spain tend to leave collective bargaining methods for the lower echelons of the firm, with individual agreements for people in managerial positions, with the inevitable outcome that, to be effective, a leader 'should' be paternalistic.

The power of the spoken word

We have just referred to the implied presence of a 'class mentality' within firms in Latin countries and their possible connection with the power of the unwritten word. A closely related issue is the existence of an official company mission and strategy, and of the company's HR policy, either written or unwritten. Table 3.10 gives explicit information on how company policies are formulated and transmitted.

Table 3.10 Percentage of firms with stated policies

Availability of:	Latin	Central	Nordic
Written Statement of Company Mission	39	55	75
Unwritten Statement of Company Policy	34	24	12
No Statement of Company Policy	14	14	9
Written HR Policies	34	44	68
Unwritten HR Policies	42	33	20
No HR Policy Statement	15	19	10

Note: Values are percentage of firms having or not having written statements of Company or HR Policies.

The results of Table 3.10 show a fairly consistent pattern:

- Very few companies in European countries admit to the non-existence of official policies.

- Most European countries acknowledge the existence of official policies with as many saying that they are in writing as that they are unwritten.
- Scandinavian countries show a definite preference for having official written policies.
- Unwritten policies are slightly more common in Latin nations than in Northern and Central European countries.

A question worth raising is about the effects of written and unwritten policy statements. I shall point out only two. Written statements exert influence by the clarity of their ideas and carefully worded formulae, while oral communications are more powerful than the written word. They contain a double element: what is being said and the relation established by saying it in the presence of the other, thereby strengthening the forceful impact of oral communications. Second, written and spoken words are related to the exercise of authority in a subtle way. The written word commits people in authority to a defined course of action publicly known and acknowledged, thus restricting their discretionary powers. By contrast, unwritten policies are presumably known by everybody, but they are binding to the extent that the legitimate authorities choose to apply them to concrete situations. So, the power of their application or no application rests with the person in authority. It has the advantage of being official; yet it is left to the discretion of the 'boss' to invoke it and apply it at will.

If this is so, it is understandable that Scandinavian firms tend to have a more objective authority structure, while Latin firms tend to depend more on the manager's personal style of exerting power. The former is often perceived as professional, with the danger of being too cold and bureaucratic. The latter is more direct, with the obvious disadvantage of appearing arbitrary and not professional enough. When it is said that Latin countries need more professional management, I wonder to what extent what is actually meant is the need to relate to one another in a more transparent, non-manipulative way.

The democratisation role of the HR function

Closely related to the exercise of authority and to communication styles prevalent in organisations are the existence and persistence of an élite mentality. In discussing the tendency to centralise HR policy decisions and the methods of recruiting and rewarding managers, reference was made to the presence of a 'class mentality' within Latin organisations. My impression is that in such organisations there is a strong selective process, determining who is relating to whom and how. In spite of their obvious advantages, recruitment methods 'by word of mouth', and rewarding systems for managers through 'personal agreements', tend to create a vicious circle that reinforces this class mentality. A typical example of this 'professional swapping' was brought to my attention recently: the HR director of Food Company A went to Insurance Company B, displacing the HR director there, who eventually, within two months, ended up in the position in Food Company A of the person who had taken his place in Insurance Company B! It is like playing professionally the game of Musical Chairs. Through all this, a feeling is maintained and strengthened that one belongs to a privileged 'in-group' of a few qualified people well known to one another and going from one organisation to another, sure that they will always be wanted. This 'smugness' runs counter to the HR value system.

Furthermore, the attitude of firms in Latin countries to training is another example of having to depend on government to do the right thing. The results of Table 3.7 and 3.8 showed that firms in Central European and Nordic countries allocated more money per day of training than in Latin countries. With the exception of France, HR departments in Latin countries had to make do with less for more days of training. The impression that training is at best a tolerated activity is too strong to be discounted. One wonders what would be the situation in France had there not been this official patronage towards training. It is indeed paradoxical that while the French government has given so many economic incentives to encourage training, the Spanish government in 1990 was considering personal training as a taxable activity. What is a matter of concern is that organisations in both countries must be controlled from above and told what to do on something so vital as training and development.

What has just been mentioned may cast some doubt on whether organisations in Latin countries are run in a democratic spirit. I am inclined to think that Latin nations are democratic mostly politically, and still have a long way to go towards living by a genuine democratic spirit in all spheres of their life beyond the political. Some of the results already explained seem to point in this direction; there may be some historical reasons, too. After all, the history of Latin countries from the Renaissance to the present has not been an easy walk to democracy. Obviously, I am not pleading here that firms be run according to a parliamentary model. The parliamentary system is one thing; the democratic spirit is another, more fundamental and basic.

My contention is that, for all its deficiencies, the HR function springs from the democratic spirit, and that many of the difficulties experienced by the HR director and staff within a firm are large due to the peculiar position of the HR department. By its very work, it must stand between the pressure from management to achieve and get results, and the employees' natural resistances arising from their legitimate aspirations as human beings. To combine the two is to stand on the cutting edge of a sharp knife. It is almost impossible not to get hurt. Yet I believe that by standing there and getting hurt, HR departments contribute very effectively to the democratisation of a firm.

All institutions anywhere in the world are in need of more democratisation. The assumption underlying this chapter is that, because of their history, Latin countries have much more homework to do in this regard than most. Perhaps much of what I am saying is related to the Protestant ethic and the habit of hard work so glaringly absent in some regions of certain Latin countries.

CONCLUSION: A LATIN MODEL OR A STAGE OF GROWTH?

At the end of this long journey, we must pose the question: is there a Latin Model in the management of human resources?

There is no definite answer; and there may never be one. However, we have found some evidence for the existence of such a model. Its features may be not very clear or very consistent across all Latin countries; some may be even contradictory. However, if I were pushed to venture an opinion, I would very briefly emphasise the following points:

- the effort to modernise and professionalise the HR department;
- ambivalence in wishing with some reservations that HR departments play a more important role in the running of the firm;
- the need for HR professionals with a thorough grounding in organisational science and a full understanding of the psycho-social implications of organisational issues;
- a great dynamic potential of an oral culture because of its forthrightness and direct contacts among people;
- the presence of subtle hierarchical structures in firms unconsciously nurturing:
  - a docile and dependent attitude towards authority;
  - an undefined, but useful, vagueness about policy with the recognition of its existence, and the uncertainty of when it is to be applied;
- the mounting pressure for a more efficient and effective use of resources by
  - a more candid and transparent exercise of authority;
  - a greater emphasis on collaboration among people.

A key issue for employers and employees alike, in Spain and perhaps in other Latin countries too, is the realisation that social and organisational structures are primarily meant to bring and keep people together in order to achieve a set of objectives. This means that such structures are not ends in themselves, nor are they obstacles to put up with. Rather, they are to be looked upon as 'helpful instruments' to provide properly qualified and committed people with a congenial atmosphere of professional work and healthy human relations. Neither rigid bureaucracies nor anarchic explosions of enthusiasm are adequate answers to the serious problems firms have to face all over the world. I dare suggest, however, that Latin countries are in greater need of revising their views and unconscious assumptions on how organisations can be made into a well-knit network of useful channels for the expression of individual talents and aspirations.

To conclude, there is the impression that Central European and especially the Scandinavian countries are more sensitive to human issues within organisations than Latin nations. Are these different models of managing? Or are they different stages in the industrialisation process of a culture? Or both?

The approach adopted in this chapter may have given the impression that if any traits were found in the results of Latin countries, they were to be taken as evidence of a Latin Model. This need not be the case. It is possible, too, that the same traits may be found at a particular stage of any nation's socio-economic development. After all, at a very early stage financial problems are paramount in organisations; then the production problems, then the marketing problems, and later on, the problems of corporate strategy and of new technologies; and finally, the human problems. Many Central and Nordic European countries are well ahead in this process. Most regions in Latin countries are at present caught up in competitiveness issues and in the introduction of new technologies. They are now beginning to wrestle with human resource problems. Rather than of a Latin Model, therefore, we should perhaps speak of a Latin way of facing the Human Resource stage of socio-economic development. It is both a cultural set of traits and also an expected stage in a process.

REFERENCES

Freedman, A (1991) 'The Changing Human Resources Function'. Report no 950, The Conference Board, New York

Hofstede, G (1980) *Cultures Consequences: International Differences in World-related Values*, Sage Publications, London

'The Competitiveness Report-1990', (1990) The World Economic Forum, Geneva

4

HUMAN RESOURCE ASPECTS OF DECENTRALISATION AND DEVOLUTION*

Jacob Hoogendoorn, Erasmus University, Rotterdam, The Netherlands and Chris Brewster, Cranfield School of Management, UK

In this contribution we pay attention to the way in which organisations respond to an environment that is increasingly turbulent. Two of these responses, decentralisation and devolution, prove to be widespread and seem not to be limited to the present, but will most likely go on as an important process in the years to come. For human resource specialists this process creates both threats and opportunities: tasks and responsibilities could be lost to line management and thus cause a loss of influence, but the process might also facilitate concentration on those personnel tasks that really matter.

A note on terminology is necessary here. By 'decentralisation' we mean the allocation out to more local parts of the organisation of tasks formerly undertaken centrally. By 'devolution' we mean the allocation of tasks formerly undertaken by the personnel specialists to line managers. These are separate, though related, forms of organisational change.

THE CHANGING ENVIRONMENT

Customers, competitors and technologies are no longer what they used to be. Product preference, brand loyalty, consumer behaviour are only stable and predictable for a limited collection of products and services, like perhaps water and garbage collection. Other products, like beer, of which we had the impression that their life cycle would survive for

* This chapter first appeared in *Personnel Review*, Vol. 21, 1, 1992. Permission for its reproduction here is acknowledged with gratitude

generations, like beer, suddenly met new competitors, like beers without alcohol, and saw turnover and marketshare go down.

Internationalisation and globalisation imply that competitors we had never heard of enter our market and prove less ready to respect the understanding we had with traditional competitors on prices and marketshare distribution. Moreover, these competitors use more advanced technologies, have a lower cost price per product, ask lower prices from customers and still make more profit. They also invest more in research and development, are able to develop new products at a faster rate and are able to claim major market shares in high-margin, new product markets and still have healthier balance sheets as well.

And of course this is not all. New suppliers, much friendlier than our own staff, tell us we would do better to buy their products and services instead of making them ourselves and stimulate us to more frequent make-or-buy comparisons and decisions.

All these environmental developments put pressure on productivity development, quality development and product development. This means that human resource management has to devote more attention to manpower planning in order to foster productivity, performance appraisal to monitor quality and leadership styles, corporate culture and incentive policy to stimulate creativity and commitment to a high-paced product development.

Product development, new product introductions, changes in the production and sales mix, however, also imply that we need people with skills different from the skills needed previously. Flexibility and multi-skills are needed, or at least a budget for training and education to offer new skills. Unfortunately, flexibility is not only needed at this operational and individual level; it is also needed at the level of corporate strategy and human resource strategy.

MAKING AND CHANGING STRATEGIC POLICIES

In less turbulent times, policy making meant the formulation of objectives, means and time schedules on the basis of inventories of needs and possibilities, comparisons of costs and benefits and the systematic choice from a number of alternatives. Implementation of policies was not supposed to face more than the ordinary resistance to change and evaluation was possible against needs and objectives that were still more or less the same. With increasing turbulence, needs and possibilities on which policies are based change rapidly, as well as costs and benefits of activities and the nature and number of policy-alternatives. If inventories of needs and possibilities and other activities in the sphere of policy preparation take too much time, then actual policy making will take place on the basis of needs and possibilities that no longer exist. Those who are responsible for the implementation of policies created on this basis will realise that their efforts are less useful or useless, and will start to develop own policies, own objectives, means and time schedules. A major disparity between the theory of the formal central organisation and the practice of the material decentral organisation might develop this way.

Organisations which critically review their policy making will realise that they are unable to match the speed of environmental change. Reaching consensus on needs and possibilities, costs and benefits, alternatives and especially on objectives, means and time schedules, continues to take too much time as long as policy making takes place at central and high hierarchical levels. And in those cases where organisations succeed in frequently changing their central policies, this flexibility is often interpreted as a lack of consistency and of managerial control.

A faster run through the policy-making cycle, in other words, does not seem to be the answer to rapid environmental change. Improving planning activities or spending more time on planning does not seem to be the answer either, in case environmental uncertainty and unpredictability are increasing. Globalisation of policies, concentration on the main and more stable objectives, implies giving up the inspiration of a more detailed target-setting and the possibility of monitoring and appraisal of results in relation to these more specific targets.

Since doing away with policy making altogether is not a serious alternative either, (nobody would believe you really stopped it, and shareholders or trade unions would immediately claim mismanagement!) we have to decide that the only accurate answers to fast environmental change are efforts to increase flexibility and, above all, decentralisation. [Through decentralisation we formalise localised initiatives to repair the shortcomings of slow central policies and reduce the number of persons, levels and organisations involved in the altering of policies pertaining to the decentral unit.] By broadening the competences and responsibilities of decentralised management we give a most powerful motivational injection and make it easier for individuals to identify themselves into their unit ('my business', 'our business'). [By stipulating the need for self-reliance of the decentral unit, giving it an own balance sheet, profit and loss account and a clear profitability yardstick, we improve both central and decentral possibilities to monitor and appraise decentral performance.] And in case this performance is unsatisfactory, decentralisation makes it easier to cut the non-performing unit out of the organisation or to let the unit merge with the activities of other organisations)

In passing, we note that on a rather different measure of 'decentralisation' to local subsidiaries from multinational corporation headquarters (rather than our measure of decentralisation within the local organisation) a number of studies have found consistently that personnel was the least decentralised amongst the various functional areas of MNCs (Goehle 1980; Hedlund 1981; Welge 1981; Schuit *et al.* 1981; Von den Bulcke and Halsberghe 1984; Young, Hodd and Hamill 1985).

PERSONNEL ASPECTS OF DECENTRALISATION AND DEVOLVEMENT: EVIDENCE FROM THE NETHERLANDS

The transfer of responsibilities to decentral management needs good preparation and support by personnel management. Activities that are necessary involve the appraisal of potential for an increase in job requirements, the registration of interest and motivation for such a broadening of responsibilities, the setting-up of training activities to support new tasks and the appraisal of performance for those who meet new tasks and requirements.

Besides these more routine personnel tasks, personnel management may be required to intervene in order to prevent communication problems and the loss of synergy. Communication problems may easily arise if decentralisation is perceived as the freedom to stop communication within a group and to stop cooperation, loyalty and solidarity. So, for instance, liberalisation of purchasing policies might imply that purchase benefits are booked to be offset by losses in the rates of capital utilisation at sister-companies within a group. Especially when we also look at the costs of a drop in the utilisation rate, such as costs of negotiation, dismissals, image loss, loss of customers, loss of labour market status and productivity losses due to conflict, uncontrolled decentralisation and liberalisation may become a costly affair.

[Decentralisation risks are also present if central tasks are allocated to decentral employees who already have a full, or more than full, workload.] In such a case the new, formerly central tasks get a low priority from those who are decentrally responsible; in effect, this may imply that decentralisation equals a liquidation of tasks or at least a serious loss in the quality of performance.]

When we look at the decentralisation of personnel tasks, the risk of quality losses seems clearly present. In a Dutch survey (Petter, Schuchman, van Voorneveld and Yspeert 1990) decentralisation proved to be a widespread phenomenon: 58.7 per cent of the respondents had gone through decentralisation processes during the 1985–1990 period and 66.7 per cent expected more decentralisation during the 1990–1995 period. (Centralisation had been experienced by 6.7 per cent and was expected by 12.9 per cent in the years to come.) In the past five years 34.2 per cent had seen no change, but for the next five years only 19.1 per cent expected no change.

In most of these cases decentralisation was not only a deconcentration of personnel officers from central to decentral desks, but was also a transfer of personnel staff tasks to line management, ie in our terms, devolvement. That this transfer could not be expected to be a success was definitely the conviction of the respondents, the personnel and organisation managers of larger organisations. They were in the majority (73.8 per cent) confident that line managers were interested in personnel tasks, although 22.7 per cent lacked this confidence. However, another majority (77.3 per cent) thought that line management did not have the personnel management knowledge and skills to properly execute personnel tasks; only 16 per cent thought that these skills and knowledge were sufficiently available.

Another answer was just as alarming: 59.1 per cent thought that line management had not sufficient time to take responsibility for personnel tasks, whereas 33.8 per cent thought that time would not create a problem. Finally readiness to give personnel tasks more priority was not expected by 62.6 per cent, while 29.3 per cent expected line management to be ready to do so.

A training firm which observed these survey results came to the optimistic conclusion that the absence of personnel management knowledge and skills among line managers could be the hole in the market they had been looking for. After a major mail-out and a response of less than 1 to 1000, they concluded that line managers did not only have no time for personnel tasks, but even had no time for training to learn the skills needed.

Another survey, in the Netherlands, examined the appraisal of the performance of personnel managers by line management. Results in this survey were not more positive than in the previous one: 57.9 per cent of the line managers were dissatisfied and had the opinion that the personnel departments were poor (Tissen, 1991). This dissatisfaction may contribute to a process of contracting out of activities, a logical follow-up if the possibilities of decentralisation and delegation are exhausted. This contracting out of tasks is growing rapidly: 27 per cent of Dutch organisations spend more than half a million guilders on services by external parties in domains like training and education, job evaluation, salary administration, recruitment and selection and outplacement (Petter, Schuchman, van Voorneveld and Yspeert 1990). The external job growth in personnel jobs seems bigger now than internal job growth.

PERSONNEL ASPECTS OF DEVOLVEMENT ACROSS EUROPE

Against these examples from one country we set data from ten different European countries, where we attempted to assess the extent of devolvement on a comparative basis.

Defining and identifying devolvement is far from straightforward, but two issues seem to be indicative: the extent to which line managers are involved in certain HR practices; and the related issue of how many personnel specialists there are for given total numbers of employees. (There are, of course, many related issues; we have already, for example, noted in the Dutch case the issue of the degree to which line managers are trained to undertake these responsibilities.) We established a straightforward ordering of the degree of devolvement common to each country by ranking every country on each of the six items and then conflating the rankings. Though this loses some of the detail, it does provide a comparative rating of the various countries. The results show some fascinating variations.

Denmark and Switzerland are revealed as the two countries in which devolvement is most typical. Denmark is consistently ranked first or second on all issues. Switzerland is always amongst the four countries with most widespread devolution — except on industrial relations, where most of the countries are clustered at the 'less devolved' end of the spectrum.

Sweden and the Netherlands are next in line with less widespread devolution, but still consistently above the mean level. Interestingly, both countries rate amongst those where most organisations have increased the authority of line managers in recent years. They would appear to be moving fast, and consistently, towards greater devolution.

Five of the ten countries (in order, Germany, Spain, France, Norway and the UK) then form a block of countries at, or just below, the 'devolution average'. There are some variations within this group despite the close overall ranking. Over the last three years Germany has had, on all issues, fewest organisations devolving responsibility further to the line managers. This fits the common stereotypes of German employers as conservative and stable. Spain has the greatest variation: it is the most devolved country on pay issues, the least devolved on health and safety and with a wide range on other issues. This is perhaps not surprising in a country which has only comparatively recently emerged from a long period of Fascist dictatorship and with a booming and highly differentiated economy. Consistency in such circumstances is difficult. Amongst the other countries, France would count as having a considerably more controlling personnel function except for a high devolvement ranking on pay and conditions; Norway, like Sweden although not as fast, is moving rapidly in the direction of devolution; and the UK, despite a substantial feeling amongst managers in the country that line management now has more authority, is ranked as one of the least devolved countries in our sample.

Table 4.1 Devolvement of personnel functions — ten-country ranking

High	DK	CH	S	NL	D	E	F	N	UK	I	Low

Italy is a case on its own. It is, by a clear margin, the country in which fewest organisations have devolved authority for HR issues to the line. It ranks at the least devolved end on five of the six items — and second from the end on the other one. Furthermore, as one might expect given that finding, it is one of the few countries to match Germany in making the least move towards decentralisation over the last three years.

Table 4.2 Devolvement and proportion of personnel functionaries

Devolvement	DK	CH	S	NL	D	E	F	N	UK	I
Personnel functionaries per 1000 employees	10.7	12.5	15.6	18.5	14.5	14.9	13.8	12.8	13.9	18.2

There is, as one would expect, a close correlation between the devolvement ranking and the number of personnel specialists per thousand employees on average. Table 4.2 indicates clearly, for example, that the two most devolved countries, Denmark and Switzerland, have the lowest number of personnel specialists; the least centralised country, Italy, one of the highest number. Switzerland and the Netherlands stand out as being amongst the more devolved countries, but still having considerable numbers of personnel specialists.

These rankings show an interesting contrast with the influence of national or regional level bargaining on pay (Hegewisch 1991). Table 4.3 uses the example of manual workers' pay; pay for other levels is more complex to illustrate as the categories often vary between countries, but shows similar rankings. The northern European countries (Germany*, Denmark, Norway, Netherlands, and Sweden) are most likely to have pay bargaining centralised above the organisational level. In broad terms there is a distinct (though low level) correlation between centralisation of pay bargaining outside the organisation, and devolution within it. This raises two interesting alternative explanations. One is that the perceptions of devolution that we have reported above — for a range of HR topics — are not reflected in reality: that it only seems as if there is devolution, but it is, in practice, highly circumscribed. The other explanation is that it is within a clearly established and predictable framework of labour costs that line managers are best able to accept and undertake a substantial role in human resource matters. The authors of this chapter lean towards the second explanation, but accept that our evidence leaves this an open question.

Table 4.3 Devolvement and pay determination for manual workers

Devolvement	DK	CH	S	NL	D	E	F	N	UK	I
Pay determination above organisational level (manual workers) %	79	—	76	78	—	59	41	99	45	61

Interestingly, we find little evidence that organisations are training their line managers to handle human resource issues. There is no clear correlation between the amount of training in human resource issues received by managers and devolution. We identified the number of organisations which had trained at least a third of the managers in such HR techniques as performance appraisal, communications, delegation, motivation and team-building. In none of these topics are the numbers in any country which had done such training correlated with the devolution

---

* Germany is excluded from the percentages as the question was not asked in that country. The researchers, and the advisory panel there, believed that since nearly all pay bargaining in Germany is conducted at the national industry level the question would be seen as irrelevant.

ranking. Denmark, for example, the most devolved country, is amongst those countries where line managers are least trained; Norway and the UK have considerable numbers of organisations training over a third of their managers in HR techniques, even though they are amongst the least devolved.

At the national comparative level it is clear that devolution of personnel functions is a widespread phenomenon, that it varies by degree in the different countries, but that there is some evidence of a common trend, across Europe, towards increases in devolution.

BACK TO THE CORE?

As decentralisation processes gather speed, only a few tasks tend to survive centrally. If the central capacity available for these tasks is also limited, then we are forced to concentrate on those tasks that are most important and cannot easily be decentralised. Such tasks could, for instance, be management development tasks and tasks related to company-wide collective bargaining duties. Next we have strategic tasks like environmental scanning, competitor analysis and corporate comparisons of human resource policies. Then there are also tasks to do with giving a central incentive to decentral policy development and evaluation of the quality of decentral human resource policies. Another task that might continue centrally is the provision of human resource information.

Where the responsibility for the personnel information system remains central, clear divisions of tasks are necessary for central and decentral inputs, download possibilities for central inputs, upload possibilities for decentral inputs, guarantees against illegal access and abuse of information, and the use of expertise that is either centrally or decentrally available. Most important, however, is that limited capacity forces us to determine what the most important personnel tasks are. In looking for these most important themes, projects or tasks, we should nevertheless not have the illusion that once we have determined what is the most important now will still be the most important next year. A survey looking to rank 25 tasks and 75 requirements for knowledge, skills and attitudes and also looking to indicate ranking expectations for the same items after five years, showed that 96 out of 100 items changed place (Hoogendoorn, 1987). Evidently information needs will change should there be a change in human resource management priorities. The advantage of a serious decentralisation process is that we no longer have to pretend that central and decentral human resource priorities are identical. Nor do we have to strike a compromise in case central and decentral priorities seem to be inconsistent. Indeed, that means that a loss of uniformity in HR policies within one company may occur. For personnel management this implies another task: to explain that central and decentral environment and organisation ask for different policies and to explain that pluriformity is not the same as injustice!

REFERENCES

Goehle, DG (1980) 'Decision Making in Multinational Corporations', University of Michigan research paper, Ann Arbor, MI

Hedlund, G (1981) 'Autonomy of Subsidiaries and Formalisation of Headquarters-Subsidiary Relations in Swedish MNCs', in Otterbeck, L (ed), *The Management of Headquarters-Subsidiary Relations in Multinational Corporations*, Gower, Aldershot

Hegewisch, A (1991) 'The Decentralisation of Pay Bargaining: European Comparisons', *Personnel Review*, vol 20, no 6, pp 29–36

Hoogendoorn, J (1987) 'Veranderende eisen aan personeelmanagement', in Maandblad, PW (ed), *Voor personeelmanagement en arbeidsverhoudingen*

Petter, JHL, Schuchman, E, van Voorneveld, H and Yspeert, K (1990) Carrieres in PZ, Report, Graduate School of Management, Erasmus University, Rotterdam

Schuit, J *et al.* (1981) *Centralisatie versus decentralisatie in internationale ondernemingen: een multifunctionele benadering*, Erasmus University, Rotterdam

Tissen, R (1991) *Mensen beter managen*, Kluwer, Deventer

Van den Bulke, D and Halsberghe, E (1984) Employment Decision-making in Multinational Enterprises: Survey Results from Belgium, Working Paper 32, International Labour Office, Geneva

Young, S, Hood, N and Hamill, J (1985) Decision Making in Foreign-owned Multinational Subsidiaries in the United Kingdom, Working Paper 35, International Labour Office, Geneva

5

THE DECENTRALISATION OF PAY BARGAINING: EUROPEAN COMPARISONS*

Ariane Hegewisch, Cranfield School of

Management, UK

For most organisations labour costs are the major element of operating costs, and for this reason alone reward policies play a crucial role in the strategic behaviour of organisations. Furthermore, the pay package is one of the most obvious and visible expressions of the employment relationship; it is the main issue in the exchange between employer and employee, expressing the connection between the labour market, the individual's work and the performance of the employing organisation itself. It expresses internal hierarchies, defines performance and plays a role in motivating and rewarding.

However, more than almost any other tool of human resource management, pay policies have been the subject of collective bargaining and employment legislation. Particularly during the seventies, strong trade unions in Europe were able to keep pay in the arena of collective bargaining. Furthermore, inflationary pressures made pay policies one of the key elements in macro-economic policy, hence restricting the extent to which pay policies were available as a tool in human resource management (Baglioni 1990, Marsden 1989).

During the last decade, factors such as high levels of unemployment and the decline in manufacturing employment combined to reduce the traditional power-base of trade unions in many European countries, a trend supported in some states by employment legislation which reduced the power of collective action. At the same time the general level of inflation remained low and, with lower absolute increases required to

* This chapter first appeared in *Personnel Review*, vol. 20, 6, 1991. Permission for its reproduction here is acknowledged with gratitude.

maintain real wages, there was increased scope for employers to link pay policies to profitability, productivity and individual performance.

Received good practice in human resource management now stresses the need to make pay more responsive to individual and company performance and to remove it from the collective bargaining arena into the field of individual accountability (see, for example, Armstrong and Murlis 1989; Gilbert 1991). In practice this has translated into recommendations for a greater share of performance-related pay elements in the pay package and recommendations for a decentralisation of decision-making on pay issues so that pay determination can be more closely harmonised with the financial performance of the employer and reflect local labour market conditions.

The Price Waterhouse Cranfield Project enables us to establish how widespread these trends are among British employers, and whether Britain is following similar trends as other European countries. The survey examines pay practices from several angles: levels of negotiations on pay; performance-related pay elements, and the changing responsibility of line managers for pay issues.

LEVELS OF PAY NEGOTIATIONS

The last decade has seen a dramatic change in pay bargaining in Britain, prompting some observers to speak of 'the culmination of a process of collapse of multi-employer bargaining' (Purcell 1991, p 37). The pay of manual workers traditionally is most influenced by national or industrywide collective bargaining. While overall still over a third of UK respondents are involved in national or industrywide collective bargaining, this is now increasingly restricted to the public sector. Less than a quarter of private sector employers say that they are involved in national or industry-wide collective bargaining over basic pay, whereas over 80 per cent of public sector employers negotiate at this level. See Table 5.1.

Throughout this chapter and in all tables the following definitions are used:

- Private sector organisations are those which classified themselves as 'publicly limited company', 'trust or co-operative' or 'other private sector'. The number of private sector respondents for each country is: Denmark, 294; France, 796; Germany, 817; Italy, 166; Netherlands, 171; Norway, 120; Spain, 259; Sweden, 169; Switzerland, 168; UK, 1029.
- Public sector respondents here are defined as public administration

only (including local and central government; public healthcare; higher education). The number of public sector respondents for each country is: Denmark, 141; France, 66; Germany, 20; Italy, 2; Netherlands, 42; Norway, 111; Spain, 21; Sweden, 92; Switzerland, 18; UK, 314.

- Responses from nationalised industries, other public corporations and respondents who just classified themselves as 'other' are not included in private/public sector breakdowns.

A look at the manufacturing industry shows the extent of the decline in this practice. Only 10 per cent of metal manufacturing employers in 1990–91 say they bargain at national level, reflecting the collapse of the national agreement of the Engineering Employers Federation in 1990; in the remaining manufacturing industry the proportion is higher at 26 per cent. This presents a dramatic fall since 1984 when, according to the WIRS survey* (even if the two surveys are not strictly comparable) the proportion of national or regional bargaining for manual workers was still 50 per cent in the manufacturing industry (Millward and Stevens 1986, p 232). The decline might be even steeper if the exclusion of small employers in the PWCP survey is taken into account; according to the PWCP data, national or industrywide collective bargaining is twice as important for employers with 2000 and more employees as it is for employers with between 200 and 500 employees (32 per cent and 16 per cent respectively).

As can be seen from Table 5.2, Britain and France are alone in the low level of national or industrywide bargaining. In both France and Britain, employers' federations have strongly encouraged the move away from multi-employer bargaining. For example, CNPF, the French employers' federation, since 1984 has refused to issue central pay guidelines in order to encourage company level bargaining. According to CNPF, the numbers of company level agreements in France rose from 2000 in 1982 to 6400 in 1988. Similarly to CNPF, the French engineering employers' federation, UIMM, has also not set a rate in central negotiations since 1987. This

---

* The PWCP survey was addressed to the highest organisational level within organisations; it includes subsidiaries and divisions, but not single establishments. The WIRS surveys, on the other hand, carried out interviews at establishment/workplace level; therefore company-level information cannot be compared. The PWCP survey asked respondents to indicate all levels of pay determination involved in decisions on basic pay. The WIRS survey had an additional question asking which level had been the most important in the last pay round; this question was not included in the PWCP questionnaire.

Table 5.1 Determination of basic pay for manual workers in the UK (percentage of organisations)

	Total	Manufacture (metal)	Manufacture (other)	Public Sector
National/industry	22	10	26	82
Regional	9	7	12	4
Company	37	37	38	15
Establishment/site	40	62	44	11
Individual	8	12	4	1%

Note: Respondents: private sector= 1029; metal manufacturing:259; other manufacturing: 241; retail, hotel and catering: 145; banking and finance: 123; public sector= 314

Table 5.2 Levels of basic pay determination in the private sector for manual workers (percentage of organisations)

Country	DK	E	F	I	N	NL	S	UK
National/industrywide collective bargaining	53	42	24	59	66	75	69	22
Regional collective bargaining	23	19	11	2	18	na	6	7
Company	6	21	50	45	24	24	36	37
Establishment/site	8	17	27	12	21	8	15	40
Individual	13	8	16	9	20	9	12	8

Note: Respondents as in 'private sector' definition, p 87

support for local bargaining, however, does not extend to managerial staff where UIMM continues to provide reference points for salary scales and increments. This is interesting as managerial and executive pay in other countries is generally the most decentralised area of white-collar settlements. It gives an indication of the resilience of the traditionally hierarchical approach to pay in France, which is strongly linked to educational attainments, age and seniority (IDS Focus 1989).

In European countries other than France and the UK, multi-employer bargaining continues to predominate. In Sweden, for example, in 1983 the engineering employers' federation VF started to sign agreements with individual white-collar unions, as well as with the manual metal workers' union. In 1984 the general employers' federation SAF only concluded industry-level agreements with the manual workers union federation LO.

However, the pattern for the rest of the decade was rather mixed, with centralised accords in some years and industry-specific bargaining in others. After announcing their permanent withdrawal from national negotiations in 1990, SAF subsequently agreed for 1991–92 for example to a national policy which limited pay increases to 4.2 per cent and prohibited local wage bargaining (EIRR 1991). Commentators expect that the newly elected Conservative government will dissolve these national tripartite bodies for the next pay round in 1992 (Söderström 1992). As can be seen from Table 5.2, company level bargaining in Sweden is quite significant for manual workers; this illustrates the fact that the central accords operate by establishing a wage floor rather than the going rate which is negotiated on top: 'Many blue collar workers in private industry and commerce earn more through the combination of local agreement excesses and individual wage supplements, collectively known as wage drift, than they do as a result of central agreements.' (Ahlén 1989 pp. 337).

In Denmark, the combination of a conservative government since the early 1980s and high unemployment have similarly weakened the central bargaining structures for white and blue collar unions, with an increase in industrywide bargaining. However, company level bargaining is much less significant than in Norway or Sweden.

COMPANY AND ESTABLISHMENT LEVEL PAY DETERMINATION

In all countries, company level bargaining is more frequent than pay determination at establishment or plant level. This is so for all staff groups; the only exception is pay determination for manual workers in the UK. Basic pay negotiations directly with the individual are relatively rare for manual workers, but become increasingly significant as one moves up the non-manual staff hierarchies. Interestingly, the lowest level of individual bargaining for the managerial group takes place in France where less than a third of respondents overall, and only 38 per cent of private sector respondents negotiate with managers directly. The general response across the other countries varies from 39 per cent in the Netherlands to 83 per cent in Switzerland. This again confirms the continued strength of notions of managerial hierarchy and comparability in France, mentioned above. Individual pay determinations are not limited to managerial staff; over a quarter of employers in Denmark, Italy, Norway and Sweden, and two-thirds of employers in Switzerland, say that individual negotiations play a role in the determination of basic pay of clerical staff.

Overall, however, the extent of decentralisation of pay determination to local level, and consequently a direct response to local performance or labour market conditions, remains limited. This is confirmed by a related aspect of pay determinations, the locus of control of pay decisions within organisations.

Table 5.3 Level at which pay policies are mainly determined within corporations and multi-site organisations (percentage of organisations)

Country	CH	D	DK	E	F	I	N	NL	S	UK
International HQ	23	13	11	15	8	21	5	13	3	11
National HQ	54	45	53	64	57	67	66	55	49	42
Subsidiary	17	35	27	10	24	6	19	16	31	17
Site/establishment	5	8	9	11	11	6	10	10	18	23

Note: Respondents: CH= 133; D= 521; DK= 223; E= 137; F= 578; I= 140; N= 83; NL= 83; S= 143; UK= 734

The survey shows that across Europe the majority of multi-divisional or multi-site private sector employers continue to take major policy decisions on pay matters at national or international headquarters (see Table 5.3). The highest level of decentralisation to subsidiary level within companies (35 per cent) can be found in Germany which arguably has experienced less pressure on established bargaining levels than most other countries in the study. Thus the comparatively high level of decision-making at subsidiary level is more likely to be an expression of the existing German industrial relations system, which places the responsibility for the negotiations of the exact implementation of centrally determined 'framework' agreements at the level of the workplace, rather than an expression of a more recent change towards more local accountability. Framework agreements in Germany are negotiated between industrial trade unions and employers' federations and are binding on all employers who are members of the relevant employers' federation, thus covering nine out of ten employers. While there have been some highly publicised decisions by certain employers, notably in the publishing industry, to leave the employers' federation and negotiate directly with relevant trade unions, these have remained marginal.

The highest level of centralisation can be found in Italy and Spain. In the case of the latter, this is probably a sign of Spain's relatively recent economic development and the predominance of foreign multinational companies among larger firms who are exerting tighter control over their Spanish operations.

The move towards decentralisation of decision-making again seems to have gone furthest in the UK, where over a quarter of private sector respondents say that the establishment or site is the main locus for pay policy decisions. However, this proportion is much lower than the number of employers who say that pay is determined at establishment or site level. This result thus confirms the research by Marginson *et al.* about the extent of headquarters control over the outcomes of decentralised pay bargaining, leading to so-called 'establishment illusion' (Marginson *et al.* 1988, pp 251) where a functional shift in bargaining structures is not accompanied by an actual decentralisation of power. It could also be interpreted as support for the assumption that the decentralisation of the bargaining process has been accompanied by a streamlining of pay policy decisions and the introduction of tighter financial control systems (Brown and Walsh 1991, p 51). As the PWCP survey addressed the organisational level, rather than establishments or sites within companies, it is not possible to compare the perceptions of respondents from plant and headquarters levels, and thus compare, as Marginson *et al.* did, whether perceptions of the implications and the extent of a shift in power differed between headquarters and plant level managers. In so far as the survey reflects only the views of managers in headquarters or subsidiaries who, according to Marginson, tend to see the decentralisation as more limited in practice, the results are more likely not to show 'establishment illusion' and to illustrate a real increase in decentralisation.

VARIABLE AND PERFORMANCE-RELATED PAY

Thus it appears, both from the PWCP survey and from other research, that the extent of responsiveness to local conditions, especially labour market conditions, remains limited in the determination of basic pay levels. Apart from the negotiations of annual wage increases, however, employers have various other instruments for responding to labour market pressures, such as the level at which new recruits are appointed, benefit packages and performance-related pay. Over two-thirds of employers in Italy, the Netherlands, Spain, and the UK had increased pay and benefits in response to recruitment difficulties (see Table 5.4). Only in the Scandinavian countries is this proportion less than 50 per cent, and even there this course has been taken by at least four out of ten employers.

The figures also show the particular competitive labour market pressures faced by public sector employers in most European countries. Germany provides an interesting exception to the general trend. The German public sector has faced comparatively less pressures for reforms

Table 5.4 Offer of increased pay and benefits in response to recruitment difficulties (percentage of organisations)

Country	Private sector	Public sector
Denmark	44	53
France	63	44
Germany	60	5
Italy	78	na
Netherlands	68	65
Norway	33	64
Spain	73	37
Sweden	39	40
Switzerland	59	45
UK	68	74

Note: For respondent numbers, see p 87

of personnel practices than other European countries. Mobility between the private and the public sector is comparatively low. In addition, since the 1960s German public sector legislation explicitly prevents regionally negotiated pay additions in response to labour market pressures, because these were seen as contrary to the general principle of public service (Blenk 1987, p 51).

Our data does not establish clearly what forms the pay and benefit increases have taken. However, there is also a strong trend toward the greater importance of variable pay elements in the reward package, with a positive correlation between those organisations who say that variable pay increased and those who used pay and benefits in response to recruitment difficulties.

Over half of private sector respondents in France, Germany, Italy, Spain, Sweden and Switzerland said that variable pay had become more important in the total pay package during the last three years (see Table 5.5). One indication of the use of variable pay in response to economic circumstances is the drop between the first and second years of the survey in the number of Swedish private sector respondents increasing variable pay from 82 per cent in 1989–90 to 57 per cent in 1990–91. In the Swedish public sector the proportion of respondents increasing variable pay fell from 93 per cent to 48 per cent of public sector employers. In 1989–90 Sweden was operating with a very tight labour market with rates of unemployment around 1 per cent. Since then Sweden, like the UK,

Table 5.5 Variable pay: a steady rise (percentage of organisations)

Country	Private sector	Public sector
Denmark	32	85
France	51	22
Germany	54	17
Italy	67	na
Netherlands	29	48
Norway	40	9
Spain	60	57
Sweden	57	48
Switzerland	57	40
UK	45	56

Denmark and Norway, has faced a severe recession and rapidly rising rates of unemployment.

The differences between private and public sector trends confirm the developments in the use of pay and benefits for recruitment purposes. The different size of the trends between public and private sector employers in countries such as Denmark, the Netherlands and the UK point again to the competitive labour market pressures which public sector employers have been under. These have induced public sector employers to think of innovative ways of responding to private sector pay trends; they also illustrate various reform programmes aimed at public sector management, and the introduction of some private sector practices. Such pressures for reforms have been less marked in countries such as Germany and France. In France, moreover, public sector employers operate within quite strictly cash limited budgets which make it harder to increase the share of variable pay.

MERIT AND PERFORMANCE-RELATED PAY

Maybe the most interesting development in the area of variable pay is the extent of merit and/or performance-related pay (Table 5.6). Merit/performance-related pay is particularly frequent in France, Italy, Switzerland and the UK, whereas the practice remains rather marginal in the Scandinavian countries. While merit/performance-related pay is predictably most frequent among the managerial and professional staff groups, in countries such as France, Italy and the UK it is no longer limited to them. For example, 42 per cent of French private sector respondents in 1989–1990 said that they used merit pay *individualisation* in the remuneration of manual workers, 32 per cent of Italian private sector employers, and — slightly lower but still substantial — 27 per cent of UK private sector employers. The number of employers who include clerical workers is even higher.

The extent of all-merit increases appears to be limited. The PWCP survey itself did not establish whether or not employers had introduced all-merit increases, but a recent survey by IRS found that 17 per cent of UK companies use all-merit increases, whereas the majority of employers have schemes where pay increases are based on a mixture of a general cost-of-living increase and an individual performance-related increase. IRS also found that in 1990 companies with all-merit increases on average allocated slightly under 10 per cent of the pay bill to merit increases, while in companies with a mixed system the proportion fell to 2 per cent (IRS 1991, p 43). In other words, most merit awards remain rather marginal in relation to the total wage package.

In France, it is estimated that merit-increases account for a quarter to a third of total annual increases. Contrary to practice in the UK, individual increases in France also tend to reflect formally the acquisition of training and educational qualifications (IDS Focus 1989, p 7). In Italy, the use of merit pay has grown similarly rapidly; it is estimated that between 1983 and 1988 the share of merit-pay in the wage package of white-collar workers increased from 13 per cent to 20 per cent, much higher than in France or the UK (IDS Focus 1989, p 10). However, there is less evidence that the introduction of merit pay has brought about a fundamental shift towards a performance culture. Rather it has been used as a response to centrally negotiated pay structures which in France as well as in Italy in the late 1970s and early 1980s emphasised the pay levels of lower paid workers and thus led to a flattening of differentials and wage scales (Marsden 1989, IDS Focus 1989). There is also evidence to show the labour market sensitivity of merit pay, given, for example, that merit pay in the Paris region is much higher than in other regions of France (IDS Focus 1989, p 7).

The practice of merit and performance-pay is no longer limited to the private sector. This is especially so in the UK where recent attempts to introduce private sector criteria for cost-effectiveness and profitability into public sector management have led to the introduction of performance criteria, particularly for pay decisions concerning managerial staff. Sixty-three per cent of employers in public administration in the UK said that they use merit pay in the managerial group, and even for clerical staff this proportion is 23 per cent. In this area the UK has developed much faster than France where in 1989–90 only 21 per cent of public sector employers had introduced merit/performance-related pay for managerial staff (Hegewisch 1991, p 7). The French government had also tried to introduce merit pay into the public sector but, after severe industrial relations problems in the late 1980s, slowed down its efforts.

Table 5.6   Merit/performance-related pay (percentage of organisations per staff group)

	CH	D	DK	E	F[†][*]	I	N	NL	S	UK
Managerial	65	24	14	48	70	85	18	27	13	68
Professional/	66	42	18	58		86	16	29	12	58
Technical[@]	62	41[#]							12	
Clerical	57	38	13	39	60	72	11	27	11	46
Manual[#]	56	32	19	33	41	32	15	27	32	23

[*]French figures are for 1989–90
[†]In France, 'managerial' (*Cadre*) includes some professional staff; clerical (ETAM) includes some technical and supervisory staff;
[@]In all countries apart from CH and S, 'professional/ technical' are one category; in CH and S the two categories are listed separately.
[#]In D, 'manual' only refers to semi- and unskilled workers; the frequency for skilled workers (*Facharbeiter*) is given in the 'technical' row.

LINE MANAGEMENT RESPONSIBILITY FOR PAY ISSUES

The growth of performance-related pay and of decentralised and individual bargaining puts greater responsibility on individual line managers. Unsurprisingly, then, the responsibility of line managers for pay issues has increased over the last three years. The trend is most marked in Sweden where 55 per cent of employers say that line management responsibility has increased. The numbers are high because Sweden has traditionally had very centralised bargaining structures and has only recently begun to move away from them. In the context of the debates on the shift of power entailed in the decentralisation of bargaining, the low British response is particularly interesting, confirming perhaps the hypothesis that the decentralisation of bargaining, has not been accompanied by an equivalent decentralisation of decision-making power.

The results for the public sector once again illustrate the pressures on public sector management practices, particularly in the Netherlands, Sweden and the UK, and the isolation from such pressures in Germany.

Table 5.7   Increase in line management responsibility for pay issues over the last three years (percentage of organisations)

Country	Private sector	Public sector
Denmark	16	21
France	45	21
Germany	15	2
Italy	35	na
Netherlands	30	39
Norway	30	29
Spain	40	45
Sweden	55	87
Switzerland	38	10
UK	23	39

Note: For respondents, see p 87

CHANGE IN THE MANAGEMENT RELATIONSHIP

What is at issue in the discussions of the decentralisation of pay bargaining, however, is not only whether there has been an increase in the responsiveness of bargaining to local corporate performance and labour market conditions. Equally important is the effect of such a change on the employment relation and the role of line managers. This issue is touched on by Kinnie in a recent article where he criticises the focus of the British decentralisation debates on the issue of whether there has been a real or illusionary change in the distribution of decision-making power between headquarters and establishment managers. Kinnie points out that such a focus on 'organisational aspects of changes to management and bargaining structures' neglects the 'distinct industrial relations perspective which considers how such changes were perceived by both managers at various levels and employees and their representatives', and the interest that local as well as headquarters managers have in protecting the impressions of establishment autonomy in bargaining (Kinnie 1989, p 32).

Arguably, the motivation for decentralisation is as much a greater responsiveness to local economic circumstances as a shift in the control over the employment relationship from employees and their representatives to managers, a reassertion of 'management's right to manage'. Indeed, the introduction of merit and performance-related pay is often discussed in this context. Even if, as many studies show, managers are often reluctant to use this tool — as evidenced for example by the persistent averaging of employees as 'above average' in performance ratings — the performance review by line managers of their subordinates nevertheless reinforces traditional work hierarchies. Incidentally, this is one of the reasons why some management gurus, such as Rosabeth Kanter, are critical of merit pay (IDS Top Pay Unit 1990, p 10); she feels it is conservative, unfair, expensive and often demotivates employees.

It should be noted that the introduction of merit or performance-related pay schemes is often just as much aimed at a change in the behaviour of managers (to make them more target-conscious and focus their attention on employee management) as it is at a change in employee performance and attitudes.

Decentralisation of pay bargaining involves major changes in resource allocation for the bargaining partners, particularly for trade unions, as is confirmed, for example, by Jackson and Leopold (1990) in their case study of the introduction of plant level bargaining in Coats Viyella. The decentralisation of collective bargaining to local levels leaves employee representatives with a formal role, even if the fragmentation of bargaining puts great strains on trade union resources. Merit/performance-related pay, however, individualises bargaining to such an extent that it almost excludes trade unions. The role of trade unions changes from active bargaining partner to support for individual employees during appeals, even if (IRS 1991), most organisations with merit pay schemes do not have formal appeal procedures, and an overall monitoring of the pay outcomes.

In general, the discussion of changes in pay determination might benefit from a greater integration of the analysis of developments in formal negotiations with discussions of their impact on the employee relationship. This is particularly so with regard to variable and perfor-mance-related pay. The extent of increase in variable pay, and of merit/performance-related pay in countries such as France, Italy and the UK, or of individually negotiated pay as in Sweden, also indicate that there is likely to have been a response to labour market pressures. In other words, the absence of formal regional bargaining in most countries does not preclude geographical responsiveness to labour market pressures, even if this is often achieved by more *ad hoc* means.

CONCLUSION

Compared with other European countries, the decentralisation of pay bargaining away from nationally negotiated rates to company or even plant level bargaining has gone furthest in the UK. This is particularly so considering the continually high level of trade union membership and trade union recognition in Britain in comparison, for example, with France, where there also has been an increase in company level bargaining. However, France and the UK are not alone in having seen pressures for decentralisation in existing bargaining structures, even if elsewhere these have not led to the break-up of multi-employer bargaining structures. Germany appears to be the only country to have been relatively immune to these trends.

Additionally, employers across Europe, in the public as well as private sector, are putting greater emphasis on variable pay elements in the remuneration package and appear to be supplementing traditional, collectively negotiated pay policies with more individually determined pay packages and a greater emphasis on performance-related elements. It remains to be seen whether these trends represent long-term shifts in the nature of reward policies or whether they merely are the expression of a more short-term response to labour market shortages.

REFERENCES

Ahlén, K (1989) 'Swedish collective bargaining under pressure: inter-union rivalry and incomes policies', *British Journal of Industrial Relations*, vol 27–3, Nov, pp 330–46

Armstrong, J and Murlis, H (1991) *Reward Management: A Handbook of Salary Administration*, 3rd ed, Kogan Page

Baglioni, G (1990) 'Industrial relations in Europe in the 1980s', in Baglioni and Crouch, C. (eds.), *European Industrial Relations: The challenge of flexibility*, Sage, London

Blenk, W (1987) 'Labour relations in the public service in the FRG', in Treu, T (ed), *Public Service Labour Relations: recent trends and future prospects*, ILO, Geneva

Brown, W and Walsh, J (1991) 'Pay determination in Britain in the 1980s; the anatomy of decentralisation' *Oxford Review of Economic Policy*, vol 7, no 1, pp 44–59

European Industrial Relations Review (EIRR) (1991) 'Sweden: Industrial Relations Background', September, pp 24–8

Gilbert, R (1991) 'Pay flexibility in the private sector', in Public Finance Foundation, *International Pay Policies*, Discussion paper 39 (Conference proceedings)

Hegewisch, A (1991) 'European comparisons in reward policies: the findings of the first Price Waterhouse Cranfield Survey', Cranfield School of Management Working paper SWP 65/91

IDS Focus (1989) 'The European view', No 53; December

IDS Top Pay Unit (1988) 'Paying for Performance', Research file 9, July

IDS Top Pay Unit, (1990) 'Putting pay into practice'; Research file 15, July

Industrial Relations Services, (1991) *Pay and Gender in Britain*, IRS/EOC

Jackson, M and Leopold, J (1990) 'Casting off from national negotiations', *Personnel Management*, April

Kinnie, N (1989) 'The decentralisation of industrial relations? — Recent research considered', *Personnel Review*, vol 19, no 3, pp 28–34

Marsden, D (1989) 'Developments of pay level patterns and flexibility in Western Europe', paper to the Eighth World Congress of the International Industrial Relations Conference, Brussels

Marginson, P, Edwards, P, Martin, R, Purcell, J and Sisson, K (1988) *Beyond the Workplace*, Blackwell, Oxford

Millward, N and Stevens, M (1986) *British workplace industrial relations 1980 to 1984*, Gower, Aldershot

Purcell, J (1991) 'The rediscovery of the management prerogative: The management of labour relations in the 1980s', *Oxford Review of Economic Policy*, vol 7, no 1, pp 33–43

Söderström, M (1992) 'Sweden' in Brewster, Hegewisch, Holden, Lockhart (eds), *The European Human Resource Management Guide*, Academic Press, London

6

DOES STRATEGIC TRAINING POLICY EXIST? SOME EVIDENCE FROM TEN EUROPEAN COUNTRIES[*]

Len Holden, De Montfort University, UK and Yves Livian, ESC LYON, France

INTRODUCTION

The burgeoning literature on training and development is testimony to the fact that companies and organisations recognise its increasing importance. Emerging from that interest over the past ten years has been the evolution of Human Resource Development (HRD) as a subject in its own right (Hall 1984; Cacioppe, Warren-Langford and Bell 1990) and Management Development has probably received even greater attention in recent years (Sisson and Storey 1988; Storey 1989; Storey 1990). The development of HRD has far reaching implications for the whole human resource function, affecting both external and internal human resourcing. It explicitly affects a range of policies including manpower planning, recruitment, job design, career path planning, management succession and implicitly influences many more HR policy areas.

From early this century leaders of organisations have been conscious of the value added effect of training in both the short and long term (Gospel 1991). Unions and workers have also been conscious of the importance of training in setting apart and upgrading individuals into skilled craft occupations and jealously guarding those positions by allowing entry only through apprentice training. However, deskilling through technological change has eventually led to the realisation that training itself must not be seen to be a barrier to creating effective organisations, but can be used strategically by both unions and

* This chapter first appeared in *Personnel Review*, vol. 21, 1, 1992. Permission for its reproduction here is acknowledged with gratitude.

management towards a mutually rewarding outcome (Bassett 1986; Lloyd 1990).

The oft-quoted examples of Germany, Sweden and Japan have been used to illustrate the beneficial effects that large investments in training, applied in a mutually cooperative atmosphere between employers and employees, can have on the efficiency of an organisation (Wickens 1987; Lane 1989; Lundmark and Söderström 1989; Le Boterf 1989). There has been an even stronger interest in management development and in recent years a series of writers pointed to the gap between good management practice and the existing status quo (Handy *et al.* 1988; Storey 1988; Barsoux and Lawrence 1990; Tovey 1991). The Price Waterhouse Cranfield Survey (1990) and subsequent in-depth analysis (Holden 1991) have been able to shed some light on the position and activities of training and development across Europe in the period covering late 1989 and early 1990. This paper attempts a deeper analysis of the 1991 Price Waterhouse Cranfield Survey.

THE SURVEY FINDINGS

Training as a recruitment strategy?

The 1990 Price Waterhouse Cranfield Survey on Strategic Human Resource Management (Report 1990) clearly showed that in five European countries (France, Germany, Spain, Sweden and the UK) great interest was expressed in the increased use of training; and the 1991 survey (extended to an additional five countries: Denmark, Italy, Netherlands, Norway, Switzerland plus the original five) has confirmed that view across Western Europe (Report 1991).

Personnel managers in organisations in all ten countries consistently listed training and development as one of the most important objectives of their function for the next three years. In addition, it is apparent that personnel managers are using training much more as a recruitment strategy. In all countries, with the exception of Germany and Sweden, training for new employees was cited as the most popular means used to aid recruitment out of a choice of eleven options.

Equally, using training to aid the solution of resourcing problems was not only seen in the external context. Internal resourcing in the form of retraining existing employees was the second most popular recruiting option in Denmark, Spain and UK; the third most popular in France, Netherlands and Sweden; the fourth in Germany, Italy and Norway and the sixth in Switzerland. Interestingly, 'retraining existing employees' was

Table 6.1 Most popular measures to aid recruitment (percentage)

	CH	D	DK	E	F	I	N	NL	S	UK
Training new employees	90	56	68	73	80	87	66	70	55	80
Retrain existing employees	67	57	52	70	44	58	51	63	55	74

more popular in Germany than 'training for new employees'; this may be due to the strong emphasis on training already given in German organisations and national legislative structure for external vocational education, so it is not perceived as an option to use in this manner (Rose and Wignanek, 1990). A similar explanation can account for the perceived lower emphasis on recruitment through training by Swedish personnel managers.

INVESTMENT IN TRAINING

Organisations in all countries have increased training expenditure over the last three years for all categories of employees (Table 6.2). This confirms the trends indicated in the first survey, but on a wider European scale.

While this is encouraging, the emphasis on the increases in training investment tend to be towards the upper echelons of the organisation, particularly management. Marked exceptions are France and the Nether-

Table 6.2 Increases in money spent on training per employee (allowing for inflation) over the last three years

	CH	D	DK	E	F	I	N	NL	S	UK
Management	74	61	51	61	64	62	49	63	70	66
Prof/Technical	68	68	50	70	65	74	43	66	48	59
Technical(S/CH) D[*]	66	43	ca	ca	ca	ca	ca	ca	58	ca
Clerical	35	39	39	58	ca	58	33	54	46	46
Manual	34	17	33	50	60	50	36	65	49	41

ca = included in category above

[*] = skilled craft workers.

lands, which show a much more even distribution of expenditure between employee categories.

A more detailed investigation of how much is being spent on training reveals a less optimistic picture. When asked how much is spent on training as a proportion of wages and salaries, only Sweden and particularly France emerge with more than a quarter of organisations spending considerably above 4 per cent (Table 6.3).

Table 6.3 Proportion of annual wages and salaries spent on training (percentages)

	CH	D	DK	E	F	I	N	NL	S	UK
0.01 – 2.0 per cent	64	61	66	76	25	76	63	65	57	62
2.01 – 4.0 per cent	26	24	20	14	43	15	17	20	19	21
4.01 and above	11	16	13	10	32	9	19	16	25	18

With the exception of France, the majority of organisations in all other nations spend less than 2 per cent of their budgets on training. What is particularly remakable is the ignorance of personnel managers of training expenditures (Table 6.4), and this lack of knowledge can have serious implications for the implementation of effective HRD. There are, however, problems in this area for even the most conscientious personnel managers. The difficulties of costing training accurately can be singularly problematic and the issue can be muddied by the inclusion of travel, subsistence and sundry costs. This, together with the problem of control of budgets by line managers and the need to communicate training expenditure to the central personnel function, provides further difficulties – a theme to which we will later return.

Table 6.4 Organisations that don't know how much they spend on training (percentages)

	CH	D	DK	E	F	I	N	NL	S	UK
per cent	25	42	33	18	2	24	30	23	44	38

France is the one country that seems most cognisant of organisational expenditure on training, explained largely by the fact that legislation exists which compels organisations to spend 1.2 per cent of the annual salaries and wages on training. Those that do not meet these requirements are subject to taxation (Voisin 1988; Gordon 1990). Of equal concern is the limited time given over to training, as Table 6.5 shows.

Table 6.5 Average number of days of training per year (percentage of organisations)

	CH	D	DK	E	F	I	N	NL	S	UK
Per manager										
Less than 5	60	59	51	32	59	56	46	61	57	69
5–10	32	30	38	40	33	37	41	28	35	23
over 10	9	11	11	29	9	8	12	11	8	8
Don't know	22	33	47	30	23	7	47	26	40	36
Per professional/ technical employee										
Less than 5	80	72	55	30	63	55	48	58	61	64
5–10	15	19	34	40	30	35	37	29	32	27
over 10	5	9	11	30	7	10	15	13	7	9
Don't know	25	32	47	28	24	6	47	25	40	38
Per clerical employee										
Less than 5	93	88	80	57	ca	82	81	84	91	86
5–10	6	8	15	24	ca	14	17	14	9	11
over 10	1	4	5	19	ca	4	2	2	0	3
Don't know	32	38	47	30	ca	11	50	26	40	38
Per manual employee										
Less than 5	93	87	83	59	74	81	75	75	98	81
5–10	5	9	12	22	20	14	17	17	2	13
over 10	2	4	5	19	6	5	8	8	0	6
Don't know	31	39	47	30	24	14	52	27	40	39

With the exception of Spain, only one-tenth of organisations provide training of ten days or more for managers and professional and technical employees. That figure becomes on average considerably less when applied to clerical and manual workers, again with the exception of Spain. While there need to be considerably more resources in terms of time for all categories of employees, there seems to be an emphasis on giving training to the upper echelons in most organisations, perhaps to the detriment of clerical and manual workers. With increasing emphasis on customer care and TQM, this could well be a false economy.

The Spanish data is interesting in that it alone indicates a higher degree of time allocation given over to training. This is probably due to response to the vibrant economic growth throughout the 1980s, when training and re-training was used as recruitment strategy in a labour shortage market for particular occupational categories. While some regions of Spain experienced as high as 16 per cent unemployment, boom areas such as

Barcelona where economic growth is high experienced severe labour shortages (Bruton 1990). As one Spanish survey panel member stated, 'Given the increasing responsibilities of management, one week per year seems barely adequate to fulfil their multifarious training needs' (Survey Report 1991). If one looks further down the organisation in the other countries, it would seem that there is still some considerable way to go in convincing leaders of organisations of the need for more training. Recession in the UK, for example, has affected training budgets adversely in many organisations (Coughlan 1991; Brindle 1991; Keeler 1991).

One interesting observation of the power that legislation can have is that in France, where companies must disclose expenditure budgets on training, few organisations do not know this data. However, there is no legislation which requires companies to disclose the amount of training days, and in this area the French are as ignorant as most of their European counterparts. Nevertheless, it is generally agreed that the legal requirement to spend 1.2 per cent of wages and salaries on training has had a beneficial effect on training in France since its introduction (Dayan, Gehin, Verdier 1986).

ASSESSMENT OF TRAINING NEEDS

A systematic assessment is important in order to clarify and identify the training needs of individuals and groups, which in turn can be integrated into future human resource planning. The 1990 survey revealed a high percentage of personnel managers in organisations claiming to systematically assess employee training needs, and the 1991 survey reveals a similar picture (Table 6.6).

Table 6.6 Do you systematically analyse employee training needs?

	CH	D	DK	E	F	I	N	NL	S	UK
per cent	74	55	56	72	85	79	63	68	76	80

Whilst this appears to be impressive, it must be borne in mind that many well-known good practice organisations responded to our survey and of these nearly half in Germany and Denmark, nearly one third in Norway and the Netherlands and around a quarter in Switzerland, Sweden, Spain, Italy and UK did *not* systematically analyse their training needs! Recent research in France has revealed that a prominent French banking organisation achieved rather negative results after a large investment in an extensive training programme, primarily because of the failure to analyse the training needs within the organisations. There was thus an inability to relate the training investment to the overall HR and business strategy. The authors suggest that this is much more representative of the way organisations operate than their management teams would care to admit (Livian and Sarnin 1991; Courpasson and Livian 1991).

Of those that did, a high use is made of line management requests and employee requests, both informal methods of assessment. While these methods are valid and give a valuable perspective from the point where training is delivered, use of these methods alone can lead to unsystematic appraisal, particularly if we bear in mind that considerable ignorance exists concerning training investment in many organisations. This would seem to suggest that information is not being reliably relayed back to the central personnel function, which should take considerable responsibility for the formulation of HR and HRD strategy.

Table 6.7 Most important method of analysing training needs

	CH	D	DK	E	F	I	N	NL	S	UK
Analyses of business plans	10	12	27	30	41	39	39	20	36	22
Training audits	19	39	19	8	0	9	1	31	1	16
Line Management requests	36	36	44	45	0	35	35	19	18	20
Performance Appraisal	21	10	8	8	n/a	13	22	24	38	35
Employee Requests	9	3	2	9	31	4	2	7	7	6

Note: Categories in full: Analysis of projected business/service plans; Training Audits; Line management requests; Performance appraisal; Employee requests.

When asked what assessment methods were the most important, a mixed picture emerges with Switzerland, Denmark and Spain relying on 'line manager requests' and the other seven countries opting for more formal methods. Germany and the Netherlands favour 'training audits'; France, Italy and Norway opt for 'analysis of business plans'; and Sweden and UK go for 'performance appraisal.' The multiple uses of assessment are praiseworthy and, if the information is well coordinated, can provide an excellent insight into the training weaknesses and strengths of organisations.

Table 6.8 Organisations monitoring the effectiveness of training

	CH	D	DK	E	F	I	N	NL	S	UK
per cent	80	61	35	74	66	80	64	67	58	84

MONITORING TRAINING

With the exception of Denmark, the majority of organisations in most countries monitor the effectiveness of training. However, just under half in Sweden, a third in Germany, France, Norway and the Netherlands, a quarter in Switzerland, Spain and Italy do *not* monitor the effectiveness of training; the UK is the exception with only 16 per cent (Table 6.8).

The way in which training is monitored is also instructive, as Table 6.9 shows.

Table 6.9 How organisations monitor the effectiveness of their training

	CH	D	DK	E	F	I	N	NL	S	UK
Tests	48	39	45	52	36	39	19	60	51	45
Formal evaluation immediately after training	90	73	90	80	84	73	71	79	89	89
Formal evaluation some months after training	35	33	49	51	53	44	28	40	47	61
Informal feedback from line managers	93	92	92	92	92	97	99	97	93	97
Informal feedback from line managers	90	92	93	91	92	97	98	98	93	96

It is notoriously difficult to evaluate the effect that training has on an organisation in terms of added value. It is universally acknowledged that training is of value, but there has yet to appear an effective way of directly measuring its efficacy in terms of increased efficiency, let alone in terms of profit (Fairbairns 1991). What can be done is to attempt to assess the effect on the person who has undergone training. Has she or he increased their work-related knowledge? Do they do their job more efficiently? This can be measured to some degree in fairly concrete operations, like learning to use a piece of equipment such as a computer, but is very much more difficult to measure in terms of the mental processes of understanding more abstract concepts, such as increased motivation or the understanding of the abstract relation between work process and the organisation as an entity. The instruments cited in Table 6.9 can therefore prove to be rather blunt in diagnostic terms. However, they are not totally without value and tests and formal evaluation are, at the least, susceptible to measurement (Barbier 1986; Fairbairns 1991).

Only in three countries, Sweden, Netherlands and Spain, did more than 50 per cent of organisations use tests. Formal evaluation was much more popular immediately after training, but trailed off considerably some months after training. By far the most used method of monitoring the effectiveness of training was by informal feedback from both line managers and trainees. Whilst this is important, it once again raises the problem of considerable reliance on subjective sources of information.

This may be compounded by the trend in organisations to decentralise functions to the line management. Our survey in both years has shown that responsibility for training and development by line management has considerably increased over the last three years, and that line management is increasingly responsible for making (and helping to make) policy decisions in such areas as training (see Tables 6.10 and 6.11).

Table 6.10 Increased responsibility of line management in training and development

	CH	D	DK	E	F	I	N	NL	S	UK
percentages	48	31	35	53	60	36	54	56	69	47

Table 6.11 With whom primary responsibility lies for training and development policies

	CH	D	DK	E	F	I	N	NL	S	UK
Line management	12	11	23	11	5	2	10	7	14	5
Line mgt with HR	50	36	41	21	33	12	43	40	52	24
HR with line mgt	30	37	28	50	53	68	37	44	31	57
HR department	6	17	7	16	6	16	6	91	2	11

Few organisations let the HR department alone decide policy and the approved option by our panel members in most countries was to favour 'line managers with the HR department.' (Price Waterhouse Cranfield Survey Report 1991). While this is undoubtedly the best practice, it puts considerable strain and responsibility on the line manager to perform the role with increasing efficiency, not only in carrying out effective monitoring, but ensuring that the information is relayed back to the HR central function, which can act as a guide to overall HR policy within the organisation in terms of being regionally, nationally, and globally strategic in the formulation of HR plans and management succession and other strategic policies.

MANAGEMENT DEVELOPMENT

We have already referred to the increased emphasis and the recognition of the importance of management development in organisations, and Table 6.12 highlights some of the more popular management development techniques used by our survey respondents.

Table 6.12 Examples of management development techniques regularly used (% of organisations)

	CH	D	DK	E	F	I	N	NL	S	UK
Formal career plan	20	12	13	28	7	34	12	24	22	27
Performance appraisal	84	58	29	49	56	76	63	87	90	84
Succession plans	50	48	11	27	17	39	41	17	42	43
Planned job rotation	13	12	23	21	8	32	28	22	24	19
High flier schemes	33	21	28	39	44	28	38	24	41	29

As we would expect, formal career plans are not widely used, but the diversity of the rates obtained by such a 'classical' management tool as performance appraisal is more surprising. Where a large majority of Swedish, Swiss, Dutch and British companies regularly use this evaluation, it is less true in France, Spain and Germany and very rare in Denmark. The use of appraisal could be viewed as one of the major tools for identifying training needs, which appears to be the case only in Sweden and the UK.

A trend in management training is to have less general management courses and more individual and company specific programmes. Whatever the forms of training, the context is clearly favourable to the increase of money spent on management training: organisations which have increased this budget account for 51 per cent in Denmark to 74 per cent in Switzerland (Table 6.13).

Table 6.13 Organisations that have increased money spent on management training

	CH	D	DK	E	F	I	N	NL	S	UK
percentages	74	61	51	61	64	62	49	63	70	66

We have already noted (Table 6.5) the relatively low amount of time given over to training in all employee categories including managers, and with the exception of Spain at 32 per cent and the Netherlands at 46 per cent, over 50 per cent of the other eight countries gave only five days or less per year for management training. Equally surprising is the high number of personnel managers and their equivalents across Europe who do not know how many days are given over to training.

Another indicator that the desire for training is greater than evidence of its existence is the fact that performance appraisal emerges as a key management development technique in the majority of organisations (Table 6.12) and yet Table 6.14 indicates that considerably fewer managers have been trained in its use.

Table 6.14 Subjects in which at least a third of managers have been trained (% of organisations)

	CH	D	DK	E	F	I	N	NL	S	UK
Performance appraisal	69	32	19	31	36	45	64	69	73	70
Staff communication	69	45	43	48	53	49	63	57	64	54
Motivation	76	64	41	44	33	47	59	46	55	47
Delegation	56	42	35	30	22	34	53	35	46	40
Team building	39	25	22	39	25	29	36	39	51	49
Foreign languages	24	27	18	56	28	49	27	27	11	6

Perhaps the least surprising, but nevertheless disturbing, finding for the UK is the reluctance of organisations to invest in language training. These findings confirm the trend indicated in the 1990 survey (Price Waterhouse

Table 6.15 Main training requirements in the next three years

	CH	D	DK	E	F	I	N	NL	S	UK
Business administration and strategy	12	11	12	15	10	7	20	8	13	10
Computers and new technology	18	16	17	18	13	12	14	10	12	13
People Management and supervision	27	25	14	13	28	13	20	23	20	21
Management of change	10	8	16	6	12	16	15	12	16	16

Cranfield Project 1990) and the findings of an earlier survey by Tyson (1989). Given the exhortation in the UK to increase international awareness 'after considerable publicity about the coming opportunities in Europe, it is perhaps surprising that the level of training in languages is so low' (Tyson 1989).

Further evidence of the high priority given to management development in organisations is furnished in Table 6.15. Of eleven options specified as constituting possible main training requirements in the next three years, 'people management' and the 'management of change' emerged as clear preferences, together with 'business administration and strategy'. All of these areas are closely related to management development.

CONCLUSION

Our evidence confirms the 1990 findings that training and development is given a high priority in the human resource function in most organisations throughout Europe. There is, however, considerable evidence from much of our data which suggests that this is more an aspiration than apparent in the day-to-day organisation. While expenditure in training has increased, particularly in management development, there are still many organisations, with the exception of the Swedish and notably the French, spending below 2 per cent of their salaries and wages budgets on training.

This analysis is reinforced by the relatively low number of days given over per annum to training in most organisations across Europe. We would further argue that training cannot be seen to be a true 'investment', since most organisations do not know how much they spend.

We have also noted that most organisations claim to analyse systematically their training needs and monitor the effectiveness of their training and while a variety of methods both formal and informal are used, emphasis is placed on line manager requests in both instances. We believe that this can produce a dichotomy between the decentralised role and increasing responsibility of line managers, and the centralised role of the personnel function which must act as an interpreter of organisation-wide information and creator of human resource policies. The desire to empower the line manager may lead to sacrifices by the central personnel function to ensure that relevant information is being relayed back. This is clearly shown by the ignorance displayed by many organisations on training investment in terms of money and time. If this is the case, as some evidence from France suggests (Courpasson and Livian 1991), then it is highly doubtful that HR policy making can be seen to be strategic.

This suggests that the assessment of training needs and the monitoring of training effectiveness needs to be distinguished at least on two levels — the workplace and at organisational or establishment level. The mutual interchange of information requires the existence of adequate data or record-keeping systems combined with effective channels of communication.

A problem thrown up by the data in 1990 and confirmed again this year is the relatively poor performance of the training function in German organisations (Holden 1991) when it has long been recognised that the German system is hailed as an example which the UK should emulate, particularly in the area of vocational training (Lane 1990). Similarly, Spanish organisations register the highest percentage responses in many training areas.

The Spanish data can be seen to represent a positive reaction to the sustained growth which has taken place in the Spanish economy in the 1980s and recently. The interest in training is obviously a reflection of the recognised needs to train and develop employees to meet the demands of a rapidly changing business environment. Equally, training has been used as a human resource tool to help alleviate recruitment difficulties in shortage areas (Price Waterhouse Cranfield Survey Report 1990). However, it must be remembered that the Spanish education and training system both institutionally and within private companies has a long way to go before they are said to be on a par with their Northern neighbours.

The German data can be explained by the fact that a great degree of training already exists through state supportive systems and mutual cooperation with employers within a legislative framework. Lane (1990) has recently argued that human resource management is decisively shaped by societal institutional frameworks, particularly by the system of vocational education.

In this respect Britain's fragmented training structures are not as supportive in the human resource context as those of Germany and Sweden (Holden 1991). There is already evidence of the problems facing the newly instituted voluntary systems of ET and TECs (Keeler 1991) and there is a growing body of opinion which believes that the government must introduce an element of compulsion. The French legislation which compels organisations to spend part of their wages and salary budgets on training seems to have had a favourable effect on increasing French awareness of and, more importantly, investment in training.

REFERENCES

Barbier, J M (1986) *L'évaluation d'information*, PUF, Paris

Barsoux, J-L and Lawrence P (1990) *Management in France*, Cassell, London

Bassett P (1986) *Strike Free: New Industrial Relations in Britain*, Macmillan, London, pp 30, 68, 71–2

Brindle D (1991) 'NHS Training Scheme Frozen', *Guardian* 26 June

Bruton K (1990) 'The Business Culture in Spain' in Randlesome C (ed), *Business Cultures in Europe*, Heinemann, Oxford, pp 214–69

Cacioppe, R, Warren-Langford, P and Bell L (1990) 'Trends in Human Resource Development and Training', *Asia Pacific Human Resource Management*, May, pp 55–67

Coughlan D (1991) 'The Disappearing Trainees' *Daily Telegraph*, 9 May

Courpasson, D and Livian, Y-F (1991) 'Training for Strategic Change: Some Conditions of Effectiveness. A Case in the Banking Sector in France.' Paper presented at the 6th Workshop of Strategic Human Resource Management EIASM, St. Gallen, Switzerland, March

Dayan, JL, Gehin, JP and Verdier, E (1986) 'La formation continue dans l'industrie', *Formation — Emploi*, no 16, pp 7–36

Fairbairns, J (1991) 'Plugging the Gap in Training Needs Analysis' *Personnel Management*, February, pp 43–5

Gordon, C (1990) 'The Business Culture in France' in Randlesome C (ed), *Business Cultures in Europe*, Heinemann, Oxford, pp 58–105

Gospel, H (ed) (1991) *Industrial Training and Technological Innovation: A Comparative and Historical Study*, Routledge, London

Hall, DT (1984) 'Human Resource Development and Organisational Effectiveness' in Fombrun, CJ Tichy, NM and Devanna, MA (eds), *Strategic Human Resource Management*, John Wiley and Sons, New York, pp 159–81

Handy, C, Gordon, C, Gow, I and Randlesome, C (1988) *Making Managers*, Pitman, London

Holden, L (1991) 'European Trends in Training and Development' *The International Journal of Human Resource Management*, vol 2, no 2, Sept. pp 113–31

Keeler, D (1991) 'Drifting Off Course', *Personnel Today*, 24 September

Lane, C (1989) *Management and Labour in Europe*, Edward Elgar, Aldershot

Lane, C (1990) 'Vocational training and new production concepts in Germany: some lessons for Britain,' *Industrial Relations Journal*, vol 21, no 1, Winter, pp 247–59

Le Boterf, G (1989) *Comment investir en formation*, Ed d'Organisation, Paris

Livian, Y-F and Sarnin, P (1991) 'Changements stratégiques et pratiques de formation dans le PME: résultats d'une recherche récente', *Ressources Humaines*, mai, pp 43,44

Lloyd, J (1990) *Light and Liberty: The History of the EEPTU*, Weidenfeld and Nicolson, London, pp 634–64

Lundmark, A and Söderström M (1989) *The Economics of Training and Personnel Development in Organisations — An Empirical Study and a Conceptual Framework*, IPF paper, Uppsala University, Sweden

Price Waterhouse Cranfield Project (1990) *Report on International Strategic Human Resource Management*, Price Waterhouse, London

Price Waterhouse Cranfield Project (1991) *Report on International Strategic Human Resource Management*, Cranfield School of Management, Cranfield

Rose, R and Wignanek G (1990) *Training Without Trainers: How Germany avoids the supply-side bottleneck*, Anglo-German Foundation, London, pp 13–19

Sisson, K and Storey, J (1988) 'Developing Effective Managers: A Review of the Issues and an Agenda for Research', *Personnel Review*, 17/4, pp 3–8

Storey, J (1989) 'Management Development: A Literature Review and Implications for Future Research. Part 1: Conceptualisations and Practices', *Personnel Review*, 18/6, pp 3–19

Storey, J (1990) 'Management Development: A Literature Review and Implications for Future Research. Part 2: Profiles and Contexts', *Personnel Review*, 19/1, pp 3–19

Tovey, L (1991) *Management Development and Training in Large UK Businesses*, Harbridge House, London, pp 9,10, 95,96

Tyson, S (1989) '1992: An Investigation of Strategies for Management Development' Paper presented at the seminar 'Europe Without Frontiers' Amsterdam, November

Voisin, A (1988) 'L'investissment formation: un état de la recherche' *Education Permanente*, 95, pp 63–76

Wickens, P (1987) *The Road to Nissan*, Macmillan, London

7

THE CHALLENGE OF MANAGEMENT DEVELOPMENT IN WESTERN EUROPE IN THE 1990s[*]

Martin Hilb, University of St Gallen, Switzerland

THE CURRENT STATE OF HRD IN WESTERN EUROPE

The development of human resources is of considerable importance to the evolution of Europe in the 1990s. The current state is best reflected by the results of the Price Waterhouse Cranfield Project survey (1991). Relevant data from this research are first assessed prior to an examination of future trends and tendencies.

The overall position in Western Europe with respect to HRM may be summarised as follows: in most countries and companies selection, appraisal, reward and development of human resources are neither strategically oriented enough nor integrated with one another, nor evaluated in an objective way. Moreover, even a written personnel policy is available only in a minority of companies within the big five European countries, as reflected in Figure 7.1.

However, based on this survey, human resource development (HRD) is considered the most important personnel function in all main European countries. It is thus more important than: compensation, which ranks as the second most important function in Germany and Switzerland; industrial relations, which ranks as the second most important in France, Italy, Spain and the Netherlands; and productivity management, which ranks as the second most important in the UK.

HRD practices are clearly influenced by labour markets, national culture and legislation. The following results can be understood within this context. First of all, the varied importance of training is reflected by the percentage of the companies' total compensation costs spent for

* This chapter first appeared in the *International Journal of Human Resource Management*, Vol 3, 3, 1992. Permission for its reproduction is acknowledged with gratitude.

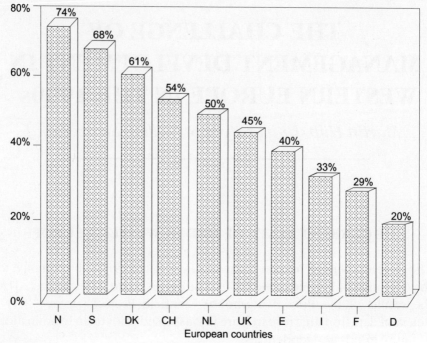

Figure 7.1 Percentage of companies in ten European countries with a written personnel policy

training. This figure differs from country to country: for example, 75 per cent of the French companies but only 24 per cent of the Spanish and Italian companies spend more than 2 per cent of their total compensation budgets for training. Moreover, there are five topics which are listed as the key training needs across the ten countries: leadership; communication technology; strategic management; total quality management; and innovative teambuilding.

The use of on-the-job career development instruments also varies from country to country. For instance, job rotation is used in 32 per cent of Italian companies, but in only 8 per cent of the French companies. Individual career plans for the 'high flyers' are used in 44 per cent of the French companies, but in only 22 per cent of the German firms. And the assessment centre is used in 22 per cent of the British, but in only 3 per cent of the Norwegian companies. In addition, 66 per cent of the Swiss companies, but only 31 per cent of the Danish firms, favour promoting internal candidates instead of external people for vacant management positions.

THE FUTURE TRENDS OF HRD IN WESTERN EUROPE

As stated before, HRM in general and HRD in particular are still handled at a very low development level in most European countries. Consequently, there are many opportunities for European companies to overcome this situation in a boundary-free Europe. Based on our practical experience and research (Hilb 1985) with HRM in Japan, the US and Europe, we have identified six possible HRD trends for the 1990s.

1. From operational training to the strategic development of human resources

Management training and development is worthless unless there is first a clear strategic company vision (Tichy 1983). Figure 7.2 illustrates this statement.

Strategic human resource development has to be based on a holistic company mission which must be developed by the whole management team (including the HR Executive) in consensus (Hilb 1986). As Figure 7.2 illustrates, the human resource development concept has not only to be based on the company mission, but also linked to the other key human resource instruments (such as selection, appraisal and reward).

2. From the one-dimensional to a three-dimensional approach of human resource development

The traditional career is still promotion. With the flattening of organisational structures and the change of corporate values (Hilb 1986), the definition of human resource management needs to be broadened (see Figure 7.3) (Schein 1978). In many western European countries more and more executives no longer value promotion as a career incentive: 'Higher is not always nicer!'. When you ask third and fourth level executives of large corporate HQ of European multinational companies: 'What was the best job during your career?', many executives answer, 'When I was general manager of a subsidiary and able to influence overall results. Here at corporate head office I feel alienated from the customer, the products . . . the action!'.

Therefore, in addition to promotion, multinational companies in Western Europe have two other important career development paths to offer:

a) Geographical, functional and divisional job rotation within the company or with outsiders such as suppliers, customers or joint-venture partners.

b) Permanent job enrichment, which can be achieved by introducing a constructive HR controlling policy such as: 'Whenever there is a vacancy, the personnel structure has to be reviewed in order to clarify

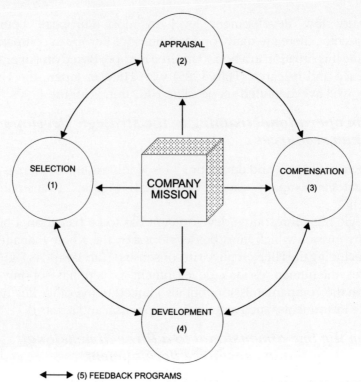

Figure 7.2 The strategic and integrated management of Human Resources

the possibility of *eliminating this position* fully or in part by: first, *enriching other jobs* with important elements; second, *automating* as much as possible *the routine* responsibilities; and third, *discounting the unnecessary* portion of the position.'

3. From the development of only a cadre of people (called 'management development', MD) to an overall development of all human resources (called HRD)

Too many companies still provide development possibilities only to a cadre of people (and call it MD), and therefore do not utilise their rich, non-managerial talents. The fact that there are so many 'head-hunters' operating throughout Western Europe indicates that most companies have failed in developing their own human resources in the interest of the people and the company. More and more European companies are likely to move away from the short-term view. for instance, 'These days you can't afford to wait for someone to grow into the job', by introducing a long-term 80:20 policy, such as 'It is our policy to fill job vacancies by the

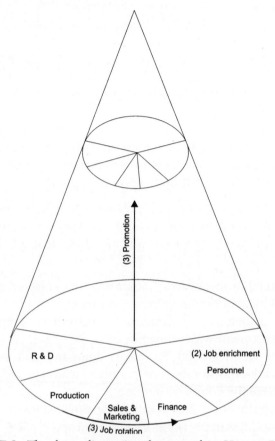

Figure 7.3 The three-dimensional approach to Human Resource Development

promotion or rotation of motivated and qualified employees within our company. Only in exceptional cases (20 per cent), such as for bottom jobs or when we enter a new business field where the properly qualified individual is not available within our company, should we go outside the organisation.' And it should be stressed that this company policy helps employees on all levels of the organisation to develop to their greatest potential and thus make the best use of all their abilities in the interest of both the individuals and the company.

4. From an ethnocentric to a Eurocentric approach to human resource development

With regard to career development policies, a multinational company can choose from four options (Herman and Perlmutter 1979):

- ethnocentric, where all key positions abroad are filled by HQ-country nationals;
- polycentric, where all key positions abroad are filled by local nationals;
- geocentric, where all key positions abroad are filled by third-country nationals; and
- regio- (ie Euro-centric, where all key positions abroad are filled by the foremost talented individual within the European operation, regardless of nationality. Figure 7.4 illustrates that the most advanced policy is the regio-(Euro-)centric development approach.

Despite high transfer costs and potential problems to re-integrate expatriates back into their home country at the end of their careers, the Eurocentric approach is the most advanced because of the following advantages:

1. It uses the rich European-wide human resources instead of concentrating only on local or home-country resources.
2. It enables a better identification of subsidiary employees with corporate European-wide strategies.
3. It creates a well-rounded European company culture which can benefit from the transferable comparative advantages of all European cultures where the company operates.
4. It enables employees in the various European locations to have greater career possibilities in the boundary-free Europe.
5. It develops 'Transnational capabilities ... (to manage across national boundaries) retaining local flexibility while achieving global integration. More than anything else, this HR policy allows greater linkage of

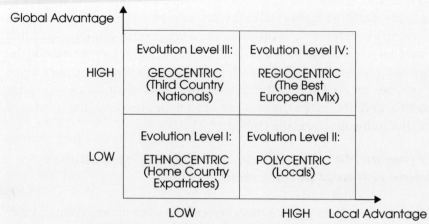

Figure 7.4 Evolution levels of international HRD

local operations (in Europe) to each other and in so doing, better leveraging local and central capabilities' (Bartlett and Ghoshal 1988).

5: From a single-man-orientated to a dual-career and family-orientated development of human resources

In Europe, more women are likely to work during most stages of their family life. 'The dual-income (and dual-development) household is well on its way to becoming the norm of the future, creating a need for new relations between home and work and thus demanding changes in both areas' (Mathison 1989). Multinational companies have to offer dual-career possibilities (including appropriate extensive cross-cultural training for the whole family) by assisting the partner who is not an employee in finding an attractive position with other organisations at the new location, as well as appropriate education programmes for the children of the expatriate. The change of traditional 'work ethic' includes key trends which 'de-emphasize the importance of material wealth as a motivator of work activity, pressures for resistance to authority, desire to realise the balance between work and other aspects of life, and increased concern with finding intrinsically interesting and personally rewarding work' (Mathison 1989, p 149). Employee opinion surveys conducted by the author in various European countries (Hilb 1985a) have shown that companies must continue to provide fair compensation and benefits, employment security and a pleasant working environment. However, if companies wish to motivate the new generation of young, individual, freedom-minded employees ('YIFFIES') (Deutschman 1990) they will have to provide in addition:

- jobs which include usefulness, joy and freedom to act;
- superiors who act as exemplary coaches; and
- permanent useful learning experiences on the job.

6. From a past-orientated to a future-orientated approach to human resources development

Based on the results of the European HRM survey, most companies in Western Europe have not yet introduced programmes for the potential review of individuals. There is no doubt that, in addition to past-orientated performance appraisal programmes, companies need individual potential appraisal programmes in order to evaluate the future talents of all their employees. Companies will be able to develop European human resource portfolios (Figure 7.5), which better illustrate further and current numbers of employees with a specific level of performance and potential.

Bottom-up executive reviews of human resource portfolios will include the establishment of suitable action plans such as:

- changes in job assignments and organisation structures including job rotations and job enrichment;
- development of individual and dual career plans for high-potential individuals with outstanding performance and family consensus for relocation;
- proactive out-placement activities for people with no potential and continuous weak performance;
- complementary training programme, mentoring, counselling, coaching and innovative teambuilding, serving both the self-interests of the employees and the needs of the organisation.

Moreover, these action plans should cover all levels of career transitions, including:

- the initial employee entry into the organisation;
- the employee transition from being a specialist to a generalist;
- the employee transition from technical work to management;
- the employee transition from fully work-involved to being more accommodating with regard to family concerns;
- the employee transition from being 'on the way up' to 'levelling off'; and last but not least
- the employee transition from being employed to becoming (partly or fully) retired.

CONCLUSION

The field of HRM in general, and HRD in particular, is 'in a stage of adolescence, international HRM and HRD is still at the infancy stage' and I would add that Eurocentric strategic HRM has just been born because of the dynamics created by Fortress Europe 92. In the area of human resource development in Western Europe, 'there are three types of companies: first, those who make things happen, second, those who watch things happen, and third, those who wonder what happened'.

It is the responsibility of top management within each company to decide whether they want to become the masters of change in Europe or its casualties.

Potential for advancement \ Performance in present job	Total	0%	2%	24%	64%	10%	100%
① Promotable now					• 2%	• 3%	5%
② Promotable in the near future				• 5%	●18%	● 6%	29%
③ Can be broadened			●	●14%	●44%	. 1%	59%
④ Limited			• 2%	• 5%			7%
		Ⓔ Unsatisfactory	Ⓓ Improvement needed	Ⓒ Good	Ⓑ Very good	Ⓐ Outstanding	Total

Figure 7.5   Example of a European HR portfolio

REFERENCES

Barlett, CA and Ghoshal, S (1988) 'Organizing for Worldwide Effectiveness: The Fundamental Solution', *California Management Review*, 31, 1, pp 54–74

Deutschman, A (1990) 'What 25-Year-Olds Want', *Fortune*, August, p 43

Herman, DS and Perlmutter, HV (1979) *Multinational Organizational Development*, Addison Wesley, Reading

Hilb, M (1985) *Personalpolitik fur Multinationale Unternehmen*, Industrielle Organisation, Zurich

Hilb, M (1985a) *Diagnose-Instrumente zur Peronalund Organisationsentwicklung*, Haupt, Bern

Hilb, M (1986) *Japanese and American Multinational Companies: Business Strategies*, Sophia UICC, Tokyo

Hilb, M (1986b) 'Die dreidimensionale Unternehmungsmission', *Management Forum*, 1/2, Physica, Vienna

Mathison, DL (1989) *Managerial Incidents and Cases*, Mathison, London

Price Waterhouse Cranfield Project (1991) on International Strategic Human Resource Management 1991 Report, Cranfield School of Management, Cranfield

Schein, E (1978) *Career Dynamics*, Addison Wesley, Reading

Tichy, N M (1983) *Managing Strategic Change*, John Wiley, New York

8

HUMAN RESOURCE MANAGEMENT IN EUROPE: EVIDENCE FROM TEN COUNTRIES[*]

*Chris Brewster, Cranfield School of Management, UK
and Henrik Holt Larsen, Copenhagen Business School,
Denmark*

THEORETIC BACKGROUND

The concept of human resource management (HRM), and the associated concept of strategic human resource management, is being debated increasingly in the literature and used increasingly within employing organisations. The history of the concept of HRM has been summarised elsewhere (Storey 1989; Hendry and Pettigrew 1990; Beaumont 1991; Freedman 1991). It developed initially from work in the United States of America in the 1960s and 1970s and since the mid 1980s has been an ever more visible feature of the academic literature, of consultancy services and of organisational terminology, particularly in the USA and Great Britain.

This chapter attempts to assess some key aspects of the concept and its practical manifestation in Europe. This is not a straightforward task: there are both conceptual and methodological difficulties. On the conceptual side, the concept of HRM is far from clearly established in the literature: different authorities imply or state different definitions and draw on different evidence. On the methodological side, there are inherent problems in assessing the concept and in identifying relevant data.

Conceptual issues

We have addressed the conceptual issues in two ways. First, the focus we

---

* A version of this chapter first appeared in the *International Journal of Human Resource Management*, Vol 3, 3, 1992. Permission for its reproduction here is acknowledged with gratitude.

have taken is limited. This chapter is concerned with human resource management at what has been termed the 'programmes' level (Schuler 1992) and is not concerned with the amorphous issues of culture and ethos raised at the philosophical level, nor with the day-to-day administration of practice and process. HR programmes have been defined, somewhat tautologically, as the effect of HR efforts on organisational structure. 'These efforts', it is argued, 'have in common the fact that they they are generated by strategic intentions and directions the firm is taking and that they involve human resource management issues, ie that they are major people-related business issues that require a major organisational effort to address. They also share the reality of having strategic goals that are used to target and measure the effectiveness of the HR programme' (Schuler 1992). At this level, therefore, our focus is on the way that organisations equip themselves to handle HR issues and the correlation of activities in this area with the overall strategic directions that the organisation is taking.

Second, we have attempted to sidestep some of the more etymological debates about what HRM means by identifying elements which have widespread acceptance as constituent parts of the definition of HRM (eg Mahoney and Deckop 1986; Guest 1990; Hendry and Pettigrew 1990).

The classical typology of the HRM field is four-fold: the acquisition, maintenance, motivation and development of human resources (for example, DeCenzo and Robbins, 1988). Others have slightly different perspectives, like Storey *et al.* (1989) who define a five-step HRM cycle: selection, performance, appraisal, rewards and development. Beer *et al.* (1985) who have contributed considerably to the legitimisation of the HRM field in general, stress the crucial role of the employee in HRM. Thus they propose a focus on the following four areas: employee influence, human resource flow (into, through, and out from the organisation), reward systems and work systems.

Some critics of HRM have argued that the concept is hardly distinguish-able from the term 'personnel management'. Legge, for example, asks

> Why the language of HRM has gained the currency it appears to have — not least among management groups themselves? After all . . . there is little real difference between normative HRM and personnel management models and, in practice, it is probable that managing employee relations in the vast majority of companies remains a pragmatic activity, whether labelled personnel management or HRM. Furthermore, many of the techniques of HRM can be found in any personnel management textbook of a decade ago (Legge 1989, p 40).

However, regardless of whether one defines HRM as a very narrow concept or 'a whole array of recent managerial initiatives including measures to increase the flexible utilisation of the labour resource and other measures which are largely directed at the individual employee' (ibid p.41), two paradoxical elements in particular stand out as common to many analyses of HRM — integration and devolvement.

By *integration* we mean the degree to which the HRM issues are considered as part of the formulation of business strategies (see Schreyögg 1987; Butler 1988; Wohlegemuth 1988; Guest 1989). There is — in research as well as in the business community — an increasing understanding of the mutual relationship between business strategy and HRM (Storey *et al.*, 1989; Freedman, 1991). As more organisations become knowledge, service or hi-tech oriented, the more human behaviour becomes a competitive factor. Employing highly skilled, professional staff with pronounced expectations of the work environment necessitates a job structure with challenge and responsibility, a communication pattern with unfiltered upward and downward information flows, and a career management system providing multi-level and multi-type career tracks.

According to Lengnick-Hall and Lengnick-Hall (1988), such an integration of business strategy and HRM has several advantages:

> First, integration provides a broader range of solutions for solving complex organisational problems. Second, integration ensures that human, financial, and technological resources are given consideration in setting goals and assessing implementation capabilities. Third, through integration organisations must explicitly consider the individuals who comprise them and must implement policies. Finally, reciprocity in integrating human resources and strategic concerns limits the subordination of strategic considerations to human resource preferences and the neglect of human resources as a vital source of organisational competence and competitive advantage (pp 459–560).

Nevertheless, much is still unknown about the dialectic relationship between strategy and HRM. Also, there is a widespread — although not very realistic — belief that HRM is the dependent variable and the business strategy the independent variable in this relationship. We, however, reject the approach (see Fombrun, Tichy and Devanna 1984; Miller 1989) that HRM should in some sense 'follow' business strategy. We are conscious of too many examples where business strategies have failed, precisely because they failed to take account of the cost of labour or the lack of appropriate skills or an inability to integrate workforces. A few examples of the link between HRM and business strategy will illustrate this point:

1. If a company is too domestically oriented (which is a strategic problem) it can establish an expatriation or 'inpatriation' programme. An overseas secondment or the 'import' of an overseas person to the headquarters stimulates the international flavour of the organisation. Thus, a HRM method (expatriation) is used in response to a strategic problem (Brewster 1991).

2. A national nuclear research centre was employing a vast number of highly skilled engineers and other technical staff. However, when the government decided to abandon nuclear power plants, there was no use for this specialised staff. Rather than making all staff redundant, the organisation redefined its business strategy and took up alternative energy sources, space research and industrial thermodynamics. The staff were retrained, and the organisation is today very profitable and successful. A strategic decision is used to solve a HRM problem.

3. A company in the mobile telephone industry found that business was booming. It decided to double production at its plant a little way north of London. In the event, they found it impossible to recruit enough skilled employees because of substantial competition for such labour in the area. After 18 months of failing to produce enough products for the market, they opened a new plant in Scotland. A strategic decision was frustrated by a HRM problem and had to be changed.

In Figure 8.1 below, the arrows 1 and 2 illustrate how the integrative approach links business strategy and HRM. Arrows 3 and 4, however, illustrate how solutions to strategy and HRM problems are found within the two sectors, respectively. They thus illustrate the traditional approach where top executives are dealing with strategic issues (problems and solutions) only, and personnel managers are dealing with personnel issues only.

This chapter examines the extent to which business strategy and HRM are integrated in a range of European countries.

The other factor we are considering is *devolvement*. By this we mean the degree to which HRM practice involves and gives responsibility to line managers rather than personnel specialists.* There is an increasing recognition of this issue in the literature (see, for example, Torrington 1989; Walker 1989; Schuler 1990, 1991; Freedman 1991). With the closer link between strategy development and human resource development, line managers are given a primary responsibility for HRM. It is argued that

---

* This discussion is about the allocation of HR tasks to managers who are not HR specialists. We distinguish this from a related, but entirely separate, discussion about decentralisation. For details of that debate, see Chapter by Hoogendoorn and Brewster.

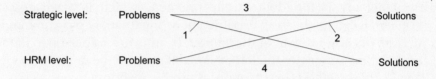

Figure 8.1 HRM and business strategy

within the major areas of HRM (attracting, retaining, motivating and developing staff) the line manager needs to be aware of the synergy between human, financial and physical resources; for him or her, allocating time, money and energy to the development of subordinate staff is an investment in enhanced effectiveness and future success; and there is no way this responsibility can be picked up by the human resource manager. The HRM function is seen as playing the role of coordinator and catalyst for the activities of line managers — a 'management team player . . . working (jointly) with the line manager solving people-related business issues' (Schuler 1990, p 51).

Devolvement is driven by both organisational and effectiveness criteria. Organisationally, it is now widely believed that responsibilities should be located at appropriate places within the organisation which means, increasingly, with line management rather than specialist functions. For most organisations the most expensive item of operating costs is the employees. Hence, in cost or profit centre based organisations (in the private or public sectors), there is pressure to include the management of the human resource in line management responsibilities.

Effectively, it is only by motivating and committing the workforce that value can be added to other resources. It is line managers, not specialist staff functions, who are in frequent, often constant, contact with employees. For most employees it is their immediate superiors who represent the management of the company. Providing these managers with the authority and responsibility to control and reward their employees makes them more effective people managers.

We have called these two elements paradoxical because they might seem, on first consideration, to be inconsistent. Integration is often linked with centralisation and senior management responsibility: devolvement with decentralisation and the passing of responsibility to junior management levels. How can both elements be central to the concept? Further consideration, however, reveals this to be a true paradox, inconsistent only on the surface and capable of resolution by disaggregating HRM into policy and practice. Integration is a *policy* issue, requiring the close involvement of HRM specialists with senior line management in the development of business policy. On the basis of such involvement, policies can be created which relate HRM and the business strategy to each other, allowing HRM *practices* to be more easily understood and undertaken by line managers.

The integration/devolvement matrix

The two dimensions can be plotted on a simple matrix (Figure 8.2).* The theoretic models which it provides allow analysis of both the role of the specialist HR department and the positioning of human resource management as a general managerial activity.

In the bottom left-hand corner of Figure 8.2, the integration of HRM with business strategy is low and there is little devolvement of HRM to the line. We have termed this position the *Professional Mechanic* to emphasise the specialist, but limited, skills and interests of its practitioners. This is the almost classical model of the 'professional' HR manager: as with other professions (law, medicine) the manager sees himself or herself as having 'higher' imperatives, above those of the organisation. Like the other professions, this specialist believes that there are many areas of the specialism which are beyond the understanding of untrained people, and which only the specialists can handle. The result, in this theoretic model, is an increasing distance from the strategic interests of the business, an increasing obsession with the mechanical requirements of the function (with increasing work overload) and an ever-greater isolation from other members of the management team.

Moving to the bottom right-hand corner of Figure 8.2, the integration of HRM with business strategy remains low, but HRM is devolved, substantially, to line management. This position we have termed the *Wild West*. Here every manager is free to develop his or her own style of relationship with employees and in extreme cases would have the power to 'hire and fire', to reward and to invest in employees as they wished. The potential for incoherence, inconsistency and a strong employee reaction is obvious.

In the top left-hand corner of Figure 8.2, the integration of HRM with business strategy is high and the personnel or HRM function has retained authority to itself. We have called this the position of the *Guarded Strategist*. The specialists are powerful figures in the organisation, working with senior managers to develop corporate strategy and

---

* An early version of the matrix appears in Brewster C and Connock S (1985) *Industrial Relations: Cost-Effective Strategies*, Hutchinson, London

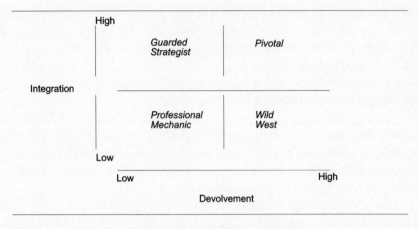

Figure 8.2 Models of HRM

operating in large and influential departments controlling such issues as how many, and who, is employed, who is developed and how the reward system operates. The personnel specialists have few problems other than coping with an enormous workload. For other managers, however, this can be a situation of considerable inefficiency and frustration. The line managers find many aspects of relationships with subordinates are in practice abrogated by the personnel function: the weaker managers will welcome the chance to slough off their responsibilities, whilst simultaneously having someone else to blame for all failures; the better managers will be frustrated.

The top right-hand corner of Figure 8.2 represents the position where HRM is fully integrated with business strategy and there is extensive devolvement of HRM to line management. In this model, the senior personnel specialists operate as catalysts, facilitators and coordinators at the policy level of the organisation. They have small, powerful departments monitoring and advising on developments in the human resource area; probably departments which are accessible in career terms to line management. The concentration on the development and monitoring of policy is correlated with the devolution of responsibility and authority to carry out the policy to line management. We have called this position *Pivotal* on the grounds that small, highly respected personnel departments at the policy-making level of the organisation can exert a powerful, disproportionate influence. The problems that the organisation faces in this model are concerned mainly with resourcing the department itself with high-calibre HR specialists who understand the way the business operates; and with training and developing line managers to handle HRM effectively.

Methodological issues

We addressed the methodological issues by taking proxy data. To establish full details of HRM integration or devolvement in an organisation could only be achieved by means of longitudinal ethnographic study: and would then be applicable only for the one, or few, organisations so studied. We wished to take a much broader, internationally comparative, view. We decided, therefore, to use data from the Price Waterhouse Cranfield Project and to adopt surrogate measures of the two elements. (We examine the limitations this imposes at the end of this chapter.)

THE EVIDENCE

Integration

As proxies of integration, we took findings in three areas: HR specialist involvement in the main policy-making forum of the organisation (Board of Directors or equivalent); HR specialist involvement in the development of corporate strategy; and whether or not such strategies are linked with HR policies which are translated into targets and evaluated. The first two items require little explanation. In European countries personnel or HR specialists rarely reach the very highest positions in employing organisations (Coulson-Thomas 1990; Coulson-Thomas and Wakeham 1991). Of course, the degree of HR access to CEO and similar positions varies by country and would appear to be more common in Scandinavia. It is also true that there are numerous CEOs who may not have come from the personnel function, but exhibit a particular interest in HRM. However, these are still exceptions. In practice, an informed HR input to top-level debates is most likely only where there is an organisational structure which provides for the head of the HR functions to be present at the key policy-making forum. Our third proxy item, targeted and evaluated HR policies, requires more explanation. We argue that a full integration of HR into business strategy can only occur where this function, like production, marketing, finance, has set targets against which it is measured. The assumption here is that aspects of business strategy which are seen as important by an organisation's top team are monitored against set objectives.

Tables 8.1 and 8.2 indicate the proportion of companies with an HR presence at the level of the Board (or equivalent); and the role that such Board-level HR specialists play in the development of corporate strategy. These show significant differences across Europe. In most countries a

Table 8.1 Head of Personnel or Human Resources function on the main Board of directors or equivalent (per cent)

CH	D	DK	E	F	I	N	NL	S	UK
58	19	53	80	83	18	67	44	87	47

Code:
CH	=	Switzerland	I =	Italy
D	=	Germany	N =	Norway
DK	=	Denmark	NL =	Netherlands
E	=	Spain	S =	Sweden
F	=	France	UK =	United Kingdom

clear majority of organisations have an HR presence at the top strategic level: as many as four out of five organisations in Sweden, France and Spain. However, in some countries, notably Germany* and Italy, the HR function is only rarely represented at Board level.

When we examine personnel department involvement in the development of corporate strategy, the picture changes somewhat. In Germany and Italy, our respondents tell us that human resource issues are taken into account from the outset in the development of corporate strategy by more organisations than the number who have Board-level reputation for the HR function: companies apparently consult with non-Board HR specialists at the earliest stage of formulating corporate strategy. In the Netherlands and UK, HR influence from the outset approximately mirrors Board level involvement. In the other six countries, there are considerable numbers of HR specialists with a place on the Board who, nevertheless, are not involved in the development of corporate strategy until a later stage.

In only three Northern European countries, Sweden, Germany and Norway, do more than half the organisations involve the head of HR in the formulation of corporate strategy from the outset. Otherwise, between a third and a half of all organisations in all the other countries have an early HR involvement at this critical level.

The next stage in the analysis of integration is to examine those organisations who have formal HR strategies which the organisation takes

---

* Our data is collected from what was West Germany and our analysis refers to that part of the state. Comparable data is currently being collected for the eastern *Länder* (project funded by the Anglo German Foundation) should prove a fascinating comparison.

Table 8.2 HR Involvement in development of corporate strategy (%)

	CH	D	DK	E	F	I	N	NL	S	UK
from the outset	48	55	42	46	50	32	54	48	59	43
consultative	20	19	30	21	22	23	24	31	28	27
implementation	6	6	9	8	12	17	6	8	4	8
not consulted	14	8	4	2	2	3	4	3	5	7
don't know/missing	12	13	15	23	13	25	11	12	6	15

seriously enough to translate into work programmes and deadlines and to monitor. The figures for HR strategies are given in Table 8.3. Again they show considerable variation. In Germany only 20 per cent of organisations have a written personnel or HR strategy, with 43 per cent claiming to have an 'unwritten strategy'. In Norway, at the other extreme, 74 per cent of organisations have a written strategy and a further 16 per cent have an 'unwritten strategy'. There is a broad correlation between having the head of the HR group on the Board, or equivalent, and having a written HR strategy. Perhaps Board membership encourages HR specialists to feel that formalised strategies are as important for their function as for other areas of the business. The noticeable exceptions to this broad correlation are in the Latin countries of Spain, France and Italy. In Spain and France, Board-level representation is high, but formal policies exist in only half as many organisations: and in Italy, formal strategies exist in twice as many organisations as have Board-level representation for the HR function.

Table 8.3 Personnel/HR management strategy (%)

Country	CH	D	DK	E	F	I	N	NL	S	UK
written	58	20	61	40	29	33	74	54	68	45
unwritten	32	43	22	40	46	40	16	30	23	27
no strategy	9	32	14	15	17	11	6	12	10	22
don't know/missing	1	5	3	4	8	16	3	4	0	6

The ten countries differ in the degree to which they are likely to translate their HR strategies into work programmes and plans. Nearly all the German organisations with written HR strategies go on to operationalise them; only half the Danish organisations do so. However, there is little change in the general order of integration (see Table 8.4).

Table 8.4 Organisations with written HR strategy translated into work programmes and deadlines (%)

CH	D	DK	E	F	I	N	NL	S	UK
42	18	36	36	25	32	46	34	45	38

There is considerably greater variation when this operationalising of strategies is taken one step further, to identify what proportion of these organisations evaluates the personnel department (Table 8.5). On this measure both the UK and Italy move up the order quite sharply; Norway moves down a considerable way. It appears that though personnel departments in UK and Italian organisations are less likely to be integrated into the business, they are considerably more likely, where they are integrated, to have their performance monitored.

Table 8.5 Organisations with written HR strategy translated into work programmes and deadlines where performance of personnel department is systematically evaluated (%)

CH	D	DK	E	F	I	N	NL	S	UK
24	8	18	23	16	27	21	19	27	27

This raises the issue of the rationale for such monitoring. The assumption made earlier was that organisations tend to measure what is important to them; hence the evaluation of the personnel or HR department would indicate a degree of seriousness being accorded to the function. An alternative explanation is that these departments are having to prove their value, whereas in countries where they are less commonly measured their value is taken for granted.

When comparing the general ordering of the countries on these criteria, some other anomalies, besides those on evaluation, stand out. Spain appears to be one of the least consistent countries, being near the top of the scale on Board membership, much further down in terms of written HR strategies and their translation into work programmes, and otherwise in central positions. This volatility is understandable given the dramatic and comparatively recent change from Fascism to democracy in Spain and the subsequent attempts of the personnel function to clarify its new role.

Other anomalies in the rank ordering of the countries concern France's high rating on Board membership and early involvement in the creation of corporate strategy compared to its much lower rating on the HR strategy issues. It is arguable that this fits in with stereotypes (supported by some evidence, see Laurent 1983 and Hofstede 1980) of France as a rigidly hierarchical country: the influential senior HR specialists do not want their autonomy restricted by written policies. Denmark tends to be almost the opposite to France, ranking in the bottom half on Board membership and early involvement in corporate strategy formulation, but tending to be higher in formalising and following through on HR strategies. The final anomaly concerns Germany's high rating on early involvement compared to its low ranking elsewhere. This may argue for alternative approaches to influencing corporate strategy; a point to which we have alluded already and to which we return in our discussion at the end of this chapter.

Overall, by combining the data in these tables we have established a ranking of typical organisations for each country (Figure 8.3).*

Figure 8.3 Relative integration ranking for ten European countries

It is important to be clear about the meaning of Figure 8.3: it shows the formal steps taken by organisations (on average) in each country towards integrating their HR strategies and corporate strategies. Almost by definition, it tells us little about those aspects of integration which we might call 'psychological': whether the atmosphere and culture of the organisation means that people issues are intrinsically taken into account in all decisions. We address this issue further in our discussion section.

---

* The wider definition of 'integration' rather than 'involvement' explains the marginally different ordering here from that in Bournois 1991 and in Brewster and Bournois (Chapter 2).

Devolvement

Defining and identifying devolvement is more straightforward than defining integration. Two issues seem to be indicative: the extent to which line managers are involved in certain HR practices; and the related issue of how many personnel specialists there are for given total numbers of employees.

On the first issue we asked our respondents to identify the position of their own organisation on six issues: pay and benefits; recruitment and selection; training and development; industrial relations; health and safety; and workforce expansion or reduction. In each case organisations were rated according to whether primary responsibility for major policy decisions rested with line management; line management with personnel or HR department support; the personnel or HR function with line management support; or with the personnel or HR department alone. The resultant rankings were then conflated to provide an overall comparison. The advantages of this approach are that, whilst it loses some of the detail, it provides a simple means of analysis and generates a comparative rating of the various countries (see Hoogendoorn and Brewster, Chapter 4).

Italy is a case on its own. It is, by a clear margin, the country in which fewest organisations have devolved authority for HR issues to the line. It ranks at the least devolved end on five of the six items — and second from the end on the other one.

On the second issue of proportions of personnel specialists to total numbers of employees, our rationale is that the more personnel specialists employed in a central staff function, the less devolvement there is of personnel management to line managers. (There are, of course, many related issues such as, for example, the degree to which line managers are trained to undertake these responsibilities.) One should be cautious about accepting a direct relationship, but in practice there is, as one would expect, a close correlation between the devolvement ranking and the number of personnel specialists per thousand employees on average.

Table 8.6 indicates clearly, for example, that the two most devolved countries, Denmark and Switzerland, have the lowest number of personnel specialists and the least centralised country, Italy, one of the highest number. Switzerland and the Netherlands stand out as being at the more devolved end of the spectrum, but still having considerable numbers of personnel specialists. These somewhat conflicting results illustrate that a high level of devolvement can occur in quite different (and not overlapping) situations. Thus, two organisations, one with a very

Table 8.6 Devolvement and proportion of personnel functionaries

Devolvement	I	UK	N	F	E	D	NL	S	CH	DK
Personnel functionaries per 1000 employees	18.2	13.9	12.8	13.8	14.9	14.5	18.5	15.6	12.5	10.7

positive and one with a very negative perception of HRM, might both be characterised by a high level of devolvement. The former organisation might find HRM too important to be dealt with by a central staff function, whereas the latter might find it a waste of resources in the first place to invest in human resources (including establishing a HRM function).

These rankings show an interesting contrast with the influence of national or regional level bargaining on pay (see Hoogendoorn and Brewster, Chapter 4).

Interestingly, we find little evidence that organisations are providing any formal training to help their line managers to handle human resource issues. There is no clear correlation between the amount of training in human resource issues that managers have received and devolution. We identified the number of organisations which had trained at least a third of the managers in such HR techniques as performance appraisal, communications, delegation, motivation and team building.

Table 8.7 Areas in which at least a third of managers trained (%)

Country	DK	N	S	UK	F	E	I	D	NL	CH
Performance appraisal	19	64	73	70	36	31	45	32	69	69
Staff communication	43	63	64	54	53	48	49	45	57	69
Delegation	35	53	46	40	22	30	34	42	35	56
Motivation	41	59	55	47	33	44	47	64	46	76
Team building	22	36	51	49	25	39	29	25	39	39

In none of these topics are the numbers in any country which has done such training correlated with the devolution ranking (Table 8.7). These somewhat conflicting results also raise different explanations. An obvious one is that line managers are just not being trained to undertake an HR role. There is statistical evidence, from the Netherlands, that this is the case in some instances (Hoogendoorn and Brewster, Chapter 4). The

Rank order *increase* in line management responsibility	Rank order % organisations with 1/3 line managers trained
S	CH
NL	S
E	N
F	NL
N	UK
I	I
UK	E
CH	D
DK	F
D	DK

Figure 8.4 Increases in line management responsibility in relation to having at least one-third of line managers trained (rankings)

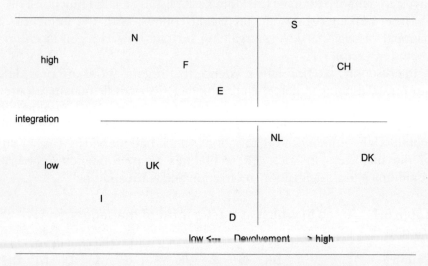

Figure 8.5 Models of HRM: ten European countries

second is that the most devolved countries have established a situation where line managers are actually able to perform the HRM responsibility: consequently, there is no need for training. The third interpretation is that a manager who is actively undertaking the HRM task gets so much experiential learning that no formal training is needed. A fourth explanation is that linking the degree of devolvement and the amount of training is a false perspective in the first place. Rather, one should look at the correlation between the *increase* in line management responsibility and training.

To investigate this last explanation, we have ranked the ten European countries according to the increase in line management responsibility for the specific HRM tasks noted above. Here, Sweden, the Netherlands, Spain and France come at the top (in the order mentioned). At the bottom one finds Denmark and Germany. If you rank the countries according to the percentage of managers having received training in management disciplines (performance appraisal, communication, motivation etc), seven out of ten countries end up with a somewhat similar ranking (Figure 8.4). The exceptions are Switzerland, representing one of the lowest increases in line management responsibility for HRM issues, but the largest proportion of companies providing training in management areas; and two of the 'Latin countries', France and Spain, which come into line with Italy on training despite being above that country on devolvement.

DISCUSSION

By plotting our analyses of the data on this model we can establish the position of the typical organisation in each country (see Figure 8.5). We can see examples of the four potential cases in our model.

Two countries, Switzerland and Sweden, fall into the category where the typical organisation has HR comparatively highly integrated with business strategy and with a substantial degree of devolvement. A second pair (Denmark and the Netherlands) falls squarely into the model that we have called the 'Wild West': devolvement is comparatively high (a little lower for the Netherlands, which is close to the middle on both measures) but integration is relatively low. A third group (Italy, the UK and Germany) are clearly 'mechanics' in our model. Personnel departments here are centralised, devolve much less, but are not, generally, integrated at the business strategy level. Spain, France and Norway fall into our remaining quadrant. They have human resources comparatively well integrated into the business strategy of the organisation, but have retained responsibility for the management of personnel issues within a specialist function.

Our study has revealed that we can meaningfully characterise HRM practices in ten European countries by the degree of integration of HRM and business strategy and the degree of devolvement of responsibility for HRM to line management. Our rationale for focusing on countries (rather than, say, sector or size variables) is thus confirmed.

In general, the influence of national cultures, national laws, national governmental agencies and national trade unions makes this level of analysis defensible and makes our analysis valuable to practitioners and commentators who have to operate in, and advise on, organisational issues in the various countries. We are more confident of this in Western Europe, where each of these countries has existed for centuries, than we might be elsewhere. We are aware, though, that this is not an unqualified categorisation — an issue brought home to us by the fact that our data in Germany does not include what was East Germany and now forms the eastern *Länder* of that country.

We do not imply, of course, that all organisations in every country fit the 'typical' model: indeed there will probably be a range of all kinds of organisation in each country. Nevertheless, the country tendencies are clear.

Relationship to other research

The matching of the two dimensions (integration and devolvement) created four cells in our matrix. Current received wisdom implies that high levels of integration and devolvement are advantageous. We are reluctant to conclude that the ideal position is necessarily in the top right-hand corner of the diagram. A number of external factors, including the national culture, have an impact on the appropriateness of a given location. Thus what is ideal in one cultural environment might be very unsuccessful in another environment. Further research is needed to analyse these environmental factors. Intriguingly, our data tends to give some support to the view that the pivotal position is linked to success. A diagonal line taking in the four countries nearest to the top right-hand corner of the diagram would include four of the five richest countries, measured by GDP per capita, in Europe.

We have argued that the two dimensions used tend to separate the various countries. Thus it becomes relevant to compare our research with studies of national cultures, such as those of Hofstede (1980, 1991), Laurent (1983) and Adler (1991). Hofstede's four cultural dimensions have had a great impact on the study of intercultural differences. It can be hypothesised that there is a co-variance between our dimension 'devolvement' and his dimension 'uncertainty avoidance'. An organisation devolving a considerable degree of HRM responsibility to line management must unavoidably expect a certain heterogeneity in HRM practice. Some organisations find it difficult to live with different practice, informal decision making procedures and sub-optimisation. Other organisations find this uncertainty unavoidable — or challenging! Along the same lines, one could argue that there is a relationship between devolvement and 'individualism/collectivism'. Collectivism should be expected to occur in organisations with a high degree of devolvement.

These conclusions are just tentative and could be the subject of further research.

Comparisons with the national cultures research shows that Sweden and Switzerland are similar in having a lower power distance index and higher individuality than most (Hofstede 1980, 1983). They are both countries with a disproportionately high number of MNCs (though a categorisation using only private sector data makes little difference to their location in this quadrant). Both countries are amongst those with the longest-term view of business (European Management Forum 1986).

The two countries in the bottom right-hand quadrant, Denmark and the Netherlands, have much in common in a cultural sense. Both Hofstede (1980, 1983) and Laurent (1983) show them scoring similarly on the different measures they use.

The countries in the left-hand quadrants do not fit together so easily relative to the research into national cultures. In the top left-hand quadrant Norway is culturally very similar to Sweden. It has, however, a much less devolved attitude towards HR. It has little cultural similarity with the two Latin countries of France and Spain (see also Filella 1991). Spain's position near the centre of the matrix represents a cancelling-out of widely differing scores on both axes. This is in distinction to the other countries where scores on either axis tend to be consistent. It is a country in a period of considerable flux arising from its relatively recent adoption of democracy, fast economic growth and late accession to the EC. The role of the HR department clearly reflects this.

The bottom left-hand quadrant also contains some culturally disparate countries. The only things they have in common are a relatively high 'achievement' culture (in Hofstede 1980, 1983 and also in a study by Trompenaars 1991) and a propensity to role formalisation (Laurent 1983). The position of the UK and Italy probably reflects an historical focus on a more antagonistic industrial relations role for personnel specialists, a low status for personnel departments and increasing attempts to establish a specific, and separate, competence for personnel specialists as a result. Those who have studied personnel management in Germany (see Ackermann 1986; Pieper 1990; Lawrence 1991; Gaugler and Wiltz 1992) point to the mechanistic nature of the function in that country. The strong adherence to a detailed legal and/or quasi-legal basis for the employment relationship, in the context of powerful works councils and a cooperative, and open, approach to trade unions, means that the personnel function is both isolated from corporate strategy-making and yet seen as the 'keeper of the law'; having to approve all actions in the human resources arena.

At the same time there is general acknowledgement that Germany has working conditions and practices which are amongst the most favourable to employees in Europe, one of the most educated and trained workforces, one of the highest degrees of worker involvement and a general tendency to include human resource issues in all major decisions (Randlesome 1990). This makes us question some aspects of the HRM concept as it has come to us in Europe from its originators in the USA. One of the central assumptions is that HRM is distinguished by the integration of personnel issues with business strategies. There is little evidence from our data that this takes place at the corporate level in one of the most successful countries in Europe. We would argue, unsupported by our evidence and therefore tentatively, that in the German case the integration of personnel issues in the collective cultural consciousness and in legislation may be more important than direct integration into corporate strategy.

Limitations of the study

It is useful to point out both the conceptual and methodological limitations of our research — and therefore potentially of our findings.

Conceptually, we have argued that an integration of business strategy and HRM is seen as a crucial element of strategic HRM. We have rejected the belief that business strategy by definition comes first, ie is the independent variable. In some organisations and/or situations, it will be appropriate to begin with the HRM strategy and form the business strategy around this. Such a 'competency-driven, or qualification based, strategy' may be typical, for example, in research or service oriented organisations which are very dependent on their human capital. We have also argued that the reasons for a particular level of devolvement might be somewhat diffuse and even conflicting. A high degree of devolvement to line management is not necessarily a reflection of a very conscious belief (and confidence) in the value of HRM. It is likely that organisations who do stress the importance of human resources choose to devolve a considerable part of HRM to line management. However, the opposite can be true as well. If an organisation does not stress the importance of human resources, perhaps no HRM function is established and responsibility is 'dumped' on line management.

Furthermore, our analysis has concentrated on national differences at the expense of sectoral, size or ownership differences. We believe our data has confirmed the value of such an approach, but we recognise that further analyses along these lines will enrich the contribution of this material.

Methodologically, there are three main limitations to our study. First, our data is limited to organisations with more than 200 employees. It is likely that small organisations have quite different approaches to integration and devolvement. Second, our objective of comparing organisational HR policies and practices across national boundaries has led us to collect data through a broad, representative, and large-scale survey. We have, therefore, had to use a limited number of general, surrogate measures to identify levels of integration and involvement. It is possible (though we believe it to be unlikely) that more qualitative measures within organisations may find, on a consistent, nationally determined basis, that the senior personnel specialists responding to our survey have provided information which is in some way biased by their position. It would be interesting to know, for example, whether senior line managers or even personnel specialists outside headquarters share our respondents' perceptions of HR functional involvement, or their perceptions of the extent to which authority in HR issues has been devolved to the line management. It is also possible that more detailed, case-study style, analysis of particular organisations will find better measures of integration and devolvement. Third, the rankings are relative, not absolute. It may well be, for example, that typical organisations in Sweden and Switzerland have a far from 'pivotal' approach to HRM. What we can say is that they are closer to it than the other eight countries for which we have data.

In summary, then, the data presented here shows clear national differences throughout Europe. It indicates that if the desired model is that of a close integration of HR with corporate strategy at the business level and the sharing of personnel responsibilities with line managers, Sweden and Switzerland, and to a lesser extent Norway and Denmark, approximate most closely to this 'pivotal' model of the HR function. However, the analysis also indicates that the 'American' model may not fit comfortably with the reality of HRM in Europe. It is interesting to note that the combination of high integration and high devolvement is in fact rare in the US. There, consciousness about strategy (and HRM) has been given a high profile, but the American culture does not generally favour devolvement and informal work procedures. This illustrates the need for us Europeans to build up our own, culturally adapted theory of HRM. We believe that our data provides a valuable basis for this next step.

REFERENCES

Ackermann, KF (1986) 'A Contingency Model of HRM Strategy — Empirical Research findings Reconsidered', *Management Forum*, vol 6, pp 65–117

Adler, N (1991) *International Dimensions of Organisational Behaviour* (2nd ed) PWS-Kent, Boston

Beaumont, PB (1991) 'The US Human Resource Management Literature: A Review', in Salaman *et al.* (eds) *Human Resource Strategies*, Open University, Milton Keynes

Beer, M, Lawrence, PR, Mills, QN and Walton, RE (1985) *Human Resource Management*, Free Press, New York

Bournois, F (1991) 'Gestion des RH en Europe: données comparées' *Revue Française de Gestion*, mars-avril-mai, pp 68–83

Brewster, C and Bournois, F (1991) 'A European Perspective on Human Resource Management', *Personnel Review*, vol 20, 6, pp 4–13

Brewster, C and Connock, S (1985) *Industrial Relations: Cost-Effective Strategies*, Hutchinson Business Books, London

Brewster, C, Hegewisch, A and Lockhart, T (1991), 'Researching Human Resource Management: the methodology of the Price Waterhouse Cranfield Project on European Trends', *Personnel Review*, vol 20, 6 pp 36–40

Brewster, C (1991) *The Management of Expatriates*, Kogan Page, London

Butler, JE (1988) 'Human Resource Management as a driving force in business strategy', *Journal of General Management*, vol 13, 4, pp 88–102

Conrad, P and Pieper, R (1990) 'HRM in the Federal Republic of Germany' in Pieper, R (ed), *HRM: An International Comparison*, Walter de Gruyter, Berlin

Cook, R and Armstrong, M (1990) 'The search for strategic HRM' *Personnel Management*, December, pp 30–33

Coulson-Thomas, C and Wakeham, A (1991) *The Effective Board: current practice myths and realities*, Institute of Directors, London

Coulson-Thomas, C (1990) *Professional development of and for the Board*, Institute of Directors, London

DeCenzo, DA and Robbins, SP (1988) *Personnel/Human Resource Management*, (3rd ed), Prentice Hall, Englewood Cliffs, N J

European Management Forum (1986), *Report on International Industrial Competitiveness*, EMF, Geneva

Filella, J (1991) 'Is there a Latin model in the management of human resources?' *Personnel Review*, vol 20, 6, pp 14–23

Fombrun, C Tichy, N and Devanna, M (1984) (eds) *Strategic human resource management*, John Wiley, New York

Freedman, A (1991) *The Changing Human Resources Function*, The Conference Board, New York

Gaugler, E and Wiltz, S (1992) 'Germany' in Brewster C, Hegewisch A, Holden L, Lockhart T (eds) *European Guide to Human Resource Management*, Academic Press, London

Guest, D (1990) 'HRM and the American Dream' *Journal of Management Studies*, vol 27, 4, pp 377–397

Guest, D (1989) 'Personnel and HRM: can you tell the difference?' *Personnel Management*, January, pp 48–51

Hendry, C and Pettigrew, A (1990) 'HRM: an agenda for the 1990s' *International Journal of Human Resource Management*, vol 1, 1, pp 17–25

Hofstede, G (1991) *Cultures and Organisations*, McGraw Hill, London

Hofstede, G (1983) 'The Cultural Relativity of Organisational Practices and Theories', *Journal of International Business Studies*, vol 13, 3, pp 75–90

Hofstede, G (1980) *Cultures Consequences: international differences in work-related values*, Sage, Beverley Hills

Hoogendoorn, J and Brewster, C (1992) 'Human Resource Aspects of Decentralisation and Devolution', *Personnel Review*, vol 21, pp 4–11

Laurent, A (1983) 'The Cultural Diversity of Western Conceptions of Management', *International Studies of Management and Organisation*, vol 13, 1–2, pp 75–96

Lawrence, P (1991) 'The personnel function: an Anglo-German comparison' in Brewster C and Tyson S (eds) *International Comparisons in Human Resource Management*, Pitman, London

Legge, K (1989) 'Human Resource Management: A Critical Analysis', in Storey J (ed) *New Perspectives on Human Resource Management*, Routledge, London

Lengnick-Hall, CA and Lengnick-Hall, ML (1988) 'Strategic Human Resources Management: A Review of the Literature and a Proposed Typology', *Academy of Management Review*, vol 13, 3, pp 454–70

Mahoney, T and Deckop, JR (1986) 'Evolution of concept and practice in personnel administration/human resource management' *Journal of Management*, vol 12, 2, pp 223–41

Miller, P (1989) 'Strategic HRM: what it is and what it isn't', *Personnel Management*, February, pp 46–51

Quinn Mill, D and Balbaky, M (1985) 'Planning for morale and culture' in Walton

R and Lawrence P (eds) *Human Resource Management — Trends and Challenges*, Harvard Business School Press, Boston, Mass

Randlesome, C (1990) *Business Cultures in Europe*, Heinemann, Oxford

Schein, E (1987) 'Increasing organisational effectiveness through better human resource planning and development', *Sloan Management Review*, vol 19, 1, pp 1–20

Schreyögg, G (1987) 'Verschlüsselte Botschaften Neue Perspektiven einer Strategischen Personalführung', *Zeischrift Führung und Organisation*, vol 56, 3, pp 151–58

Schuler RS (1992) 'Strategic Human Resource Management: Linking the People with the Strategic Needs of the Business' *Organisational Dynamics*, summer, pp 18–31

Schuler, RS (1990) 'Repositioning the Human Resource Function: Transformation or Demise?' *Academy of Management Executive*, vol 4, 3, pp 49–60

Storey, J (ed) (1989) *New Perspectives on Human Resource Management*, Routledge, London

Torrington, D (1989) 'Human Resource Management and the Personnel Function', in Storey J (ed), *New Perspectives on Human Resource Management*, Routledge, London

Trompenaars, F (1991) quoted in Hampden-Turner C, 'Towards a multi-cultural approach to creating wealth and value'. Paper presented to the Fifteenth EAPM Conference, Istanbul, June 1991

Watson, JW (1989) 'Human Resource Roles for the '90s', *Human Resource Planning*, March, Vol 12.1, pp 55–61

Wohlgemuth, AC (1988) 'Human Resources Management und die wirkungsvolle Vermaschung mit der Unternehmungspolitik', *Management-Zeitschrift Industrielle Organisation*, vol 56, 2, pp 115–118

9

HR MANAGEMENT: AN INTERNATIONAL COMPARISON

Eduard Gaugler, Mannheim University, Germany

An international comparison of HR management is no easy undertaking. To be sure, the literature includes a wealth of information and accounts of personal experiences in connection with HR management around the world. These accounts, however, are highly individual and cannot be considered complete. This article, too, falls short. It would be impossible for the present comparison to include every country, or even to discuss HR in all the most important industrialised countries of the world. Thus this review restricts itself to a discussion of a few selected aspects of international HR management.

First, we will note the similarities in HR management around the world. Next, we will examine how HR management differs from country to country. And finally, we will draw some conclusions from these similarities and differences.

BASIC HR FUNCTIONS THE WORLD OVER

Every organisation requires human labour to attain its goals and to fulfil its obligations. No company can do without personnel. Maintaining the supply of labour in an organisation requires that appropriate measures be taken by the management. The HR function therefore plays an essential role in the management of both medium-size and large companies throughout the world.

HR management encompasses various basic functions. First and foremost, it is the function of HR management to procure staff for the company. These people should be available, in the required numbers and with the qualifications needed for the work to be done, as and when the company needs them. It is also the object of HR management to procure them economically. This does not mean that salaries, wages, and fringe

---

benefits should be as low as possible; it means that the ratio between compensation costs and the employees' contribution to the work of the company should be as favourable as possible.

This point leads us on to discuss the second basic function of HR: managing employee compensation. Employee compensation is a central cost category for most companies. And because compensation levels influence employee attitudes, performances, and productivity, they have a major impact on organisational success. Moreover, the level of labour costs affects the competitive strength of the company on the local market, and the differing levels of labour costs play a major role in determining the international competitive strength of companies. The management of compensation systems is therefore a critical responsibility of HR management in several countries.

Another basic function of HR management is company leadership. Employees in all companies are not only interested in receiving high wages or salaries and generous fringe benefits; they also expect just treatment from their employers. Employee expectations include acceptable working conditions (safe and comfortable workplaces and reasonable hours of work, etc), appropriate work assignments, the opportunity to use their own abilities in their work (prospects for promotion), and good relations with their colleagues and supervisors. HR management therefore includes fostering humane working conditions, developing the staff's abilities, creating a positive work climate, and encouraging supervisors to adopt a fair attitude and style of leadership with their employees. The HR department should motivate the employees to make as great a contribution as they can to the attainment of company objectives, while showing that the company respects the human dignity of its employees.

Employment at the organisation is a major part of most employees' lives. There may be many links between their work in the company and their other spheres of life (their families, their leisure activities, etc). The company's responsibility for its employees may therefore extend beyond their involvement in the company's operations. In these instances, the social responsibility of the HR department extends to some of the employees' spare-time activities and to their families. It is particularly important here for HR to avoid having a negative influence on the employees' personal lives, and to offer assistance with their personal well-being. The company should not interfere, however, with the employee who wishes to maintain his or her privacy.

A MODERN CONCEPT OF HR

The above description of the basic HR functions represents the view that prevails in economically developed countries. There is no doubt that 100 — or even 50 — years ago, the concept of HR, even in the most progressive countries, was far more limited. The responsibilities of the HR department have expanded significantly in recent decades, for numerous reasons, and have won wider recognition and greater respect from employees in other departments.

In the more highly developed countries, at least, this concept of HR management is now widespread. In the less highly developed countries, interest in modern HR management is growing. And there are signs of a modern interpretation of the role of HR in various socialist countries as well.

Obviously, the concept of HR's role varies somewhat from country to country. But the conviction that HR management represents a basic element of general management is probably held everywhere. HR is as much a part of the modern-day concept of management as marketing, finance, and public relations. HR management is not viewed as simply an ancillary function of management, but as one of the central functions of management at all levels. There is ever-increasing recognition that the success of a company depends in large part on the success of its HR management.

CULTURAL DIFFERENCES AND HR

An international comparison of HR practices clearly indicates that the basic functions of HR management are given different weights in different countries, and that they are also carried out differently. The concept of HR management varies, as do the activities undertaken within the framework of HR management. Many reasons have been given for these differences. For many years, management scientists — and, in particular, theorists of international management — have been tackling the question of whether and to what extent cultural differences between various countries affect managerial practices.

Some researchers deny the influence of culture on management. As they see it, management involves a set combination of functions which have a particular, immutable nature and are carried out independently of the culture of the country concerned. They believe that in particular the economic duties of management are independent of the country's culture.

Other researchers, by contrast, adopt the 'cross cultural approach', which assumes that there are connections between culture and management in any country. These researchers emphasise that differences in HR management in different countries reflect differences between those countries' cultures. The idea that a country's culture influences its management practices, is being supported to an increasing degree by new theoretical arguments. Numerous empirical investigations in many countries have also found that the cultural characteristics of any one country can influence management in general and HR management in particular.

In short, a comparison of international HR management practices yields the following conclusions:

- It is generally recognised throughout the world that HR management is a basic element of general management.
- HR management is receiving increasing recognition and respect.
- The practice of HR management differs from country to country, and many management scientists believe that these differences reflect cultural differences among these countries (cross-cultural approach).

Whether or not we take the cross-cultural approach to our study of international HR management, we need to recognise that different cultures do in fact have different HR management styles. Let us examine a number of factors that may contribute to these differences.

CULTURAL FACTORS

In recent years, a number of countries in the Far East have recorded great economic success, and this has led to close examination of these countries' management practices. Research has not been restricted to examining the particular management techniques in these countries, such as '*ringi*' and '*nemawashi*' in Japan. It has also explored the roots of modern-day management in the history of thought in these countries.

The Far East, for example, did not experience an Age of Enlightenment as Europe did; and Marxism and Socialism have had little or no influence in Japan. The cultural background of the Far East, with its emphasis on the family and the great significance of the patriarchal system, is also markedly different from that of Western societies. These factors have all been studied as possible keys to the present-day success of Far Eastern management.

The Japanese view of the individual's relationship to the society has major implications for HR management in Japan. The human being is seen primarily as a member of a group, and the concept of the independent individual is given much less attention there than it is in the West. This difference may help explain, for example, why Japanese measures that are used to increase motivation are aimed primarily at the working group. In the West, by contrast, measures to increase motivation generally focus on the individual worker.

Cross-cultural HR management

When employees from one culture are employed at an organisation that is governed by another culture's management practices, the differences between the two cultures may become painfully evident. Two to three decades ago, for example, the economic sector of the Federal Republic of Germany recruited several million workers from foreign countries, among them Greece and Turkey. Many of those Greek and Turkish workers' general upbringings and educations were incompatible with the culture of the modern German workplace. The workers had difficulty in gaining the acceptance of their German colleagues and supervisors. the HR department, which was accustomed to dealing with a fairly homogenous workforce, was confronted for the first time with the conflicts that inevitably arise from diversity. They found themselves largely unable to understand the foreigners' attitudes and reactions.

Many organisations, however, recognise that the HR staff needs to be familiar with the employees' cultural background in order to manage effectively. The US companies that established themselves in Germany after the Second World War learned to function with US experts and managers in their German branches; and they learned to operate their HR departments with German staffs. Similarly, the German companies that are now establishing branches in the United States engage mainly US experts and managers for their HR management in those branches. And Japanese and Korean companies entrust Germans with their HR management in their larger branches in the Federal Republic of Germany. These companies' top managements recognise the importance of having an HR staff that is compatible with the employees throughout the company. An HR staff that shares the employees' cultural background is more likely to be sensitive to the employees' needs and expectations in the workplace — and is thus more likely to manage the company successfully.

ETHNIC DIVERSITY

In many countries, the local workforce itself is quite diverse. Many companies have found that a diverse workforce can enrich the organisation's creativity and innovative spirit. But diversity can also make special demands on the HR staff. In the Federal Republic of Germany, the United States, and Great Britain, for example, many HR managers are in charge of ethnically heterogeneous workforces. In Japan and Korea, by contrast, HR management is not confronted by the challenges that come from a mixed workforce.

The demands placed on HR management by an ethnically mixed workforce vary tremendously. In some companies, the workforce is well integrated and harmonious. In others, however, ethnic and/or racial tensions and a lack of communication among employees from different groups create serious obstacles to the maintenance of high performance and productivity. The HR department at such companies faces special challenges.

ECONOMIC FACTORS

HR management is a part of the general management of the company, which in turn is part of the nation's economy. The structure and the position of the national economy therefore exert an indirect influence on each company's HR management.

The differences between socialist economies and free enterprise economies, for example, are of considerable significance for HR management. In planned economy systems, the fulfilment of the government's plan by the individual organisation is of primary importance, and the HR department, like the rest of the organisation, has to serve this paramount interest. At the same time, the HR department in this kind of system must adopt an employment policy that prevents unemployment. HR management in socialist enterprises is therefore steered to a large degree toward external goals which are determined by central organs of government.

In a free enterprise system, the success and continued existence of a company depend in large part on its efficiency in competition with other domestic and foreign companies. Thus the activities of all the employees must contribute to enabling the company to work and compete successfully. Economic efficiency is therefore a goal for HR management as well.

HR and competition

Competition on the selling market varies tremendously in intensity. In the

Federal Republic of Germany, many companies are confronted on the domestic market with heavy competition both from other domestic companies and from foreign companies. On the world market, too, many German companies face keen competition. In such companies, HR management must stimulate the employees to be very flexible and highly motivated. They must encourage the employees to accept innovations which are intended to improve the company's competitive strength. HR management must also promote the creativity of the staff through suggestion systems, quality circles, and other techniques so that as many employees as possible may contribute to improving the company's market position. [Keen competition in a competitive national and international economy provides a great challenge for HR management. Countries with a protectionist trading policy, by contrast, make it possible for HR management to be relatively passive.]

HR management's contribution is especially critical in a free-market economy whose labour costs are relatively high. The majority of highly developed industrialized countries have high wage levels; many companies in these countries have to cope with very high labour costs per working hour (including wages, salaries, benefits, and other ancillary labour costs). By contrast, less developed countries usually have much lower labour costs.

High labour costs require employees to maintain a high productivity level in order for the company to remain competitive. In countries with high labour costs, HR management therefore must continually strive to improve the employees' performance. This may explain why in some highly developed countries HR accounting and HR controlling have received more and more attention in recent years: These tools allow HR management to control and increase productivity when labour costs are high and still rising.

THE INDUSTRIAL RELATIONS FACTOR

Industrial relations systems throughout the world are based on very different structures and function very differently. The great differences that exist in industrial relations in different countries provide quite different frameworks for the HR management of individual companies in those countries. Before we can judge the significance these international differences in industrial relations have for HR management, we must first examine several key factors that make up a country's industrial relations system:

- the influence of the state on the relations between employers and trade unions;
- the relationship between the employers and the trade unions; and
- the degree of employee participation in the management of the company.

In socialist countries, the state exerts a very strong influence on industrial relations. The state steers the economy in accordance with its plans, and very often the state itself functions as an employer. The trade unions in these countries are subject to the political and economic aims of the state; they are required to support the state in the fulfilment of its economic plans. Industrial action by the trade unions (ie strikes) is forbidden. The state and the Communist Party control the trade unions in the socialist countries and restrict their influence on HR management in the company.

In capitalist countries, the state usually interferes very little or not at all in the relations and negotiations between employers and trade unions. In some countries, minimum wage levels are prescribed by law. In the United States, the president can suspend industrial disputes that constitute a threat to public welfare by invoking the Taft-Hartley Act. In the Federal Republic of Germany, the state allows employers and trade unions complete freedom in the conclusion of collective labour contracts. In these countries, each company's HR management policy is influenced very strongly by the agreements reached between the employers' associations and the trade unions.

The nature of the relationship between the employer and the trade union has a significant impact on the HR manager's role. In some countries, the two sides generally reach their agreements without conflict; in others, industrial disputes are frequent. This aspect of industrial relations varies greatly even among highly developed, industrialised countries. In Japan and Switzerland industrial disputes have been rare for a long time; but such conflicts are common in Italy, Great Britain, and the United States. Frequent industrial disputes can place a great burden on HR management. They may damage the company's financial stability and strain cooperation between employees and management. Companies are therefore usually eager to reach an agreement with the trade unions quickly and without dispute. Good cooperation between management and staff is easier to achieve in the individual company if disputes between trade unions and management are rare. This cooperation has been achieved in Japan, Switzerland, the Federal Republic of Germany, the Netherlands, Denmark, and Sweden. In these countries, HR management is rarely disrupted by industrial disputes. This does not mean, however, that the trade unions in these countries are weak or that they have no influence on HR management.

Agreements between trade unions and employers generally regulate compensation, benefits, and many other working conditions. These agreements form the framework for HR management within each company. If we compare employee wages and working conditions in several countries, we will find great differences in the standards set by law and by collective labour contracts. HR management, which is bound by these standards, thus varies accordingly. Laws and contracts, however, usually set the minimum standards for the company. Management can — and often does — go beyond these minimum standards in providing benefits for its employees. Determining the benefits to be provided and administering the benefits programme are two key aspects of the HR management role.

In many countries the trade unions have representatives within individual companies. In such cases, HR management sometimes acts as a direct partner in the company's negotiations with the trade unions. In the Federal Republic of Germany, specific laws govern co-determination by employees, requiring that employees have a say in setting company policies. These include the Works Constitution Act (1972), the Co-determination Act (1976), and the ECSC Co-determination Act (1951). These laws govern the co-determination of the works council and co-determination in the supervisory board of the company. Under these rulings, the employees elect their own representatives to the works council and to the supervisory board, and there is also a vice-president for labour at the top management level. The laws on the co-determination of employees in the company largely set HR policy in many German firms. They require HR management to support the interests of the staff in the setting of management policies. As the World Congress of International Industrial Relations Association, based at the International Labour Office in Geneva, showed in meetings in Hamburg in September 1986, the German ruling on co-determination by employees has met with great acclaim throughout the world. It appears, however, that no other country in the world is willing to adopt this German model.

THE LABOUR AVAILABILITY FACTOR

The availability of a potential workforce in a given country also influences HR management practice there. In countries with tight supplies of labour, HR management is forced to take active measures so that the companies can satisfy their personnel requirements.

After the Second World War, the Federal Republic of Germany was faced with overemployment for a long time. Germany's available workforce was not large enough to meet the companies' needs. Confronted with the choice between transferring their production to other countries where manpower was available, or bringing foreign workers into Germany, many companies took the latter option. In 1973, this trend reached its peak: at that time 2.6 million foreign workers (11.6 per cent of the working population) were employed in the Federal Republic. In 1986, 1.6 million foreigners (7.7 per cent of the working population) remained in Germany; of these, 13.7 per cent were unemployed. As discussed earlier, the procurement of foreign workers in the 1960s and 1970s and their integration into the companies presented HR management in Germany with a new challenge.

In Germany, as in many other industrialised countries, there has been considerable unemployment for a number of years. Up until 1987, only Switzerland, Sweden, Norway, and Japan had very low rates of unemployment.

Yet despite high unemployment, many companies in these countries have difficulty finding the employees they need. This is because the unemployed population largely lacks the skills, training, and experience the companies require.

This situation has had a major impact on HR management. HR must continually seek new ways to attract and retain employees who have those skills and experience that are in particular demand and short supply. In countries where the shortage of qualified workers is particularly acute, HR management has an additional function. By means of employee development programmes, including extensive occupational training, the companies strive to qualify previously unskilled people for jobs that they are otherwise unable to fill. In some countries, similar training programmes have also been implemented to retrain employees for new jobs as technology renders their previous jobs obsolete. Planning and administering such training programmes are major new responsibilities for the HR department.

These training initiatives can also be applied to many developing and threshold countries. In the majority of these countries there are large numbers of unemployed people with too few qualifications for most jobs. By providing these people with professional qualifications, HR management in these countries could help alleviate the enormous unemployment that plagues their economies.

TECHNOLOGICAL FACTORS

A country's designation as developing, threshold, or highly developed corresponds in part with the educational level and professional training of its population. The designation also indicates the country's degree of technological development. In highly developed, industrialised countries, companies engage in technological research and use new technologies extensively. This reliance on technology has a significant impact on HR practices in highly developed countries.

Technology and unemployment

As mentioned earlier, many highly developed countries suffer from chronic unemployment. Much of this is structural unemployment: it results when employees lose their jobs — and cannot find new ones — because they are not skilled in new technologies. The rapid pace of technological progress requires that HR managers foresee the demands that future technologies will place on the staff and enable them to gain the qualifications required for these new technologies in good time. Providing technological training for employees is a major challenge for HR management both in highly developed countries, with rapid technological progress, and in the threshold countries as well.

HR and user friendliness

In some countries that are active in developing technological innovations, HR management has a new and very important function: contributing to the development of new technologies that are designed with safety and comfort in mind. In the Federal Republic of Germany, for example, there has been enormous progress in the design of technologies that take into consideration the requirements of the people using them. As a result, the number of industrial accidents has dropped from 2.7 million in 1960 to 1.5 million in 1985. Modern-day information and communications technologies that are predominantly used in the office and in administration are increasingly responsive to the requirements and expectations of the staff. HR management can – and should – play an increasingly large role in contributing to the responsiveness of new technology in all sectors of the company.

Making technology humane

New technologies — particularly in the information and communications areas — are resulting in new ways of organising work and assigning tasks. HR management must make sure that the new technologies are combined with humane work practices. Contributing to the humane design of technologies and of work organisation is a central function of modern HR management in the highly developed countries.

The implementation and use of modern technologies — especially automation and robots — often require major capital investments. These capital investments can be recovered most readily by using the technologies intensively. This economic objective, however, conflicts with an employee objective: the shortening of the work week. One possible solution to this problem is making the working hours of the individual employee more flexible. Several successive shifts of workers could then use the new technology each day.

In Germany, for example, flexible working schedules have met with employee approval and have also allowed for the greatest possible use of technology. Thus for both humane and economic reasons, HR management in the highly developed countries is now being called upon to develop and implement flexible employee schedules.

Above all, the continual changes in the workplace that result from technological developments require that HR be innovative and responsive to change. Modern HR management cannot remain passive toward technological development; it must be creative in its search for economical and humane solutions to HR and organisational problems.

The solutions to these problems may also prove helpful to HR management in those countries that are still on the way to mechanisation. When such solutions to problems are transposed from one country to another, consideration must of course be given to the characteristics of the companies and their respective staffs. A mere imitation that ignored the special characteristics of the countries and their cultures would be unlikely to succeed.

WHAT'S AHEAD FOR HR MANAGEMENT

The above discussion of the various roles of HR throughout the world is based on a particular concept of HR management. The roles of HR management in any company reflect the economic objectives of the company and the requirements and interests of the employees. This general description applies to HR management in developing countries, in threshold countries, and in highly developed countries. How the HR function is carried out, of course, varies greatly from country to country.

Throughout the world, however, HR management is a basic element of general management. In medium-size and large companies the functions of HR management are increasing in scope; and the complexity of these functions requires professionalism and expertise. HR management requires specialised skills and training; but this specialisation must not lead to the isolation of the HR department from the rest of management or from the rest of the staff. Regular contact between the HR staff and the rest of the employees is a prerequisite for successful HR management.

In the past, the HR role was often a 'sideline' performed by people whose principal jobs were in other departments. HR was viewed as a secondary function that did not require special knowledge or training. Today, however, it is well recognised throughout the world that HR management requires professional training. Universities and colleges in many highly developed countries and in threshold countries now offer programmes in HR management. In German-speaking countries alone (the Federal Republic, Austria, and Switzerland) there are more than 40 universities where HR management is taught. In addition, HR management programmes are offered at many technical colleges. Similar training for future HR managers is available in the United States, in Great Britain and several other European countries, in Australia, and in a number of countries in the Far East.

In fact, as a result of the dynamic development of the HR field in many countries, for some HR managers this basic training is not enough. Institutes other than universities and colleges now offer further, advanced training for HR managers and directors; they also provide forums where experienced HR people can share their experience and learn from that of their colleagues. Such meetings occur on both the national and the international levels.

On the basis of these considerations we can draw several conclusions about the necessary abilities and characteristics of HR managers. First, they must be committed to both achieving the economic goals of the company and meeting the needs of the employees. When problems arise and decisions have to be made, they must be flexible and innovative enough to find solutions that will benefit both the company and its staff. Above all, they must have the energy, foresight, and intelligence to grow and develop along with the burgeoning field of HR.

Postscript

Due to the fundamental changes which took place in Central and Eastern

Europe during the last few years, trade unions in these countries are now liberated from their dependence on the state and the Communist Party. In particular, East Germany has seen the growth there of free trade unions from western Germany. The so called *Kader* (management development and selection) policy in East German enterprises, dominated by the political objectives of the SED (the old ruling party), has disappeared since reunification. Human resource management in eastern German companies since is more and more approximating to the western German model.

Eduard Gaugler, May 1993

10

HUMAN RESOURCE MANAGEMENT IN GREECE*

Nancy Papalexandris, Athens University of Economics and Business, Greece

INTRODUCTION

The early years of the 1990s see efforts being made by all member states of the European Community to adjust to the challenge of the Single European Market. These efforts and their successful outcomes are of vital importance, particularly for the economically weaker countries of the community. As one of them, Greece is faced with the necessity to rethink its policies and strategies, in both the private and public sectors of its economy. All the functions of enterprises (marketing, finance, production) are being re-examined, restructured, and adjusted to meet the forthcoming changes.

In view of the above, it is evident that adopting a successful strategy in any economic sector or organisation depends largely on the human resources which will undertake its implementation. Many Greek firms, especially larger ones, seem to have realised this to a considerable extent. Human resource policies and practices are being re-examined in general. But, in particular, Greek firms are trying to adopt methods and techniques already successfully applied by multinational companies (MNCs) operating in the country. At the same time, there is a strong movement towards introducing human resource management (HRM) in the public sector.

This article will try:

- to present an overall picture of the current state of HRM in Greek organisations in the public sector;
- to pinpoint problems and issues facing firms and practitioners;
- to describe future challenges and prospects as they appear to be

* This chapter first appeared in *Employee Relations*, vol 14, 4, 1992. Permission for its reproduction here is acknowledged with gratitude.

emerging from the country's full integration into the European Community, and the gradual but inevitable removal of borders between its member states.

HUMAN RESOURCE MANAGEMENT IN GREEK ORGANISATIONS

Human resource management has received an ever-increasing amount of attention during the past two decades in the highly industrialised countries of the world. This has resulted in a situation where the personnel function has come to be regarded as of equal importance to production, finance or marketing. In many instances, top managers are heard to maintain, in public, that the key factor to their firm's success can be found in the quality of their human resources.

In Greece, some formalised personnel activities in selecting, appraising and remunerating employees have existed in the larger private and public sector firms for a considerable period of time. However, these activities were not geared towards assisting individuals to develop their potential, or to make a significant contribution to their organisations' effectiveness, as a result of increased job satisfaction.

In the early 1960s, there was a spectacular upturn in the economy, following the Association Agreement of Greece to the EEC and the influx of foreign multinational firms which invested in the country. Foreign firms provided a challenge to the attitudes of Greek company owners concerning the practice of management in general, and HRM staff in particular. MNCs started successfully using sophisticated management staffing techniques, which Greek firms seemed to ignore at that time. Greek firms followed their example only at a rather slow pace until the start of the 1980s.

Research studies covering this period showed that, compared to other management functions, HRM seemed to lack sophistication, and the application of modern human resource management practices was rather limited. This was seen as a reason for the low level of organisational effectiveness of Greek firms at the time. In the 1980s, and following full membership of Greece to the EEC, the situation seemed to change, as some large and progressive Greek firms applied HRM similarly to the MNCs operating in Greece.

A research study was conducted in 1986, among 25 medium to large (100–499 employees) and 25 very large (more than 500 employees) manufacturing firms in the private sector. Its main objective was to identify the methods by which companies recruit, select, appraise, promote and train their managers. A follow-up study in 1988 examined a paired sample of five larger Greek and five multinational manufacturing firms.

Finally, a survey in 1989 studied 272 firms operating in Greece, belonging to all branches of the economy (manufacturing, trade, banking, insurance, transportation, shipping, tourism, construction and various other services). These firms were selected because they had specifically developed a personnel function, employing managers to deal exclusively with personnel matters. Based on these surveys, as well as on information about the Greek managerial context in general, an overall picture of HRM activities can be presented. The term HRM will be used interchangeably with the term 'personnel management', as there is no real distinction between them in Greece.

THE ROLE AND PROFESSIONALISATION OF PERSONNEL MANAGERS

According to Kanellopoulos (1990), in almost all firms which possess a personnel department, its significance is equal to that of other departments (production, finance, marketing) and the personnel manager reports directly to the head of the company. In some MNCs, the personnel manager reports directly to the personnel manager at company headquarters.

In most cases, personnel managers are university graduates, have attended executive seminars in personnel matters, and speak at least one foreign language. Their university education typically covers economics or business administration, while a smaller percentage have studied social sciences, law, technical subjects or else have previous service in the military forces.

The educational level of personnel managers can be considered satisfactory, although economics and business graduates who studied in Greece during the 1960s and 1970s, and who are now heads of departments, will not have received any training in personnel matters. Such subjects were not included in university curricula at the time, and personnel managers' lack of academic knowledge may have been offset by attendance at training courses.

In past decades, the presence of retired military officers was significant, since it was felt that they possessed personnel skills acquired during their service. There was also a preference, in the past, for personnel managers with legal backgrounds, which was justified by the frequent changes and complexities of labour legislation. Many personnel managers, however, had no university education, but had joined their firms at low hierarchical levels and had achieved their position following long years of loyal service. The shift of qualifications among personnel managers towards more business-related subjects appears to be an encouraging sign. Nevertheless, there seems to be more need for post-experience training in the field, especially in firms located outside Athens or Salonika, where the main opportunities for training are concentrated.

Personnel managers reach their position as head of their department following an average of thirteen years' experience in the personnel function. Most of them have worked in various firms and in various departments. This is due to the fact that HRM has only recently become established in Greece, and so managers from various other departments have moved in. Another reason is the small size of firms, which means that opportunities for promotion are limited, and high levels of mobility can be seen between both departments and firms.

A range of qualities, abilities and characteristics appears to play a major role in determining the effectiveness of personnel managers. These include experience, knowledge of personnel matters and business matters in general, social and negotiation skills, an acceptable personality, interest in the job and in people. Such criteria indicate, even more, the need for special training in both personnel matters and in human skills development. This training has already started over the past years, but it needs to be further developed.

According to Kanellopoulos's 1990 survey, the activities which are considered of major importance to Greek personnel departments are:

- selection and recruitment;
- performance and appraisal;
- training and development;
- industrial relations;
- salary and wage administration.

These activities coincide with activities which are mentioned in the international literature as those important for HRM. The least important activities include:

- handling of employee suggestions and complaints;
- opinion and attitude surveys of employees;
- disciplinary action;
- working hours and shift patterns;
- transfers;
- dismissals and demotions.

These results show that personnel departments consider most important those activities which could be characterised as developmental. They rate as of least importance those which are concerned with discipline and control. The fact that employee attitude surveys are not considered important shows that there is scope for enlargement of HRM activities, especially in the area of communications and employee relations.

In the sections which follow, additional information will be presented on those activities which occupy most personnel managers' time and which are considered by them to be most important in Greek firms.

MAJOR ACTIVITIES OF PERSONNEL DEPARTMENTS

Selection and recruitment

Until recently, few Greek firms appeared to have formalised and systematic policies of selecting and recruiting to managerial posts. Today, most larger Greek, and all multinational, firms try to recruit young graduates who show managerial potential, to be able to apply subsequently a policy of staffing from within.

As a general rule, practices differ according to the size and ownership of firms. Larger Greek firms and foreign subsidiaries use a variety of sources for recruitment, including the use of consultants' services, advertisements and personal connections. This allows for a wider number of alternatives than for all Greek firms, which make extensive use of their personal contacts. For recruitment to top management positions, such as managing director and/or functional directors, foreign subsidiaries also have the alternative of accepting a manager directly from company headquarters or from other sister companies. The policy of attracting managers from other firms ('poaching') also occurs, primarily through offering a higher reward package. On the other hand, larger firms have the advantage of receiving more employment requests from various individuals at any given time, thanks to their prestige and good name in the business market; this occurs despite their compensation practices, which are not necessarily more generous than those of smaller firms.

The larger Greek firms and foreign subsidiaries are more demanding when it comes to selection. In fact, the more extensive lists of characteristics and qualifications (person specifications) which they expect from their potential employees (in contrast to smaller Greek firms) indicate clearly that such firms are in a position to demand them. Despite occasional variations in the qualifications expected, all firms set defined selection criteria. Foreign subsidiaries seem to give more weight to experience, cooperation or team spirit, as well as education in the particular field of the position concerned, followed by an MBA obtained abroad. Among Greek firms, a tendency to look for intelligence and a wide perception is apparent, together with adequate references or experiences.

In smaller firms, friends' recommendations are often taken seriously into consideration and such candidates are favoured, provided they are equal to, or not significantly worse than, other candidates. In manufacturing, it is very common to have members of the same family or their relatives working together, and this is believed to improve loyalty to the firm. Apart from blue-collar workers, where references play a major role, administrative and managerial staff undergo initial screening and selection (which, as a rule, are separate) due to the large number of candidates. An initial screening of the curriculum vitae is usually undertaken by the personnel manager, the managing director, or by an organisation consultant. Psychometric tools and personality tests are often used by consultants for higher posts. The final selection of more senior managers is usually the responsibility of the managing director, but is preceded by a series of interviews with the department head and personnel manager. Recruitment consultants are occasionally involved in initial screening, so that their personnel manager does not spend time on obviously unsuitable candidates. In some firms, apart from interviews, questionnaires are completed by the candidates to assess their perceptions, objectivity, team spirit, drive and other personal characteristics. Additional optional written tests on the specialist field of employment concerned may be administered.

In general, selection follows a strict procedure, starting from screening carried out by a personnel department (where one exists) or by a personnel bureau. It continues with interviews given by the immediate superior or the director of the position to be filled; and ends up with an interview, or just the approval of the managing director, depending on the importance of the position. Occasionally, a committee for higher managerial position is also formed in some foreign subsidiaries.

Summing up, we can conclude that selection and recruitment in Greece varies, primarily according to the size and ownership of the firm. Sophisticated practices, implemented with the assistance of business consultants or by the firms' human resource specialists, are applied by larger Greek firms and subsidiaries of foreign multinationals. On the other hand, smaller Greek firms rely most on family connections, personal contacts or newspaper advertisements, although opinions are being expressed for the situation to change drastically in favour of more sophistication and objectivity.

Performance appraisal

Performance appraisal aims at keeping a record of how well an employee is performing in her/his job. Originally, the most widely used method of performance appraisal in Greek firms, even of larger size, was the superordinate making some sort of unstructured judgment of the subordinate. Appraisal later became more formalised and comprised (in most cases) part of the routine job of the personnel department. It typically consisted of the routine measurement of employee characteristics, using checklist forms and giving grades for various character traits such as initiative, reliability, personality, etc. Today, the trend is in the direction of evaluating more what the person *does* (job behaviour) rather than what he/she *is*, although this is quite often not without difficulties.

Performance appraisal for managerial posts is increasing in sophistication, along with the growing size and professionalisation of Greek firms; the problems involved in its practice are also multiplying. According to research data, commonly found problems are the selection and measurement methods for performance evaluation criteria, as well as the impartiality of the appraiser. The main objectives of appraisal systems are detecting those employees who have undeveloped potential and are eligible for promotion, and those who are able to profit from training opportunities in order to replace superiors or ensure the expansion, diversification or succession needs of the firm. In the event of no opportunities existing for improving a manager's position, salary increases are used to compensate high-performing managers, who must also be kept informed of their organisational ranking.

A complete appraisal system was found to exist in all MNCs, which adhered to guidelines laid down by parent companies abroad. Three people were involved in the appraisal: the immediate supervisor, the personnel manager and the department manager. Appraisal was based on Management by Objectives (MBO) and target setting. It was reported that this had worked well, but mainly in marketing departments, where the planned volume of sales was an easy target to define.

In most firms, the immediate superior was required to conduct the appraisal annually, with the help of standard printed forms. Subordinates were evaluated according to certain rather general and subjective criteria, such as loyalty to the firm, integrity, hard work, theoretical knowledge and the ability to communicate with subordinates. Some more objective criteria were also used, such as meeting deadlines in preparing financial statements, or filling orders on time. This emphasis on more subjective criteria is in line with the similar approach (mentioned earlier) used by Greek firms in recruitment and selection. Some Greek firms were rather reluctant to disclose appraisal information to the employees, as this could possibly create tension; only the personnel managers and/or the chief executive had access to this information.

Firms surveyed mentioned the following difficulties in implementing appraisal programmes. When deciding to introduce performance appraisal a few years ago, one company faced conflict among top management and other managers would not agree on which criteria to include in the valuation. Personal likes and dislikes were brought up during the experimental stage of the appraisal, to such a extent that, finally, the effort was considered a waste of time and was abandoned. A second company reported that the need for an appraisal system had been realised, but the lack of job specifications and job descriptions of managers made it difficult to proceed. Most companies reported that they practised appraisal only for lower technical and some supervisory jobs; managers were perfectly adequately assessed informally or not assessed at all. They believed that there was no actual need for evaluation, as everyone knew how everyone else performed, and informal, everyday contact gave the opportunity for observation and appraisal.

While formal appraisal was not considered justifiable in smaller, family-type firms, the rather limited use of formal appraisal in larger Greek firms is due to the existence of close personal relationships and the difficulty in setting precise targets, as a result of frequent changes in the external environment of firms. Employees, especially in larger firms where unions exist, usually resent the introduction of appraisal systems, favouring seniority as the main criterion for promotion instead.

Personnel managers in most progressive firms believe that the limited utilisation of performance appraisal has implications for promotion and training. It is the less able employee who will profit from lack of appraisal, or from routine appraisal using subjective criteria. As any determination of training needs and procedures depends very much on promotion opportunities, as well as on the appraisal of managers' capabilities, a serious restriction is placed on the firms' HRM in those cases where appraisal is not carried out objectively.

Hopefully, this situation is gradually changing. Personnel managers in many Greek firms are spending time and effort to find ways of overcoming obstacles and improving the objectivity and accountability of their performance appraisal system. Efforts are being made to link payment with productivity, and MBO and target-setting are becoming more extensively practised. All these changes are believed to be very important steps, which will increase the competitiveness of Greek and, in the process, the importance of HRM.

Training and development

One of the main features emerging from HRM research in Greece is the strong belief, of almost all respondents, in the value of training as a means of improving individual, group, or company performance. In the 1986 study, 84 per cent of the top managers surveyed claimed to be enthusiastic about training. In 20 per cent of firms, there was also a specific policy for training which provided for a linkage between training, appointments to management positions, and business plans. All the MNCs, and some of the Greek firms surveyed, carried out an analytical identification of training needs, made a careful selection of training activities and methods, and set relevant criteria for training evaluation. This percentage has increased significantly in the early 1990s, as will be described later. In 1986, much variation was found in the extent of participation in training courses. Some firms sent one or two managers annually to attend a seminar. Other firms, especially foreign subsidiaries, provided training for all members of managerial status. Interviews showed that there was a significant relationship between company size and foreign ownership and the sophistication of training offered. Larger and foreign-owned firms were more likely to possess a developed in-house training function. They also had more precise criteria for the selection of participants and attracted more value to their training efforts than did smaller and Greek-owned firms.

On-the-job training programmes were found to be a small part of the total training offered, with the exception of technical training for middle managers which was provided in most manufacturing firms. Serious efforts were made in the field of accident and fire prevention. Technical managers had to act as trainers themselves, to help their subordinates in accident prevention. Publications, posters, and films were used and, in some cases, technical managers followed training seminars outside Greece to be able to communicate their knowledge to their subordinates. One company reported that its technical managers were also using class discussions, held during training events, as a means to observe which of their subordinates would be able to move up into branches all over Greece, and had organised technical demonstrations using their head-office technical managers as tutors for their regional technical personnel, as well as offering courses for their customers. Apart from acting as trainers themselves, technical managers were in close contact with machinery suppliers abroad to facilitate technical acceptance. There were exchanges of visits with relevant factories abroad under 'know-how' or consulting agreements, and frequent visits to international technical exhibitions.

Off-the-job practices included both internal and external courses. Internal courses were organized in 38 per cent of firms, including all foreign subsidiaries. Greeks who had replaced foreign nationals in top positions in these firms had continued to follow guidelines provided by the parent company, which invariably gave support to extensive training. Thus managers in foreign firms attended courses or conferences at the headquarters' training centres abroad, while junior recruits were sent to receive practical, local, on-the-job training. In-house seminars were organised locally in Greece, and a training department responsible for the coordination of activities was reported to exist in these firms.

Internal training seemed also to have gained popularity among Greek firms. Some were found to organise courses quite frequently, while the remainder invited foreign experts, or Greek consultants, once or twice a year, to conduct seminars on issues requiring immediate attention. Again, technical managers were more involved in internal training activities, receiving training in data processing, production control, and planning, stock and quality control. This training was also offered by experts sent from abroad by machinery suppliers.

External courses were used by 52 per cent of firms which did not have in-house training, as well as by 28 per cent of those which did. The two main management training centres used were the Greek Management Association and the Greek Productivity Centre, which attracted 90 per cent of training participants. A small percentage of courses was offered by private firms such as banking, insurance or computer companies, which organised training events and invited participants to increase their publicity, or to promote their own products. Attendance at management centres abroad such as Management Centre Europe, the American Management Association, the Harvard Business School, INSEAD and IMEDE, was reported by ten firms. Managers in the buying, export/import and marketing functions were reported to travel frequently to attend conferences or visit exhibitions. Firms with in-house training participated occasionally in external courses, when the topic was of interest. In some cases, where the course was thought to be useful for the whole firm, management centres were asked to make an in-house presentation. The most popular subjects were management, organisation and personnel. This is to be expected, since these areas have only recently been covered by business schools, and since the increase in the size of firms has made the organisation of the personnel function relatively more complex.

Over the past few years, the amount of internal training offered has increased considerably, as a result of subsidies provided by the European Community. Several consultancy firms have started to offer specialised training courses, at both an executive and middle management level, while lower level employees have also had exposure to general, non-technical, managerial and administrative subjects. This general increase in the quantity of training is gradually being followed up by an improvement in its quality. There is evidence today of a more systematic approach to the identification of training needs, to the measurement of training results, and to the selection of participants on the basis of learning and performance needs. Even smaller firms have realised that training can be valuable only if done on a systematic and needs-related basis, and with a subsequent critical evaluation. This, in turn, forces training agencies and training consultants to improve the quality of their services to meet competition and to satisfy a market which is much more aware today than it was a few years ago.

Employee relations, pay and benefits

Employee relations are of major importance for personnel managers, especially in larger firms. Personnel managers interviewed in the 1986 study all agreed on certain characteristics of the labour force which they had to take into careful consideration to keep industrial peace. These included:

- pressure by workers for higher wages;

- the importance of fairness in payment, and workers' expectations of various benefits;
- length of service, rather than merit, as a payment criterion and the value attached to job security;
- the unwillingness to accept orders from middle managers, and the desire to have access to grievance procedure leading to top management;
- the problem of managing an intelligent and hard-working labour force, which also displayed tendencies to question authority, to be strongly individualistic, and to have difficulty in teamwork.

In considering these characteristics, big manufacturing firms have been active in providing fringe benefits which, reportedly, have worked well in preventing labour conflict. Generally speaking, firms which can afford to do so offer as much as possible to keep their workers satisfied. In smaller firms, top management is always available to handle complaints

173

and sort out misunderstandings. Added to this is the fact that a close, almost family relationship is maintained with many members of the workforce; the owner may act as the best man at weddings, for example, or as godfather to his workers' children.

Two personnel managers in the survey reported that they always keep an open telephone line and accept calls by workers, to solve misunderstandings within the workforce or with their supervisors. These seem to occur quite often, as most supervisors have been promoted from the shopfloor and their authority is frequently questioned. In one particular firm, bad manners and insults from a supervisor to a worker caused a strike and serious loss of time and money.

Besides problems of relations between the workforce and supervisors, problems among workers themselves have often to be resolved by personnel managers. An illustrative example was given by a firm in food processing, where, whenever seasonal workers had to be employed, permanent workers unjustifiably considered them a threat to their employment, treating them in such a hostile way that the atmosphere became extremely unpleasant.

In larger firms especially, personnel managers have to cope with the strong influence of trade unions and their representatives within the firm. Strikes were not an uncommon phenomenon in larger firms during the 1980s. Besides claims by trade union representatives for higher pay, demands were made for better working conditions, and various claims pressed for involvement in management decisions.

In larger firms, working conditions are a main concern of management, and regulations exist for safety at work. Nevertheless, some accidents have occurred due to the unwillingness of workers to follow safety regulations. Personnel managers have, therefore, a very important task in educating workers about hazards and convincing them to wear necessary accessories such as glasses, helmets or rubber shoes.

Handling trade union representatives' claims and complaints requires much skill and effort on the part of personnel management. Often, investment decisions (such as the introduction of technology or plans for modernisation) can be a source of dispute between management and workers' representatives, who fear the loss of jobs. Some firms encourage the training of trade union representatives to improve mutual understanding since, when it comes to investment decisions, workers lack the necessary background knowledge to understand the situation. It was found that the growing complexity of industrial relations in larger firms, in the 1980s, had forced the more innovative firms to look for personnel managers or assistants with professional training in interpersonal skills.

However, the industrial relations climate of the 1990s appears to have changed in favour of industrial peace and better employee relations within firms. A characteristic example is the attitude of trade union leaders during collective bargaining, in 1991, between the General Confederation of Greek Workers and the Association of Greek Industries. During discussions over pay agreements, workers' representatives showed their wish to establish a basis for a continuing dialogue, to help fight recession and to establish conditions which will encourage investment and reduce unemployment.

All these developments mean that there will be more time for HRM to deal with practical problems facing employees in firms and also to take advantage of collaboration with workers' representatives, replacing the confrontation of past decades.

PUBLIC SECTOR MANAGEMENT

Even in highly industrialised countries, research evidence has shown that the lower level of performance among public sector organisations is due to the unwillingness of employees to perform as productively as in the private sector; similar evidence is manifesting itself in Greece as well. Empirical data demonstrating this phenomenon was gathered during a recent survey in Greece from employees in ministries, public organisations, public corporations and private firms. Differences in employees' attitudes towards their jobs were measured on a comparative basis. The analysis of the results has shown that employees in private firms are more satisfied and committed, are more highly motivated and show less indifference than those in public organisations.

A number of factors negatively affect the performance of employees in public sector organisations. Special issues which exist are:

- the characteristics of job content, especially the lack of variety and meaningfulness of jobs, the lack of job autonomy, the absence of feedback and results;
- the confusion and conflict between roles, policies and procedures;
- the missing link between efforts, results and rewards;
- the organisational climate, which gives little recognition for achievement and few opportunities to employees to influence their own levels of efficiency;
- the poor quality of leadership at all hierarchical levels;
- the lack of reward for goal-oriented behaviour.

These factors negatively affecting performance point to improvements which must take place in the public sector. These need to be focused mainly on the organisation of human resource management to provide:

- more effective feedback to employees, and more clarity regarding goals and responsibilities;
- more exact definition of the policies and procedures of their organisations;
- more distinct links between effort, results and rewards;
- a climate favouring recognition and competition, and which militates against job indifference and neglect.

These improvements cannot occur without the adoption of techniques such as:

- job rotation and job enrichment;
- the cultural orientation of new entrants to the organisation;
- a well understood and fair system of selection, promotion, evaluation and reward;
- the development of short, medium- and long-term goals, both at departmental and organisational levels.

Undoubtedly, for such improvements to occur, the general environment of public administration needs drastic changes. These include:

- the decrease of party influence and involvement in decision making;
- emphasis on professionalism;
- the encouragement of innovation and entrepreneurship;
- the upgrading of HRM in public administration.

During 1991, Law 1943/91 was passed in the Greek Parliament, aiming to modernise and upgrade public administration. This law provides for goal-setting, performance appraisal, strict selection procedures, linking pay with performance, extensive induction training for new entrants, and internal or external courses for all levels of employees. Furthermore, various committees are working to introduce incentives for performance (performance-related pay), to create a new appraisal system, and to put into practice generally all the ideas included in the Law. While it is still too early to say what results will eventuate from these efforts, the mere fact that public administrators have realised the need to borrow concepts and practices which are already widely practised in the private sector is a basis for optimism.

CURRENT ISSUES AND PROSPECTS

Human resource management has come a long way over the past two or three decades in Greece, since the typical personnel manager was an ex-military officer and the HRM department dealt mainly with maintaining employee records and distributing wages and salaries. Personnel is a function which can still develop and has plenty of scope to do so. Some of the issues facing HRM today, and its prospects for development, are described below.

Professionalisation of HRM in smaller and family-owned firms

Extensive training in personnel matters is needed for owners of smaller firms, and in the larger family-managed firms. In such enterprises, owners usually keep for themselves the role of personnel management, without possessing the knowledge or the skills for its effective practice. While it is true that consultants have developed a range of services, these mainly relate to employee selection and training. Much more development is needed in the areas of job descriptions, person specifications, job evaluation, payment systems and performance appraisal systems, even in the larger firms. Furthermore, special systems geared to the needs of small-firm owners in particular are needed, since 98 per cent of firms in Greece are in the small—medium size category.

Links with research and academic institutions

Research in HRM is quite a recent practice in Greece. It is however, growing in parallel with the introduction of more HRM courses in Greek universities. Already, such courses are offered at the Athens University of Economic and Business, the Piraeus University and the University of Macedonia in Salonika. Post-experience training courses are provided by management centres, consultants, and training agencies. The business studies departments of Greek academic institutions are increasingly producing articles for publication on the subject of HRM (see References). Additionally, professional bodies such as the Association of Personnel Managers and the Institute for Training and development of the Greek Management Association have organised conferences, lectures and resource projects, to further examine and bring forward personnel issues to a larger audience of company managers.

The Greek Productivity Centre organised an international conference in Greece, in June 1991, on the role of management consultants in HRM. The Department of Public Administration of Pantion University organised a symposium on personnel issues in public administration. All these activities represent encouraging signs regarding the development of a research and publication base, on which an analytical approach to practice may be built.

Identifying and developing managerial talent

The issue of identifying and developing managerial talent is yet to be tackled by Greek firms, which still rely mainly on their circle of friends and relatives for recruitment. MNCs are very active in developing managerial ability and the differences in results between them and Greek firms are often only too apparent. It is of major importance for firms to widen their sources of recruitment, especially by recruiting from universities. The Association of Greek Personnel Managers has organised career days, during which university business graduates are interviewed; these efforts, which have been very successful, need further expansion and development, to enlarge the recruitment base to the HRM function. Furthermore, consultancy firms, which at present recruit mostly for executive posts, should gradually include hiring university graduates for entry-level posts.

It is feared that the imminent removal of the borders between European countries may mean a loss of young Greek managerial talent. Many young Greek graduates possess higher degrees and an excellent knowledge of foreign languages; hence they can easily move to countries where pay and job prospects appear more favourable. Through suitable selection and appointment procedures, many promising candidates, who lack the necessary contacts and orientation, could be identified and developed early to nurture their full potential in a job that fits their abilities.

New patterns of employment and a changing workforce

Human resource managers have to realise that, in the future, they will be dealing with a more diversified workforce. Women have moved into managerial ranks and into technical specialisations, which were previously restricted to men. Moreover, the level of education (even among entry-level workers) is rising. Citizens from EC countries have the right to work in Greece, as from 1 January, 1993, and the expected influx of workers will mean a more diversified labour market. Patterns of employment are also changing, with increased job mobility among both workers and managers, and part-time employment playing a more prominent part in Greece in the formal labour market for the first time in the 1990s. Mergers and acquisitions, which occur increasingly frequently, require the integration of new employees coming from different organisational cultures; changes in technology and job requirements also require constant retraining and up-dating of skills. Hence, labour force flexibility and structural change are likely to become issues which HRM managers will need to tackle constructively in the 1990s.

All these activities further complicate the task of personnel managers, but are also challenges which cannot be met without improvements and developments in HRM techniques, policies and philosophies.

CONCLUSION

From the information presented, and the issues discussed in this article, it is apparent that HRM in Greece is in a state of rapid development, as well as fundamental change. Personnel managers enjoy a high status in most of the larger firms and deal with a range of activities similar to those exercised in industrially-developed countries. Professionalism is quite high among personnel managers who are, as a rule, university graduates with company experience in various departments. Companies which have not yet developed a personnel department can, and are, gradually starting to use the services of consultancy firms. But in the smaller and family-owned enterprises which are still numerically dominant in the Greek economy, it is evident that HRM must develop much more in order for it to take an equal place with other business functions.

More training on personnel issues is increasingly being offered at the post-experience level, while business departments of universities offer courses in HRM. Future developments may strengthen and increase the significance of HRM in Greece. The approaching single European market means increased competition for products and markets for Greek firms. This carries implications regarding the need for effective HRM, so that firms can compete effectively in the new European economic and social context. Hopefully, this is a message which most firms in Greece have received, and are taking steps to implement.

REFERENCES

Bourantas, D (1990) *Motivation, Commitment and Motivation of Employees in Public Sector Organizations*, Center of Economic Research, Athens

General Confederation of Greek Workers (1991) *National General Collective Labour Agreement*, Athens

Georgoulis, VA (1978) 'Comparative Management Study of Selected Greek and European Multinational Manufacturing Firms Operating in Greece', PhD Thesis, University of Bath

Greek Management Association (1972) *Management of Greek Firms*, Athens

Greek Management Association (1986) *Management of Greek Firms*, Athens

Hassid, J (1977) *Greece and the EEC: Comparative Study of Industrial Structure*, Institute of Economic and Industrial Research, Athens

Hassid, J (1980) *Greek Industry and the EEC: A Study of the Impact from Entry*, vol I, Institute of Economic and Industrial Research, Athens

Kanellopoulos, C (1990) *Personnel Management and Personnel Managers in Greece*, Greek Productivity Center, Athens

Nikolopoulos, A (1989) *Trade Unionism in Greek Firms*, Papazissis Publications, Athens

Papalexandris, N (1986) 'Management Development Practices in Manufacturing Firms in Greece', PhD Thesis, University of Bath

Papalexandris, N (1988) 'Factors Affecting Management Staffing and Development: The Case of Greek Firms', *European Management Journal*, vol 6, no 1, Spring

Papalexandris, N, 'A Comparative Study of Human Resource Management in Selected Greek and Foreign-owned Subsidiaries in Greece' in Brewster, C and Tyson, S (eds), *International Comparisons in Human Resource Management*, Pitman Publishing, London

Papalexandris, N and Bourantas, D (1991) 'Factors Affecting Employee Performance in Private and Public Sector Organizations in Greece'. Paper presented at the International Conference of the Greek Productivity Center, Athens, 17-18 June

Papalexandris, N and Bourantas, D (1992) 'Variables Affecting Organizational Commitment: Private versus Publicly-owned Organizations in Greece', *Journal of Managerial Psychology*, vol 7, no 1

Papavassiliou, M and Tzekinisis, C (1990) *Practical Issues in Personnel Management*, Galeos Publications, Athens

Solomon, E (1986) 'Private and Public Sector Managers: an Empirical Investigation of Job Characteristics and Organizational Climate', *Journal of Applied Psychology*, vol 71, no 2, pp 247–59

11

CHANGING MANAGEMENT APPROACHES TO EMPLOYEE RELATIONS IN IRELAND[*]

Patrick Gunnigle, University of Limerick, Eire

INTRODUCTION

A notable characteristic of management commentaries over the past decade have been the suggestion that employee relations at establishment level have undergone remarkable change. This is variously attributed to a 'new realism' among managers and employees, the development of greater linkages between business strategy and personnel policy choice or the adoption of Human Resource Management (HRM) approaches. Despite the persuasiveness of such arguments, there remains some confusion about the nature of change in employee relations.

This chapter addresses the issue of management approaches to employee relations at enterprise level. It attempts to assess the degree to which management approaches to employee relations have changed in recent years. In particular, it addresses a number of key issues in assessing the nature of change in employee relations:

1. Where is the change from?
2. Where is the change to?
3. What are the dimensions along which change might take place?
4. What is the current evidence for change?
5. What are the likely directions of future change in employee relations?

At the outset it is important to clarify what is meant by employee relations as the term itself is a source of some confusion. The traditional management focus has been on the pluralist concept of industrial relations, encompassing the premises that a basic conflict of interest exists

---

* This chapter first appeared in *Employee Relations*, vol. 14, 4, 1992. Permission for its reproduction here is acknowledged with gratitude.

between management and labour and that this conflict could be optimally handled through collective bargaining between employers and trade unions over divisive issues, particularly pay and working conditions. During the 1980s it became evident that although this definition aptly described management/worker relations in many organisations, it did not encapsulate organisations where the focus was more unitarist in perspective. This latter approach placed the emphasis on dealings with the individual employee, using various mechanisms such as elaborate communications, career development, quality circles and merit pay. This approach was often linked to a preference for non-union status. An analysis of management styles clearly needs to incorporate the total range of approaches and, in this paper, employee relations is seen in generic terms as incorporating all employer/employee interactions concerning pay, working conditions and related employment matters and includes both pluralist and unitarist models.

The meaning of management style in employee relations

Management style is interpreted as the philosophy and principles guiding management action and behaviour on labour matters. It incorporates managerial values and beliefs about how employees should be managed and forms the basis for the subsequent development of policies in areas such as collective bargaining and reward systems.

WHERE IS THE CHANGE FROM?

For the great majority of medium and large organisations, employee relations management in Ireland has traditionally been associated with a strong collectivist, industrial relations emphasis. In the terminology of the Donovan analysis of industrial relations in Britain, employee relations in Ireland have been grounded in traditional pluralist principles, aptly described thus:

> Over a wide range of industries and services, employers and unions have conducted their relations on the basis of the premises that their interests were in significant respects different and in opposition . . . These differences of interest were reconciled on an ongoing basis through collective bargaining pure and simple.
>
> (Roche 1990)

In the pluralist industrial relations model, human resource considerations rarely concern strategic decision makers; relations between management and employees are grounded in the pluralist tradition with a primary reliance on adversarial collective bargaining; and personnel policies are oriented towards short-term issues with little conscious attempt to develop linkages with business policy. Within this model, the role of the specialist personnel function is essentially reactive and short-term in perspective; industrial relations is the primary personnel activity, with the personnel function the guardian of procedures and negotiator of industrial harmony via its responsibility for managing relations with the unions. Manifestations of the pluralist tradition are high levels of union density, highly developed collective bargaining institutions at establishment level, and industrial relations as the key role of the personnel function.

WHERE IS THE CHANGE TO?

While there are numerous commentaries on the pervasiveness of change in employee relations, many of these are quite vague on what exactly has changed and the extent of such change. It is clearly important to specify the nature of change before any evaluation of its extent. At the risk of simplification, it would appear that most of the advocates of change contend that the move has been towards employee relations styles which incorporate characteristics of Human Resource Management (HRM).

A problem with this approach is that there is a great deal of discussion, but little consensus on what HRM is or on how it contrasts with traditional 'industrial relations'. I believe that most confusion stems from the tendency to view HRM styles as essentially homogenous, incorporating a specific philosophy and combination of personnel and employee relations policies. However, practice seems to indicate there are numerous variants of HRM incorporating different approaches to workforce management. A useful categorisation is developed by Keenoy (1990) who identifies three 'relatively distinct' forms of HRM:

1. *Traditional HRM* This is the most widely known form of HRM, which is characterised by a resource or investment perspective of an organisation's workforce. It is the high profile form of HRM practised by companies such as IBM, Marks & Spencer, Hewlett-Packard, Digital and Amdahl and has been affectionately labelled 'soft' HRM. An essential tenet of this model is that there is an organisational pay-off from a combination of HRM policies which emphasise consensualism and mutuality of management and employee interests. This pay-off is manifested in terms of higher levels of quality, flexibility, and commitment leading to increased competitive advantage. Related personnel polices include sophisticated selection and socialisation,

internal labour market emphasis, direct communications with employ-ees and a high-powered personnel function acting in a strategic 'change agent' mode.

2. *Industrial Relations plus HRM* This second type of HRM is characterised by moves towards greater consensualism and commit-ment in traditional unionised companies with established collective bargaining procedures. This approach, often termed 'dualism', is characteristic of management approaches in a number of Irish organisations, such as Aer Rianta and Analog Devices.

3. *Strategic HRM* This variant is characterised by the integration of human resources into the business plan to ensure that personnel policy decisions are tailored to establish competitive advantage. Such policies need not necessarily be employee-centred. Thus, while traditional HRM is characterised by the implicit assumption that employees are a resource, strategic HRM infers that personnel policies are contingent upon business policy. Such policies may either view employees as a resource or as a commodity; that is, an 'employee commitment' or 'labour control' approach may be adopted, depend-ing on business strategy.

HRM is therefore a perspective on workforce management which can take numerous forms, all of which contrast with the traditional pluralist industrial relations model. However, the degree of change differs considerably, depending on the type of HRM adopted.

Alternative management styles in employee relations

These different models are illustrative of the range of employee relations styles confronting organisations. Thus management style in employee relations may be either unitarist or pluralist, cooperative or conflictual. Styles which reflect HRM variants incorporate a greater strategic perspective on human resource issues and closer linkages with business policy, while styles reflecting traditional industrial relations are more reactive and adversarial in nature. Such choices may be expressed in terms of a typology of management styles in employee relations styles, as outlined in Table 11.1.

In reflecting upon the Irish situation, the most striking feature of the typology of management styles outlined in Table 11.1 relates to the 'sophisticated paternalist' and 'sophisticated unionised' groupings. These styles are significant because they indicate a planned and coordinated approach to employee relations management, in contrast to the other styles which are indicative of a more 'incidentalist' approach. The

Table 11.1 Typology of management styles in employee relations

1. Anti-Union
Little or no consideration given to personnel or employee relations considerations; no union or collective arrangements; managerial value system characterised by low concern for employee needs and aggressive opposition to union recognition and collective bargaining.

2. Paternalist
Characterised by a management concern for employee needs; however, preferred employee relations style rejects union recognition and collective bargaining and incorporates little sophistication in personnel policies.

3. Sophisticated Paternalist
Characterised by an emphasis on individual employee welfare and well-being; sophisticated personnel policies on recruitment, employee development, communications and rewards; rejects union recognition and collective bargaining. This approach equates to 'traditional HRM' as practised by some prominent high technology non-union companies, incorporating a resource perspective of employees whereby investment in, and equitable treatment of, employees is seen as yielding substantial benefits to the organisation.

4. Sophisticated Unionised
Characterised by an acceptance of the pluralist tradition and trade union recognition; role of trade union(s) and collective bargaining carefully prescribed by management (eg single union agreements); collective arrangements augmented by an individualist emphasis incorporating HRM-type polices (similar to sophisticated paternalists). This approach equates to a neo-pluralist model reflecting a variant of traditional pluralism augmented by HRM-type policies designed to develop greater consensualism and employee commitment.

5. Traditional Unionised
Traditional pluralist perspective characterised by adversarial industrial relations incorporating a predominant role for collective bargaining and, possibly, multi-unionism.

'traditional unionised' style equates to a basic pluralist industrial relations model and has been the most pervasive style in the majority of medium and large organisations in Ireland.

On the other hand, the 'anti-union' and 'paternalist' styles indicate opposition to the pluralist tradition, either through forthright attempts to curb or eliminate any moves towards collective representation or more subtle policies to demonstrate to employees that their best interests lie in accepting managerial prerogative. It has traditionally been argued that these styles were confined to smaller organisations and that in the event of growth they would 'succumb' to the pluralist model over time. However, recent Irish evidence points to greater opposition to unionisation in the 1980s, a growth of larger, non-union organisations adopting traditional HRM policies and the increased use of such policies in unionised organisations.

These developments, if pervasive, would indicate a significant change in Irish employee relations. In terms of management styles, such developments would be characterised by the increased adoption of either the 'sophisticated paternalist' or ' sophisticated unionised' style. The sophisticated unionised style equates to a neo-pluralist approach incorporating many of the basic characteristics of traditional pluralism, but also incorporating HRM polices designed to promote greater individualism, consensualism and commitment. The 'sophisticated paternalist' style incorporates the traditional HRM model as practised in some prominent, high technology, non-union companies. This approach is characterised by a resource perspective of employees which assumes an organisational 'pay-off' from a combination of personnel polices designed to produce high levels of quality, flexibility and commitment. This approach contrasts significantly with traditional pluralism. It is essentially unitarist in character, as there is no assumed conflict of interest between management and employees, and it seeks to develop total employee identification with the organisation. Traditional HRM policies are sometimes associated with practices designed to entice employees away from collective representation towards more individual, consensual forms of direct involvement.

WHAT ARE THE DIMENSIONS ALONG WHICH CHANGE MIGHT TAKE PLACE?

Turning to the nature of employee relations style it is suggested that there are three benchmark dimensions along which managerial styles in employee relations may differ, namely strategic integration, individualism and collectivism.

Strategic integration

This refers to the degree to which employee relations issues are part of strategic decision making and the degree to which decisions on employee relations are linked to business strategy (Table 11.2). High strategic integration involves integrating employee relations (ER) issues into strategic planning, integrating personnel/ER policies with policies in other functional areas (eg operations or marketing) and integrating policies across personnel/ER areas (eg recruitment, employee involvement, rewards). Low strategic integration is characterised by an absence of employee relations considerations in strategic planning. A consequence is that employee relations policies are essentially reactive in nature, are problem oriented and may indeed be incompatible across personnel policy areas. A traditional perception of strategic decision making is that it concerns 'primary' business issues (such as operations or finance) and any attention devoted to employee relations issues is secondary and somewhat 'incidental'. On the other hand, it is evident that some organisations incorporate human resource issues in strategy creation and take well considered strategic decisions to establish a particular employee relations style.

Table 11.2 Dimension One: strategic integration

High strategic integration	Strategic HRM	Human resource issues are an integral component of the organisation's long-term strategy and mission
	Business-led HRM	Human resource issues are dependent upon but linked to higher-order decisions on corporate mission and objectives
Low strategic integration	Traditional personnel management	Human resource issues are a peripheral management concern and are handled in an essentially reactive fashion

Individualism

The second major dimension of employee relations style is individualism (Table 11.3). This dimension refers to the degree to which management adopts an essentially individual focus in managing human resources. High individualism is characterised by management recognising the resource value of employees. It is associated with comprehensive employee development policies and adopts the ideal, typical characteristics of traditional HRM, including sophisticated recruitment and socialisation of new employees, internal labour market emphasis, attractive rewards and good employment conditions. In contrast, low individualism, or a commodity view of labour, sees employees in ultra-utilitarian terms within the overriding goal of profit maximisation. The consequent management emphasis is on tight supervisory control, restrictive job design, minimisation of labour costs and little concern for broader human resource issues, such as job satisfaction, employment security or employee commitment. Purcell (1987) suggests that paternalism, characterised by managerial values of caring, benevolence and welfare but with little emphasis on employee development or internal labour markets, is a middle ground between high and low individualism. High individualism is a central ingredient of strategic human resource management (HRM). Guest (1987, 1989) argues that a major objective of HRM-type policies is to 'develop in individual employees a feeling of commitment to the organisation', adopting the assumption that increased levels of commitment have substantial benefits for both employees (eg job satisfaction) and their organisation (eg improved performance).

Table 11.3   Dimension Two: individualism

High individualism	Employees as a resource: comprehensive employee development emphasis
Paternalism	Caring, benevolence approach; little employee development
Low individualism	Employees as commodities: no employee development

Source: adapted from Guest, D (1987)

Collectivism

The third benchmark dimension underpinning employee relations style is collectivism (Table 11.4). This refers to the degree to which management acknowledges the right of employees to collective representation and the involvement of the collective in influencing management decision making. Employee influence is an important concept: it implies that employee opinions are not only heard (ie the employee 'voice') but that institutional arrangements are put in place to ensure such views are acted upon and effectively shape management decision making. High collectivism is manifested in mechanisms for employee representation such as trade unions and/or works councils. It incorporates both the existence of such mechanisms and the spirit in which management approaches their operation, particularly the degree to which management actively supports employee involvement or alternatively seeks to minimise its impact on the organisation. The traditional HRM approach has been associated with a move from collectivism to individualism via sophisticated recruitment, rewards and employee development policies. However, individualism need not necessarily counterpoise collectivism, so that managements can develop policies to increase individualism whilst retaining established collectivist structures, including trade union recognition.

Table 11.4   Dimension Three: collectivism

High collectivism	↑	Pluralist co-operative
Adversarial collectivism		Reluctant involvement
Low collectivism	↓	Unitarist/little/no co-operation

Source: adapted from Guest, D (1987)

CURRENT TRENDS: THE EVIDENCE FOR CHANGE

Atypical employment forms

One of the most visible changes in employment practices in Ireland has been the growth of 'atypical' employment forms. Atypical employment is defined as any form of employment which deviates from the full-time, permanent format and includes self-employment, temporary and part-time work (Figure 11.1). However, this trend must be viewed in the context of broader changes in employment patterns: particularly first, the expansion in unemployment (by over 250 per cent since 1979); and second, shifting employment patterns, characterised by a fall in agriculture and manufacturing industry and growth in the service sector.

The expansion of the services sector merits particular consideration in the context of atypical employment growth. Current data indicates that 57 per cent of the Irish workforce are employed in the services with 28 per cent employed in industry and 15 per cent in agriculture. However, the growth in the services sector has been primarily restricted to private

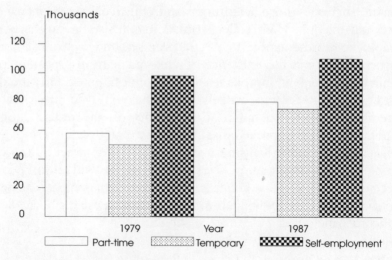

Source: Labour force surveys

Figure 11.1 Atypical employment 1979–87

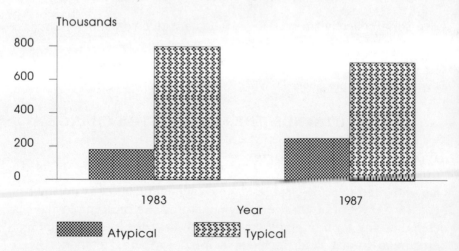

Source: Labour force surveys

Figure 11.2 Atypical/typical employment 1983–87

(professional and personal) services — areas traditionally associated with atypical employment forms. In contrast, the public sector, which is traditionally associated with typical employment forms, has undergone severe contraction in employment terms. Consequently, changes in the sectoral employment distribution have been biased towards an increase in atypical employment. It has also facilitated a rise in female employment.

However, the nature of the jobs lost and those created differ substantially. Areas of job loss, particularly manufacturing industry and the public sector, are traditionally associated with providing relatively secure, well-paid employment. In contrast, areas of employment growth, particularly personal services (eg contract cleaning, catering) are associated with more insecure, poorly paid jobs.

A second important issue is that despite the growth in atypical employment, the great majority of workers (almost 80 per cent) still work in typical employment (Figure 11.2).

Thus, while there is a definite trend towards atypical employment, the change is a gradual one and must be viewed in the context of broader economic and (particularly) labour market change.

Emergence of the 'flexible firm'

An associated issue is the suggestion that a flexible firm model is emerging, characterised by core and peripheral workforce categories. Within this scenario the 'core' is composed of full-time staff enjoying relatively secure, challenging jobs with good pay and employment conditions. On the other hand, the 'periphery' is composed of an amalgam of temporary, part-time and contract groups enjoying much less favourable pay and employment conditions, little job security or access to training and promotion. The flexible firm scenario is based on the planned development of this core/periphery employment model, together with a drive to increase flexibility in three key areas:

1. *Functional flexibility*, incorporating multi-skilling, whereby workers would develop a wide range of skills and agree to carry out work across traditional skill boundaries.
2. *Financial flexibility*, incorporating two elements: first, tying basic pay rates to labour market conditions rather than traditional comparabilities, eg new 'low pay' grades in some banks; and second, building a flexible pay element into the compensation package, such as the use of bonus or incentive payments based on a measure of individual or company performance.
3. *Numerical flexibility*, incorporating core-periphery employment patterns and using peripheral groups as a buffer to protect the core from the detrimental effects of changes in market conditions

Current Irish evidence suggests there is a definite trend towards greater flexibility. However, this is essentially confined to numerical flexibilty and may in part be a factor of the looseness of the Irish labour market and the ready availability of people willing to work in temporary or part-time jobs. Functional flexibility is essentially confined to manufacturing industry (where employment is falling). Trends towards flexibility generally seem most pervasive in the services sector. However, there is little evidence of the combination of different forms of flexibilty. Therefore, while flexibility is on the increase, there is no evidence of the existence or planned emergence of the flexible firm.

Strategic integration

Strategic HRM involves the integration of human resource considerations into wider strategic planning and the development of personnel policies to support competitive strategy. Such policies need not necessarily be employee-centred, but may be either 'hard' or 'soft' depending on the chosen route to competitive advantage. On the other hand, the more traditional industrial relations/personnel management model is essentially reactive in nature. In this model personnel and employee relations considerations are not a concern of strategic decision makers, but rather an operational issue only given priority when problems arise.

In the Irish context, a number of factors both supporting and mitigating against the adoption of HRM type approaches may be identified. Factors encouraging HRM include the emphasis on developing competitive advantage. Particularly important here is the increased emphasis on quality as the major route to competitive advantage and the adoption of total quality initatives requiring greater cooperation between management and employees, increased employee commitment and involvement. Other important factors include organisation restructuring to devolve more responsibility to strategic business units; the increasing importance of culture and mission in focusing management effort and guiding decisions on resource allocation; a possible tightening in some segments of the Irish labour market; the visibility of successful HRM models; and increased education levels of Irish management.

On the other hand, factors militating against the widespread adoption of strategic HRM include the continuing trend towards increased organisational size and diversity. Purcell (1989) argues that increased diversity leads to greater emphasis on financial control criteria, rendering human resource considerations a minor corporate concern. It is also noteworthy that despite the visibility of HRM models the majority of these are confined to high technology manufacturing. While clearly important, they are relatively small in employment terms. In 1987, total employment in US-owned industry was 38,000, while total public sector employment

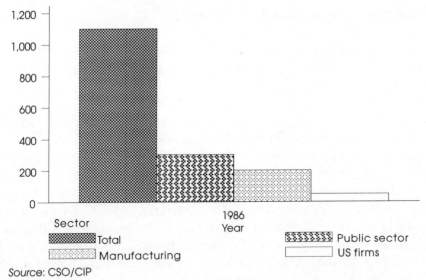

Source: CSO/CIP

Figure 11.3 Employment in public sector, manufacturing and US firms

was almost 300,000 (Figure 11.3). Thus while developments in the 'high tech' sector are important, the bulk of employment is concentrated outside this sector with the consequence that any widespread changes in employee relations style have to emanate from sectors other than high technology manufacturing. In relation to the Irish labour market, any anticipated tightening will, most likely, be slow and change will be gradual rather than dramatic. Equally, the growth of different ('atypical') employment forms, while significant, is still confined to a small proportion of the workforce.

A further mitigating factor is the traditional role of the personnel function in Irish organisations. The traditional model is grounded in pluralist industrial relations principles and characterised by low-trust relations between management and employees. Within this model conflict is institutionalised via collective bargaining, with the personnel function orchestrating this adversarial process from the management side. While consistent with the value of collectivism, this model is characterised by low strategic integration and low individualism. A more current factor, possibly limiting the adoption of strategic HRM by placing the emphasis on short-term financial criteria, is the prospect of recession in the world economy. The openness of the Irish economy, its export dependence, and the high level of multinational investment make it highly susceptible to external developments.

Proactive employee relations styles

A related issue is the development of proactive employee relations styles, incorporating HRM-type policies, among some organisations, particularly in high technology manufacturing. This development has been particularly prominent in the subsidiaries of multinational organisations. Numerous commentators have noted the impact of corporate personnel policies on the personnel and employee relations practices of subsidiaries locating in Ireland. Looking at the Irish experience, it would seem that the most visible examples of proactive HRM-type polices are in foreign-owned companies, particularly of US origin, who have established in greenfield sites since the late 1970s. The bulk of MNC investment in Ireland since the 1970s has been from the US and concentrated in newer and technologically advanced sectors, particularly electronics. Many of these MNCs originate from a culture of non-unionism and familiarity with traditional HRM practices. Consequently, they will generally pursue the non-union path in establishing plants abroad and have done so with remarkable success in the Irish context.

A particular issue in the context of evolving employee relations styles concerns trade union recognition and the future role of collective bargaining. The period since 1980 has witnessed the most serious decline in trade union density in the post-war period. However, this decline is principally attributed to macro-economic factors, most notably economic depression and increased levels of unemployment, and also changes in employment structure characterised by decline in traditionally highly unionised sectors (typical employment forms in manufacturing industry and the public sector) and growth in sectors which have traditionally posed difficulties for union penetration (particulary private services).

McGovern (1989) points to increasing opposition to union recognition in the 1980s, suggesting that management approaches to unionisation have either hardened in line with the 'anti-union' style or become 'more subtle' in attempting to avoid unionisation. He also suggests that US high technology companies have been the major exponents of the non-union route via traditional HRM-type policies in remuneration/welfare, quality of work life, employee relations and communications. Such policies collectively incorporate the 'sophisticated paternalist' style of employee relations management. Murray's (1984) study of employee relations in the manufacturing sector supports these trends in suggesting that foreign owned firms adopted more proactive and sophisticated approaches to employee relations management and gave greater resources and responsibility to the personnel function. On the issue of unionisation, the study found that US-owned companies were far more likely to be non-union, while other foreign owned companies were 'solidly unionised'. On the other hand, Gunnigle and Shivanath's (1989) study of personnel practitioners in Ireland found that European-owned organisations, particularly those of British origin, adopted more short-term, reactive approaches to personnel/ER management. While the study did not investigate in detail the reasons for variance, it has been suggested that differences in style are attributable to broader structural problems rather than ownership *per se*. In particular, it has been suggested that British companies operating in Ireland are quite different in character to most other multinationals, having located here much earlier to serve the domestic market and avoid tariffs, and have more recently suffered in the face of international competition. This has led to employment contraction and other cost reduction initiatives, resulting in more reactive short term employee relations responses.

Perhaps the most useful insights on employee relations management in foreign-owned companies comes from Scotland, where MacInnes and Sproull (1989) examined the nature of unionisation in the electronics industry. The Scottish electronics sector is widely perceived as a 'hot-bed' of high technology, non-union or single union arrangements. The study found that while there were indeed a large number of such plants, particularly those of US origin, the industry in general was not all that different from other UK manufacturing sectors. In relation to union recognition, MacInnes and Sproull found that although a large number of plants were non-union (66 per cent), the majority of these were small with a consequence that the majority of employment was in unionised plants (62.4 per cent of employment). They also found that the country of ownership did not have a significant influence on union recognition, concluding that 'about the same proportion of UK-owned and US-owned plants recognised unions'.

The authors found that age of plants was a significant influence, with companies which were established in the 1980s less likely to be unionised than those established in earlier decades. In relation to union membership, MacInnes and Sproull estimated employment density in the Scottish electronics industry to be approximately 40–44 per cent which is only slightly below the UK manufacturing industry average and higher than traditionally assumed — both in terms of density and recognition. The authors found that unionisation had no impact on employment growth. They agreed that union recognition had been more difficult in the 1980s, but argue that this is not confined to electronics or, indeed, surprising (given changes in legislation, the difficult economic environment, changes in employment structure and low inflation). They concluded that the probability of union recognition depends on three factors: size, age of establishment, and the presence/absence of single status arrangements (ie factors similar to the rest of manufacturing industry). The general conclusion of the authors is that the Scottish electronics industry is not as distinct as imagined and is quite modest in scale: consequently it would be wrong to assume that future work and employee relations patterns will be shaped by what happens in electronics:

> contrary to the normal assumption made about the electronics industry being a bastion of non-unionism, union organisation and membership is quite robust and shows no signs of falling off (MacInnes and Sproull 1990).

In analysing the development of proactive employee relations styles, there is a clear need for caution in generalising on the employee relations practices of MNCs on the basis of limited, if prominent, examples. Industrial structure and product market conditions are important factors influencing employee relations styles and related issues at establishment level (such as labour costs) and it is difficult to draw any general conclusions from current data on the Irish experience, which is largely piecemeal and anecdotal. Despite the presence of some prominent examples of managerial styles other than those based on traditional pluralism, the aggregate evidence does not point to any significant decline in unionisation or change in the traditional unionised model. However, there are indications that managements are increasingly pursuing features of the sophisticated unionised or sophisticated paternalist styles, particularly in companies established since 1970.

Less industrial conflict

Using traditional indices of strike activity (man days lost, strike frequence and workers involved), the Irish record indicates a clear upward movement in strike activity in the 1960s and 1970s and a decline in the 1980s. Figure 11.4 points to a significant decline in strike activity for much of the 1980s, but a reversal of this trend in 1989 and 1990. This decline in strike activity has generally been attributed to business cycle factors rather than significant managerial initiatives at workplace level. Recession, company closures/contraction and unemployment are major factors reducing the likely incidence of strike activity.

In analysing strike patterns of MNCs in Ireland, Kelly and Brannick (1988, 1991) contrast the records of the two major sources of foreign investment: British and US companies. While in the 1960s US companies

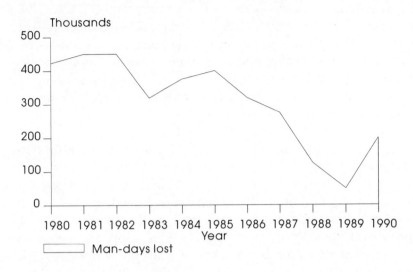

Source: UCD/Department of Labour
Figure 11.4   Strike activity 1980–90

were the most strike prone, their record has improved dramatically since the 1970s to a stage where US MNCs record very low levels of strike activity. In contrast, the strike record of British companies has deteriorated dramatically. The reasons for this deterioration have been mentioned earlier and are largely attributed to product market difficulties. In relation to the contrasting improvement of the strike record of US companies, Kelly and Brannick offer two reasons:

1. The changed industrial composition of US MNCs: most are now high technology companies in the 'newer' industrial sectors, particularly electronics and chemicals (as opposed to labour intensive companies producing standardised products in the 1960s).
2. US MNCs are predominantly based in the electronics sector, which has been to the forefront in developing innovative and proactive employee relations and HR strategies and policies.

This latter point emphasises the significance of management philosophy and practices in developing particular employee relations styles. In particular, it seems that the 'sophisticated unionised' or 'sophisticated paternalist' styles most closely equate to the approaches of US firms pursuing the HRM route. Again, it is important to add a word of caution. Product market conditions are clearly a crucially influential factor, as is the age and size of establishment. Changing product market conditions can severely alter the context within which employee relations decisions are made. High levels of volatility in some industrial sectors (such as electronics) can dramatically change the product market conditions, and other factors influencing the employee relations style adopted in organisations, and lead to changes in style; for example, a significant decline in market share may lead to employment contraction warranting a more traditional industrial relations approach.

A further issue is the potential for the development of diverse cultures in organisations requiring different employee relations styles for different workforce categories. This seems particularly likely in organisations pursuing the flexible firm route. Thus traditional ('soft') HRM policies may be adopted with the core workforce in return for high levels of functional flexibility, commitment and loyalty, while a traditional industrial relations approach may be adopted in dealings with the peripheral categories (eg 'hard-nosed' bargaining, application of grievance/disciplinary procedures, etc).

CONCLUSIONS

This chapter has attempted to sketch the main issues relating to management styles in employee relations and to assess the degree to which management approaches have changed over the past several years. Of particular significance in the Irish context is the degree to which HRM-type approaches are being adopted and replacing the traditional pluralist industrial relations model of workforce management. In evaluating current Irish developments, there is a danger of confusing notable examples of traditional HRM with widespread pervasiveness of such approaches. As discussed earlier, much of the evidence and support for strategic HRM emanates from the US. However, the context of such developments in the US is considerably different from Ireland and it seems inappropriate to simply extrapolate from the US experience and infer similar trends here. Differences in industrial and employment structure, employee relations traditions and trade union density are some of the unique factors influencing organisational approaches to managing human resources in Ireland.

Recent developments suggest a strengthening of the unitarist ideology among the management of Irish organisations and, particularly, greater opposition to union recognition, the emergence of strong non-union sector and a fall in union membership. However, the change seems to be gradual rather than dramatic and involve incremental change on the traditional industrial relations model. In terms of managerial styles in employee relations, this would infer that the thrust of any change will be towards neo-pluralist or 'sophisticated unionised' approaches. Consequently, established industrial relations institutions will remain largely intact and the traditional approach to personnel and industrial relations management will continue to have relevance in the 1990s.

In conclusion, it does seem that developments in business strategy and product markets are creating greater organisational awareness of the impact of employee relations issues on organisation performance. HRM-type approaches will continue to be adopted. Traditional HRM, incorporating the non-union route, may remain popular with some large foreign firms establishing at greenfield sites. However, the more widespread adoption of comprehensive HRM approaches would require significant change in the approach of Irish managements, particularly in integrating human resource considerations in strategic decision making. Thus, it seems more likely that where HRM initiatives are adopted, this will occur alongside, rather than in place of, traditional workforce management approaches, especially collective bargaining.

REFERENCES

Carroll, C (1985) 'Building Ireland's business; Perspectives from PIMS', Irish Management Institute

Dineen, D (1991) 'Changing employment patterns in Ireland'. Paper read to the IPA Conference on 'Industrial Relations Outlook and New Employment Patterns', Dublin

Flood, P (1989) 'Human Resource Management: Promise, Possibility and Limitations', Research Paper, University of Limerick; Gunnigle, P and Flood, P (1990) *Personnel management in Ireland: Practice, trends and developments*

Flood, P (1990) 'Atypical employment; Core-periphery manpower strategies — The implications for corporate culture', *Industrial Relations News*, no 9, 10

Guest, D (1987) 'Human resource management and industrial relations' in *Journal of Management Studies*, vol 24, no 5; Guest, D (1989) 'Human Resource Management: Its implications for Industrial Relations and Trade Unions' in Storey, J. (ed) *New Perspectives on Human Resource Management*, Routledge and Kegan Paul

Gunnigle, P and Shivanath, G (1989) 'Variations in the personnel role: Some Irish survey evidence', *Employee Relations*, vol 11

Hendry, C and Pettigrew, A (1990) 'Human resource management: An agenda for the 1990s', *International Journal of Human Resource Management*, vol 1, no 1

Keenoy, T (1990) 'HRM: A wolf in sheep's clothing', *Personnel Review*, vol 19, no 2

Kelly, A and Brannick, T (1988) 'Explaining the strike proneness of British companies in Ireland' *British Journal of Industrial Relations*, vol 26, no 4

Kelly, A and Brannick, T (1991) 'The impact of new human resource management policies on US MNC strike patterns: The case of Ireland' (Unpublished paper)

MacInnes, J and Sproull, A (1989) 'Union Recognition and Employment change in Scottish Electronics', *Industrial Relations Journal*, vol 20, no 1, spring

McGovern, P (1989) 'Union recognition and union avoidance in the 1980s' in *Industrial relations in Ireland: Contemporary issues and developments*, University College Dublin; Kelly, A and Brannick, T 'The management of human resources: New trends and the challenge to trade unions', *Arena*, August

Murray, S (1984) 'Employee relations in Irish private sector manufacturing industry', Industrial Development Authority

Purcell, J and Sisson, K (1983) in 'Strategies and practice in the management of industrial relations' in Bain, G *Industrial relations in Britain*, Blackwell, Oxford

Purcell, J (1987) 'Mapping management styles in employee relations', *Journal of Management Studies*, vol 24, no 5

Purcell, J (1989) 'The impact of corporate strategy on HRM' in Storey, J (ed) *New perspectives on Human Resource Management*, Routledge and Kegan Paul, London

Roche, B (1990) 'Industrial Relations Research in Ireland and the Trade Union Interest'. Paper presented to the Irish Congress of Trades Unions Conference on Joint Research between Trade Unions, Universities, Third Level Colleges and Research Institutes, Dublin

Suttle, S (1988) 'Labour Market Flexibility', *Industrial Relations News*, no 38

Wallace, J and Foley, J (1991) 'New style agreements in Ireland: Fact or fiction' (Unpublished)

12

RECRUITMENT, REFORM AND THE ITALIAN LABOUR MARKET*

Stefano Folletti, Giampiero Giacomello, Associazione Industriali di Bologna, and Jonathan Cooper, SAIS, Johns Hopkins University Bologna Center

INTRODUCTION

The vaunted reform of the Italian labour market which passed into Statute on 23 July 1991 as law 223 (*Riforma della Cassa Integrazione Guadagni e del Mercato del Lavoro*) provides innovative guidelines for the recruitment of blue-collar workers. It heralds a legal recognition of changing circumstances and echoes employers' calls for 'flexibility' in hiring procedures. Employers are basically happier people as a result.

However, critics of the new law have noted that the structure of the 'collocamento' or placement process, established in the infancy of the First Republic, when Italy was a largely agrarian economy with some of the highest unemployment levels in Europe, has been retained. The language of a process initiated over 40 years ago remains the same. The role of the state, as the only permissible hiring 'intermediary' between *prestatore del lavoro*, the worker, and the *datore del lavoro*, the employer, is still inviolable. Legislation has missed the opportunity to anticipate the dynamics of the Italian labour market; it has simply reacted, stepped into line, with what has already become common practice. The law has converted a *de facto* situation into a principle.

THE ITALIAN LABOUR MARKET BEFORE WORLD WAR II

Collocamento in modern Italy has controversial roots. Before 1927 and the first legislative indications of Fascist manipulation of the labour

---

* This chapter first appeared in *Personnel Review*, vol 20, 6, 1991. Permission for its reproduction here is acknowledged with gratitude.

market, recruitment was the prerogative of the *Camere de Lavoro*, the Chamber of Labour, a state organisation with an objective role in the hiring process, very like the role played today by the *ufficio di collocamento*, the state placement office. With the emerging predominance of the Fascist trade unions, the Corporazioni, the political left's position of power in labour relations was broken — a process made possible only through the extensive use of 'legalised' violence. The Corporazioni soon became the dominant actors in Italian labour relations, and the 'objective' role of the Camere di Lavoro chimerical.

On 2 October 1925 Confindustria, the National Confederation of Italian Industries, through the so-called *Patto di Palazzo Vidoni*, recognized the Fascist trade unions as the only legitimate, representative voice of Italian labour. From that moment, regardless of legal rights to form, or to enrol in, independent trade unions, the only union representation tolerated by Fascism was its own.

The state's management of the recruitment process dates from the pre-Fascist period. In practice, the Fascist unions took over the state's objective role, making membership of the trade unions and the Fascist party, practically speaking, a *sine qua non* of employment.

THE ITALIAN LABOUR MARKET IN THE REPUBLIC

Immediately after the Second World War, a decentralised system of hiring responsibilities flourished. In some provinces, the new republican trade unions, the Confederazione Generale Italiano di Lavoro (CGIL) took responsibility for local hiring, in other areas, *prefetti*, local government representatives, operated with special administrative powers.

In 1949, after the politicised split of CGIL, the Italian parliament passed the law on hiring and recruitment that still forms the basis of legislation today. The law was specifically designed to replace the fragmented system that had taken hold at the end of the War, and laid particular emphasis on the elimination of intermediation of private individuals or trade unions, in the hiring process. Offices of public administration, representatives of the state at the local government level, became the only legitimate intermediaries between *prestatori* and *datori*.

At the core of the new recruiting system was the notion of *richiesta numerica* — recruitment by number. Workers for particular jobs were selected on the basis of an ordinal list, prepared by the state's *ufficio di collocamento* (labour office) without regard for skills. Lists were drawn up of unemployed workers and priority given according to the state of need and length of time on the list. Numbers of dependants and condition of health were among the main criteria for assessing this state of need. Companies employing blue-collar labour effectively had no say in their choice of workers to hire. Employers requested a number of workers from the *ufficio di collocamento* and these were sent to the workplaces by the office according to list priority.

The exception to this general rule was the notion of *richiesta nominativa* — recruitment by name. This process gave the employer discretion to choose, literally to name, a prospective employee. In practice, the *richiesta nominativa* was extremely limited: to white-collar or technical hires; to companies employing fewer than five workers (law 264, article 14, 29 April 1949)*; to the recruitment of management in companies employing fewer than three people (article 11); to employment of somebody already employed by another company.

On May 20, 1970, law 300, the *Statuto dei Lavoratori* (the Workers' Statute) was passed by Parliament. The Statute succeeded in changing the face of Italian labour relations by establishing fundamental rights for workers. As a result, the Italian labour laws are among the most protective of the rights of workers in Europe. In addition the *Statuto dei lavoratori* increased the provisions for the use of *richiesta nominativa* to close relatives of an employer (article 34, law 300, 1970.)

Law 863, passed in 1984, extended still further the provisions for 'richiesta nominativa'. The first provision permitted the hiring of young people (15–29 years old) on training contracts for no longer than two years (articles 3 and 4, law 863, 1984). The second provision allowed for the hiring of 50 per cent of an employer's workforce needs, which would hitherto have been recruited by *richiesta numerica*, now to be hired under *richiesta nominativa* (article 6, law 863, 1984.)

Clearly, over the years, *richiesta numerica* was perceived as less and less important, and by the late 1980s practically redundant, except for the recruitment of 50 per cent of a company's unskilled labour needs. Nevertheless, the principle and the process was retained, despite the disappearance of the economic and social circumstances that had made the system desirable in the first place. The original circumstances were characterised by high unemployment, social discrimination among employees, and by a large pool of unskilled labour that was professionally interchangeable. They justified a system designed to promote access to the job market of the less protected and weak categories of workers.

---

* The rationale behind this provision lies in the importance placed on 'trust' in the relationship between top management and hired management. This concept was seen as vital in a small company.

Those circumstances simply do not apply to a country which, in 1991, is among the top six ranking industrial powers in the world.

Law 223 of 23 July 1991 goes further than any preceding law to acknowledge the redundancy of *richiesta numerica*. Article 25 states that 'any employer has the possibility to hire any worker through *richiesta nominativa*'. The general precedence of *numerica* over *nominativa* has, for the first time, been reversed.

However, the legislation has retained the old language, and retained the old structures. The state retains its central role in the hiring process. Now, provisions are laid down for *richiesta numerica* where previously they had been laid down for *nominativa*. Article 25 asserts that companies employing more than ten blue- and white-collar workers must take 12 per cent of their recruited personnel from special categories considered particularly weak or in need. These categories consist of long-term unemployed (over two years) or those dismissed as a result of extenuating company crisis. Law 223 is certainly, therefore, innovative over prior legislation as far as blue-collar or unskilled labour is concerned, but there is practically no change in the legislation for the hiring of technical, trained or white-collar workers. Given that dismissal laws (law 604 of 1966, law 300 of 1970 and law 108 of 1990) are extremely rigid in defending the workers' rights to maintain their employment, perhaps the most important feature of law 223 is the significant shift it represents in the burden of responsibility for making a 'bad' hire — from the labour office to the employer himself.

Shifting the burden of responsibility from state to employer is an argument in favour of flexibility and deregulation of the *collocamento* process. Yet that has not happened with law 223. The use of private third parties in the search and selection process for middle and top management is an increasing trend in Italy. But headhunters and recruitment agencies are still only permitted 'arm's length' responsibilities; intermediation in the recruitment process is taboo, with heavy fines for offenders. Furthermore, in comparison with most of Europe, part-time working is scarce. This is hardly surprising since part-time work legislation only entered the Statute Book in 1984. Part-time work contracts are still unusual, but significantly, 75 per cent of them have gone to women. Despite the trends, third-party temporary work agencies are still illegal.

THE LABOUR MARKET AND SKILLS SHORTAGES

Price Waterhouse Cranfield Project survey data shows four categories as the hardest to recruit in Italy: managers (22 per cent), engineers (21 per cent), qualified professional and information technical staff (12 per cent), technicians (11 per cent). Responsibility for the lack of managerial and technical talent available to Italian business is usually laid, by Italian practitioners themselves, squarely at the door of the education system.

The main criticism of Italian education is that it is struggling to respond structurally to the changing needs of the job market. Specialisation, professionalisation and automation are paramount features of modern industry, but so is flexibility. Italian high schools offer more opportunity than ever before for vocational training — from 100 children finishing secondary school at 14, about 20 per cent will go to a traditional, classics-oriented *liceo*, about 30 per cent to a technical school, and about 20 per cent to a 'professional' school. Perhaps 30 per cent will leave education entirely at that point. Yet, a 'classics snobbism' still prevails. University students are drawn predominantly from the ranks of those studying at *liceo*. More technical students are continuing their studies at university than before, but vocational training at high school generally means a job-search at 18. About 300,000 young people enter the job market each year, of whom 125,000 finish after secondary school and 75,000 finish after high school. Little has been done to bring Italy into line with the EC Resolution of 29 June 1985, which asserts that every young adult entering the job market should have attended at least one year of professional training after leaving school.

University admission is open to any student with a high school leaving certificate, the *maturita*, and this makes for high numbers of students enrolling at university; over 300,000 a year at present. Yet, once there, registered students move in and out of the system, sometimes taking time off to work or to complete military service, often taking longer to complete a degree programme than the prescribed four to six years. Seventy per cent of those enrolled simply do not finish. Finally, there are curricular problems: coursework is often theoretical and access to professors limited. There is little application of principle to practice. Students have little opportunity, unless registered in particular faculties, to benefit from 'stages' or internships.

In the period of 35 years from 1951 to 1985, the number of students enrolled at Italian universities quintupled from 226,000 to 1,113,000. In the same period the universities increased from 27 to 49 and the number of teaching faculties tripled from 15,000 to 50,000. The number of graduating students increased from 20,000 to 72,000. However, behind this qualified picture of growth and opportunity, the starker 70 per cent attrition statistic predominates.

Italy comes tenth in the European table for graduates as a proportion of its population. Other, less industrially developed European neighbours do better. The distribution of student constituencies among the universities is quite uncoordinated. As many as 150,000 students are enrolled at La Sapienza in Rome and 80,000 in Bologna, (a student body as large as that of Los Angeles in a city with a population of about half a million.) Medicine and Human Science faculties are overwhelmed by applicants, Economics and Commerce the reverse — a pattern which can be explained only by the strong bias in Italian culture and secondary education to classics and humanities.

In 1990 a belated attempt was made to establish a new relevance to the business communities of the Italian university system. The Parliament passed a law establishing the *diploma universitario*, also called a *laurea breve* or short degree. Diploma programmes have been planned specifically for applied and scientific courses to provide a ready pool of trained personnel for an Italian job market starved of engineers and economists. Yet legislation is once again looking to the practitioners to take the initiative. Exactly what constitutes a *laurea breve* has not yet been defined by Parliamentary decree. Meanwhile, major public and private sector employers are setting up their own dedicated programmes, sometimes in conjunction with particular university faculties, defining their own terms in the hope and expectation that *faits accomplis* will influence the next legislative step.

LABOUR DEVELOPMENT STRATEGIES

On the margins of recruitment legislation, for example in provisions set for the hiring of the disabled, Italy has a particularly good record. However, as a legacy of a *collocamento* system, (the *richiesta numerica*), which was originally designed to promote access to the workplace for the disadvantaged, this may be expected.

Law 482 of 2 April 1968 states that employers with a workforce of over 35 must have hired at least 15 per cent of their active workforce from a list of special categories, including military and civilian casualties of war, work invalids, blind or deaf people. Significantly, the PWCP attests to 72 per cent of Italian companies developing their human resource strategies by monitoring the disabled in their workplace (compared to 62 per cent in the UK, 42 per cent in Germany and 33 per cent in France.)

According to law 482, employers are obliged to send a list of names of all employees to the labour office every six months. This constitutes an ongoing process of supervision of companies' obligations in regard to mandatory recruitment from special categories (art.21.) Employers failing to observe the requirements for hiring the disabled, (having been given 30 days from a labour office warning), are fined up to 25,000 lire for every working day thereafter that they are under their quota (art.23).

At the qualitative level, however, Italian law is deficient and does little to encourage training or teaching of disabled employees, nor for matching a disabled employee's qualifications with job requirements. Effectively, the special category lists extend the notion of *richiesta numerica* — hiring is determined by a disabled worker's ranking. The provision on the size of the company is rigidly enforced, but 35 employees is an arbitrary cut-off point. Companies employing fewer than 35 employees are entirely excluded from the requirements. And there is no flexibility yet in the system to discriminate between, say, a manufacturing company employing more than 35 workers with a relatively large unskilled proportion of its workforce, and an electronics company of the same size which requires highly trained personnel. Such issues are now being discussed in a new bill on compulsory recruitment before Parliament.

HUMAN RESOURCES DEPARTMENT STRATEGIES

HR departments have become increasingly relevant in developing human resource strategies for Italian business in recent years. The traditional role of the personnel manager, as having purely administrative competence in effecting top management decisions on human resources, has changed radically. Strategic decision-making is now a widespread function of human resource departments, and a special competence now acknowledged in the areas of recruitment and training. This is, at least, the predominant situation in medium to large companies (MLEs, over 200 employees). In small and medium-sized companies (SMEs), which, of course, generate a significant proportion of Italy's industrial wealth, human resource strategy is still often left to the CEO, but increased training needs are ubiquitous features of business, and the importance of human resource specialists is likely to ripple down to SMEs. The 1980s were marked, as elsewhere in Europe, by rapid growth in Italy's service sector and this has had a direct influence on the numbers of skilled and expert workers needed in companies of all sizes.

In 55 per cent of MLEs in Italy the human resource department is principally responsible for selection and recruitment, in collaboration with line management. This compares to 45 per cent in the UK, 44 per cent in Germany and 43 per cent in France.

The same trend can be noted for workforce expansion. In 46 per cent of Italian MLEs workforce expansion decisions are made by the human resource department in cooperation with line management. This compares with 33 per cent in Germany, 31 per cent in France and 24 per cent in the UK.

Further, the human resource department is perceived as the sole initiator, ie without line management responsibility, for recruitment decisions in 12 per cent of Italian MLEs and for workforce expansion decisions in 18 per cent. This compares to 12 per cent and 8 per cent in the UK, 5 per cent and 13 per cent in France and 5 per cent and 11 per cent in Germany.

Although the Price Waterhouse Cranfield Project, from which this data is taken, indicates that the role and initiative of line management has not changed substantially in the last three years, the strategic positioning and decision-making responsibilities of human resource departments certainly have. These responsibilities will increase still further as a consequence of the extended discretionary provisions awarded employers under law 223. Where human resource departments previously have been largely concerned with management and technical recruitment, the new law will encourage implementation of personnel strategies for blue-collar and unskilled hiring. This implies increased workloads for human resource departments and enhanced responsibilities in strategic development. Line management, on the other hand, is now set to lose some of the responsibilities for human resource involvement that it has maintained in recent years.

Competence in larger human resource departments in Italy is beginning to be shaped around three divisions: recruitment, training and labour relations. Expansion of responsibilities and closely defined specialisations to handle that expansion will determine the near future of human resources in MLEs in Italy.

SUMMARY

The innovations introduced by law 223 of July 1991 are undoubted steps forward. Few human resource practitioners would argue about the benefits of the reform as far as it goes. Certainly, legislative recognition of the *de facto* redundancy of the *richiesta numerica* is an important feature. The controversy that the law has provoked has been for the changes wrought in the *cassa integrazione guadagni*, the state unemployment benefit fund set up to protect workers in the event of extenuating business crises, rather than in the hiring process.

However, the law is most significant for what it has not done. Like previous 'reforms', it has not changed the basic structure of hiring set up in 1949. It has not changed the nature of state responsibility in the *collocamento* process. In terms of significant reform, it has not looked long enough at the forward march of European legislation in the way of third party intermediation in recruitment. And finally, it has not looked hard enough at the practitioners of human resources, the problems in the Italian education system and above all the needs of Italian employers for a trained, flexible workforce for the twenty-first century.

REFERENCES

Cerato, L, Paracone, C, Osella, P and Ulberto, F (eds) (1991) *La Fabbrica: camminando con l'innovazione*, Ed, SIPI

Lucchini, L (ed) (1988) *La Risorsa Scuola* Sole 24 Ore

Macchiavelli, A (ed) (1991) *Sapere Minimo sull'Europa* (Confindustria), Ed, SIPI

Pera, G (1988) *Lezioni di diritto del lavoro*, Edizioni Giuffré

Price Waterhouse Cranfield Project, Italy (1991)

'Rapporto di gestione delle Formazione Professionale' (1990), Provincia di Bologna, Ed, IRS

Volpini, F (ed) (1990) *Agenda per l'Amministrazione del Personale delle Aziende Industriali*, Tandi Sapi Editore

13

CURRENT PERSPECTIVES ON HUMAN RESOURCE MANAGEMENT IN THE UNITED KINGDOM

David Guest, Birkbeck College,

University of London, UK

INTRODUCTION

Over the past decade, human resource management (HRM) has been extensively written about and studied in the United Kingdom (UK). Both writing and research have approached the topic from a variety of perspectives, providing richness and diversity but sometimes also leading to confusion. The first part of this chapter briefly describes some of these approaches. The second and main part then explores three areas of HRM policy and practice in which there appears to have been significant innovation in the UK. The final, briefer section then uses this information to consider some of the problems and issues in arriving at convincing judgements about progress in HRM and, by implication, the quality of certain types of data.

APPROACHES TO HUMAN RESOURCE MANAGEMENT

There appear to be at least six main ways in which HRM has been investigated in the UK. There is considerable overlap between them, but the different focus of each reflects a view of what is interesting and important about the subject.

1. Debate on the nature and theory of HRM

A rich seam of literature has examined the nature of HRM and whether it differs in any significant way from traditional personnel management. The central question is whether HRM is 'old wine in new bottles' or something distinctive and new (Guest 1987). A second strand in this debate has sought to distinguish between various forms of HRM. Thus Storey (1987) and later Legge (1989) separate 'hard' HRM, with its focus on strategy and utilisation of the human resource, from a 'softer' HRM with its greater emphasis of the word 'human' and its concern for people in organisations. These issues are of importance to students of HRM as a movement and as a feature of management thought. After a while the debate can become sterile, unless it is seen by the participants to serve a useful purpose. One such purpose is the provision of a template or, better still, a theoretical framework around which to test propositions about whether HRM works, why it works and under what conditions it works more or less successfully.

2. HRM and the 'new industrial relations'

There has been a debate as to whether there is any causal link between the parallel growth in attention paid to HRM and the apparent decline of trade union power and influence in the workplace. This debate has broadened into a discussion of whether there is a new industrial relations. Much obviously depends upon definitions of the new industrial relations and indeed of HRM as well as upon interpretation of complex sets of data.

Perhaps the best contemporary source of information on trends in industrial relations and related aspects of human resource management is the third Workplace Industrial Relations Survey (Millward *et al.* 1992), covering over 2000 establishments. This concluded that there had been significant change in the industrial relations system over the decade, perhaps reflected most importantly in the decline in trade union membership. Where trade unions have remained, the changes have been less marked. Nevertheless the traditional manufacturing sector has changed from being multi-enterprise to being single enterprise-based and some reform, incorporating characteristics of HRM, has often taken place at plant and enterprise level. There is an expanding non-union sector. This may include some organisations practising HRM, but may be just as likely to contain a number that are more autocratically managed. At this stage, no distinctive alternative to the traditional system of collective bargaining is emerging in these organisations.

Another feature of a possible new industrial relations has been the growing interest in employee involvement. Most companies have sought to increase employee involvement in recent years (Guest 1989; Ramsay 1991; Marchington *et al.* 1992). This can be seen as a shift towards HRM, one goal of which will often be to marginalise the trade unions by dealing directly with the workforce.

Whether or not there is anything that can sensibly be called the new industrial relations, Dunn (1990) has noted that the rhetoric of industrial relations has changed. The metaphor of trench warfare has been replaced by the idea of the new frontier, an idea much more in line with HRM.

3. HRM and performance

A third strand in research and writing on HRM has been concerned with its impact on the performance of British industry. This is closely related to industrial relations to the extent that part of the debate has concerned explanations for increases in productivity in British manufacturing industry (Metcalf 1989, Nolan and Marginson 1990). One of the possibilities that has been mooted is that productivity gains reflect a tougher management stance, demonstrated by the shake-out which occurred in the early 1980s when the greatest shifts in performance occurred and by the negotiation of flexibility deals (Marsden and Thompson 1990).

A different perspective on performance has focused on aspects of Total Quality Management (TQM) and the question of whether it can only flourish in the context of positive HRM. Case studies of organisations like Rank Xerox (Giles 1989), which in 1992 was awarded the first European Quality Prize, suggest that a quality approach to people is a key factor in successful TQM. Most organisations pursuing quality seriously are finding that they have to confront the quality of both their human resources and the quality of the treatment of these human resources. In short they need to practice HRM.

4. Comparative HRM

Another research question which has been widely explored is the extent to which HRM, and similar approaches to management of the workforce, represent a foreign import, usually American or Japanese, and if so, how far it can be successfully transplanted into the UK.

One strand of this work has sought to identify and characterise these approaches to management. With respect to Japan, this can be found in both the specific case studies of companies like Toshiba (Trevor 1988) and Nissan (Wickens 1987) and in attempts to tease out common themes across Japanese companies (Oliver and Wilkinson 1988). Similarly, American companies have been studied as cases or in groups (see, for example, Buchanan and McCalman 1989).

A number of important findings have emerged from this research. First, foreign firms operating in the UK seem more likely than many of their British-owned counterparts to have a distinctive and consistent HRM strategy, closely integrated with a 'strong' organisation culture. Second, foreign-owned firms are more likely to innovate in the field of HRM (Purcell *et al.* 1986). One example is the recent increase in forms of flexibility and sub-contracting of HRM within organisations (Adams 1991). Third, the coherence of approach and willingness to innovate appears to pay off in terms of productivity gains. Recent reviews (for example, by the CBI) of performance during the 1980s indicated that it is the foreign-owned firms which have contributed disproportionately to the productivity gains of manufacturing industry as a whole. It is therefore easy to understand the temptation for those wanting to unlock the secrets of the success of these companies in the optimistic hope of translating the lessons into practice in their own organisations.

5. HRM as strategy

For a number of writers and researchers, the distinctive and most interesting feature of HRM is its concern for strategy. One inference is that traditional personnel management can be distinguished from HRM by virtue of the way in which the former ignored, but the latter embraces, strategy.

Those interested in HRM as strategy have been particularly concerned with the link between business strategy and HRM strategy. This focus raises difficult questions for advocates of a distinctive view of the nature of HRM. In particular, by starting from strategic choice, and influenced in particular by the work of Porter (1985), it seems logical to argue for a range of HRM approaches. In America this view was presented coherently some years ago by Miles and Snow (1984). In practice it results in adopting one of two approaches. One is to say that strategic analysis points to those situations where an approach which can be distinctively labelled HRM, as opposed to traditional personnel management, is most appropriate. The other is to argue that different business strategies require different human resource strategies. There may be two or more main choices, and they can be classified in a variety of ways, but all are variants of HRM. There is thus no attempt to delineate what is, and what is not, HRM. The label, and whether HRM is different from personnel management, becomes much less important than the strategic role played by human resources and the growing recognition of the importance of formulating a coherent human resource strategy.

Following this approach, the research focuses on the process of strategic planning and implementation of these plans. The work of

Hendry and Pettigrew (1990) has been both prescriptive in presenting a model of the key factors that should be considered in understanding HR strategy and descriptive in its analysis of how strategic HRM in general and training and development in particular has evolved in a number of organisations. If the results can be generalised, they indicate that there is now more strategic thinking. There is still something of a question mark about how this is translated into performance.

6. Adoption of new HRM policy and practice

The final approach to the study of HRM in the UK, which has been of interest to academics and policy makers alike, concerns the adoption of new techniques. One way of characterising what is distinctive about HRM is to argue that it reflects adoption of a particular set of practices. Taken together, these might be described by advocates of HRM as best practice. This can either be identified from the academic literature or defined in terms of what companies, acknowledged to be at the leading edge of HRM, actually do. Often some combination of the two will be chosen. The result has been a large number of surveys of practice. In general, they indicate that there has been considerable innovation and extensive adoption of new practices across much of industry in areas such as selection techniques, employee involvement and culture change programmes. What is less clear is how extensive such innovations are within organisations, for how long they last and what impact they have.

There are, no doubt, other approaches to the study of HRM in the UK. However, those outlined above give some indication of a diverse and extensive field of study. The next section develops these strands by exploring three policy areas which serve to illustrate the UK develop ments in HRM. We will be paying particular attention to evidence on impact and effectiveness. The three areas are: selection, training and rewards. They have been chosen because they are arguably among the most central 'levers' for effective HRM, in the sense that they cover the crucial issues of getting the right people into the organisation, ensuring that they have the knowledge, skills and attitude to perform the work effectively and then providing incentives to ensure the motivation necessary for high performance. The issues of policy integration and strategy are discussed in the final section.

HRM AND DEVELOPMENTS IN SELECTION IN THE UK

If HRM involves a considerable investment in human resources, then it will pay an organisation to take care to select the right people. Recruitment and selection have always been at the heart of personnel management. HRM implies a shift away from particular concerns for job and person specifications and questions of fairness and equity, though all of these remain important, towards an emphasis on identifying people who will display high-quality performance and long-term commitment and flexibility within the organisation. Organisational psychologists have developed a body of well-supported knowledge about techniques which will facilitate identification of such people. They have also adopted the use of what they term utility analysis (Feltham 1988: Smith and George 1992), a form of cost benefit analysis, to demonstrate the considerable financial pay-off of using techniques which have a high predictive validity — that is, the ability to predict future performance. We might therefore expect to see greater use and more careful use of such techniques in industry.

It is worth noting in passing that in the field of individual assessment, as in most other aspects of HRM, Britain has tended to follow the American experience. American research has pointed to the value of selection techniques such as assessment centres, biodata, performance tests, some cognitive tests, and, from a slightly different perspective, the use of realistic job previews (Smith and George 1992). There is a debate about validity generalisation, that is, the extent to which a test which successfully predicts performance in one setting will be equally success-ful with similar types of worker in another organisation. What we might expect to see is an increase in the use of the techniques which have demonstrated the highest validity for a variety of types of staff in a variety of settings. We would also expect to see some systematic attempt to determine the value of the selection techniques used. There have been some well-publicised cases of particular organisations, often foreign-owned, using best-practice selection techniques. Among the better known examples are the Japanese car firms where large pools of applicants for production work have been carefully sifted using a battery of aptitude and performance tests. This provides an important signal about the value attached to all levels of the workforce.

There have been several surveys exploring the use of selection techniques (Robertson and Makin 1986; Bevan and Fryatt 1988; Mabey 1989; Shackleton and Newell 1991; Williams 1991). Two of the studies are of particular interest since they set out to explore trends. Shackleton and Newell (1991) provided a replication and extension of the study by Robertson and Makin (1986). The studies were conducted in 1988 and 1984 respectively. Looking just at the selection of managers, the proportion who sometimes use cognitive tests has risen from 29 per cent to 70 per cent and those who sometimes use personality tests from 36 per cent to 64 per cent. Over the same period the proportion making some use of assessment centres and biodata, which are among the more valid techniques, has risen from 21 per cent to 59 per cent and from 6 per cent to 19 per cent respectively.

Williams (1991) reports a 1991 survey in local government which follows up surveys conducted in 1986 and 1989. It is of particular interest because all the others seem to have been biased towards larger organisations of the sort typically found in *The Times* top 1000 companies. His results show that the percentage of local authorities using any sort of test moved from 42 per cent in 1986 to 49 per cent in 1989 and 51 per cent in 1991. Much the most common purpose for test use was selection, which was cited on each occasion by almost 100 per cent of authorities. Personality tests were more popular than cognitive/aptitude tests. By comparison, the Bevan and Fryatt survey among large industrial organisations found that for management levels, 65 per cent used cognitive tests for selection and 64 per cent used personality tests. It seems that across all the more recent surveys, about two-thirds of organisations make some use of tests when selecting managers. Local government has been less ready to use other valid techniques; for example, the 1991 survey revealed that assessment centres were sometimes used by 38 per cent, but only 1 per cent were using biodata. The same survey also revealed an almost total lack of systematic validation of selection techniques.

Although the various samples are not directly comparable, they all show a growth in the use of tests. At first glance this looks encouraging, but closer analysis reveals that much of the growth has occurred in the use of personality tests, rather than in the techniques with a demonstrably higher validity. While such tests may well have a role to play in assessment and can contribute to selection decisions, their independent predictive validity is less clearly established (see, for example, Lewis 1991; Smith and George 1992). It therefore appears that personnel managers are often responding to the fashion for testing. There is little evidence that the use of tests and other selection techniques is part of a coherent human resource strategy. Looking just at those who have changed their use, which in practice means those who have started to use tests, 25 per cent in local government cite as the main reason increased labour turnover and 21 per cent cite increased competition for staff. It would appear to be a technical solution to a technical problem. The Bevan and Fryatt study asked a similar question, in answer to which 21 per cent cited technical changes, 20 per cent mentioned increased competition for staff, 16 per cent referred to increased labour turnover and, more interestingly, 13 per cent cited changes in workforce composition. It may be that the questions did not encourage reference to a wider set of policy changes, but certainly few were revealed. It therefore appears that in many cases tests and other selection techniques are viewed as a narrow technical solution to a particular problem or reflect a current fashion based on limited information about what will work. This is HRM based on technique rather than strategy.

HRM AND DEVELOPMENTS IN TRAINING

The 'excellence' literature that appeared in the 1980s invariably revealed that successful companies do a lot more training than average. At the same time a series of highly publicised studies showed that training in general, and management development in particular, appeared to be badly neglected in Britain (Handy 1987; Mangham and Silver 1986). Institutional arrangements have been put in place in an attempt to rectify this, more notably in the form of the management charter and the system of national vocational qualifications.

In some respects it is possible to conceive of training and development as one of the success stories of HRM in the UK. As well as national developments, a number of companies have recognised the need to develop a coherent training and development strategy. Some of these have been carefully studied by Hendry and Pettigrew (1990). The major training expenditure survey, Training in Britain (Training Agency 1989) indicated a high level of expenditure on training by British industry. Although the data is relatively unreliable, more particularly because of its inclusion of the estimated costs of 'on the job' training, even after rigorous scrutiny (Ryan 1991) the expenditure levels appear similar to those in Germany. The Price Waterhouse Cranfield Survey showed that most UK companies, like those in other countries, claimed to have increased their spending on training in the three years up to 1990; in the UK case, this was directed mainly at management and professional training. There is also some evidence that in the recession that started in the late 1980s, companies have not cut back on training in a way that would once have been thought likely (Training Statistics 1991).

On the basis of some figures there is consequently reason for optimism that serious steps are being taken to rectify the national training problem. But scepticism about the relevance of these expenditure figures is reinforced by conflicting evidence. As Finegold (1991) notes, there is a growing array of case studies, in a variety of manufacturing and service sectors, which have found almost uniformly that British firms have a lower skilled workforce and place a lower priority on training than comparable companies in Germany, France and Japan. (p 111)

Finegold's argument is that the UK is trapped in a 'low skill equilibrium', in which training is concentrated on a few élite workers while the rest are largely ignored. There is considerable evidence to support this. The Training in Britain survey (Rigg 1990) again confirms that training in UK firms is directed primarily at the managerial and professional levels at the expense of the large mass of low skill workers. The most revealing finding from Training in Britain is that two-thirds of workers had received no training in the last three years and 42 per cent could not imagine undergoing any training for the rest of their working lives.

Sako (1990) has examined the institutional arrangements underpinning training in the UK, Japan and Germany and found significant differences, more especially in the incentive structure for enterprise training. The NIESR series of comparative studies of training practices and their impact across a variety of industries in the UK and Germany reveals a consistent and depressing pattern of interrelated factors in the UK. These include a narrow focus for skills training, a need for more inspection and supervision in the UK because of the low level and narrow range of shop-floor skills, problems in the effective use of sophisticated technology, and low productivity, with a consequent vulnerability to foreign competition (Prais and Wagner 1988; Steedman and Wagner 1987, 1989).

Not surprisingly, in the early 1990s the training problem appears to be as serious as ever. One survey revealed that even in the depths of recession, with unemployment high and rising, over 25 per cent of companies were still being held back by skills shortages (Training Statistics 1991). Even in a city like Liverpool, the problem is ever-present (Merseyside Chamber of Commerce 1991). The implication is that even if the figures on training expenditure are true, the money has not always been wisely directed and has certainly failed to alleviate the chronic UK problem of skill shortages.

Keep (1989) has argued against the dangers of being beguiled by the practices of a few excellent companies into believing that they are typical. Nissan reported a 1991 training budget of 14 per cent of its salary bill. The need to compete has forced Rover and Ford to increase training expenditure well above the national average. However, these are exceptions. Any increase in training expenditure would appear to reflect a narrow concentration on excellence among the few, rather than a broadening of the skill competence base. This, in turn, is likely to exacerbate the problems of poaching of staff and consequent pay problems. As an integrated HRM strategy, its chances of success appear bleak.

It is notoriously difficult to obtain good information on training policy and practice. At the heart of the problem lies the difficulty in defining what constitutes training when what matters most is learning, which may occur formally or informally. Indeed, effective organisations are being exhorted to become 'learning organisations', perhaps following Japanese practice, in which learning is integrated into daily working life. In such a context, measures of training time and expenditure become largely meaningless. Perhaps the best judgements can be arrived at by analysing the evidence from both surveys and case studies. Taken together these appear to suggest that while training may be taken more seriously in UK organisations, much of the investment has not been wisely directed.

HRM AND DEVELOPMENTS IN PERFORMANCE-RELATED PAY

In the first two years of the 1990s, performance-related pay (PRP) was probably the major focus of innovative activity within HRM, sometimes appearing under the umbrella of the broader concept of performance management, and challenged as a fashionable topic only by the continuing concern for quality. The reasons for this are not hard to find. PRP has been the focus of sustained political exhortation, combined with coercive action in the public sector. This, in turn, reflects a set of assumptions about economic motivation, the importance of individual rather than collective arrangements, and the desirability of mechanisms to control labour costs by paying only for performance rather than for a negotiated rate. From this it becomes clear that PRP is a central plank in an approach to motivation and performance, which sometimes reflects concern to promote a performance culture. The concept of a performance culture is also linked to the search for accountability, which has been associated with the desire to devolve management decisions to the business unit. PRP is one way of allowing greater local control over costs. Finally, PRP allows for greater individuality and accountability and therefore flexibility to reward only those who deliver performance. At the same time, this presents a major challenge to the traditional role of collective bargaining.

Several studies have charted the growth of PRP. Ingram's (1991) analysis of the CBI data bank on manufacturing industry, reveals widespread change in payment systems. This is reinforced by an ACAS

(1989) survey, based on interviews in 664 establishments, which revealed that 38 per cent had made some sort of change in their payment systems in the last three years. During that time the incidence of PRP schemes had increased by about 25 per cent. However, although about a third of the establishments used some form of PRP or merit payment for some staff, in three-quarters of them the scheme applied only to non-manual workers. One of the more recent surveys of a large sample of organisations (Bevan and Thompson 1991, 1992) reveals that about 75 per cent of organisations make some use for some staff of PRP, but that often this was not integrated into a formal performance management system.

The evidence indicates a growing use of various forms of PRP, directed mainly at non-manual workers. However the New Earnings Survey helps to put the importance of PRP in perspective. For example, the 1991 Survey showed that 35.5 per cent of male manual workers and 21.3 per cent of all workers, male and female, received some form of incentive payment. However, the amount was trivial: £10.40 out of average weekly earnings of £253.20 or 4.1 per cent of earnings. We know from these regular surveys that the proportion of the workforce receiving some sort of incentive pay has tended to decline over the years and that the amount of total pay derived from such incentives has not been large — even in the motor industry in 1990, it only represented 7.7 per cent of total earnings.

The impact of PRP can be considered from three main perspectives:

- its impact on productivity;
- its impact on industrial relations;
- perceptions and beliefs about its impact among policy makers.

In considering the evidence, it is helpful to separate share ownership and profit sharing schemes from PRP. It is also important to emphasise that the quality of the evidence is poor, being drawn mostly from interviews with senior personnel managers who are closely involved with the schemes.

The impact on productivity

In a series of detailed case studies, Wood (1991) found that PRP may increase costs, because of a tendency to give more money to the high performers rather than take it away elsewhere. Furthermore, in a number of cases, often linked to flexibility deals, it has been agreed that extra pay is given for the acquisition of new skills, but these may not be used sufficiently to justify the extra pay. In one company this had been partly overcome by changing from a 7 per cent cost of living increase plus

2.5 per cent bonus to an 8.5 per cent merit pool. This looks like an overall increase, but in fact is not. Problems of cost slippage were apparent in one organisation that moved to a system where all pay was performance-linked and could range from a 0 – 20 per cent increase. This replaced a 9 per cent basic plus 0 – 3 per cent merit payment and to avoid increased costs required very tight policing. This in turn provoked management resentment and worker opposition. The easy response is to relax the pressure. Although these cases raise questions about the costs of PRP and about its impact on wage inflation, they fail to address the issue of compensating productivity increases. For that we need better evidence on the link between pay and performance. One type of evidence we do have concerns the pay of top executives.

Those who were sceptical about any association between corporate performance and top executive pay have had their doubts convincingly confirmed in the study by Gregg, Machin and Szymanski (1993). They examined the relationship between the remuneration of the highest paid executive and company performance for 300 large UK companies. Whatever criteria of performance they used, they found only a weak relationship for much of the 1980s, which all but disappeared at the end of the 1980s and into the early 1990s.

In one of the largest surveys of the link between pay and performance, Bevan and Thompson (1992) examined the association between high-performing companies, performance management and PRP. High performance was defined as a consistent increase in pre-tax profits over the five years from 1986 to 1990. They found no association between company performance and either performance management or PRP.

The impact on industrial relations

Trade unions have generally been opposed to PRP, seeing it as a potential threat to collective bargaining. However, in recent years the unions have been on the defensive. They may not like PRP, but it is generally not an issue over which they have taken strike action and they are realistic enough to know that they cannot keep it out of all unionised workplaces. Union suspicions are partly confirmed by the ACAS survey, which found that industrial relations considerations were a major stimulus to change in payment systems. More specifically, adjustments in differentials, removal of anomalies, increasing flexibility and reducing demarcation and harmonising terms and conditions were all important.

However, changes in payment systems need not be all anti-union, since in 21 per cent of the ACAS cases, pressure from the unions was cited as a reason for change. Furthermore, attempts to use individualised PRP to drive a wedge through trade union membership have sometimes backfired. Pickard (1990) reports that personal contracts for senior managers, either in the public sector or in recently privatised companies, have failed to weaken the union, although it may be required to provide a more personal service. At British Telecom, membership of the Society of Telecom Executives actually increased by 15 per cent after management imposed PRP and followed it with personal contracts. Since not everyone agreed to personal contracts despite the financial inducements, the union retains negotiating rights. After Associated Newspapers moved to PRP and individual contracts, membership of the National Union of Journalists at the *Daily Mail* increased by 15 per cent (Pickard, *op cit*). The felt need for the security of union membership remains as strong as ever under such circumstances, raising serious doubts about claims that moves towards PRP and individual contracts are means of enhancing commitment to the company at the expense of the union.

One fear of the unions is that with PRP, pay rises become more secret, limiting their power to represent their members. However, the Central Arbitration Committee forced Selfridges, the department store, to reveal the distribution of pay under the section of the 1975 Employment Protection Act, which requires companies to disclose information required for collective bargaining. In some cases, unions might actually increase their influence, following the introduction of PRP. Metcalf and Thompson (1990) in their IMS report of 25 cases, note that not only did the unions retain their bargaining role, but that decentralisation of bargaining had sometimes actually strengthened the union hand, since local managers were less familiar with collective bargaining and the central union could identify and 'pick off' the weaker plants.

There have been several threatened disputes over the application of PRP schemes. In virtually every case they have been resolved without a strike. At ICL, the computer firm, a dispute was threatened after the introduction of PRP, when some workers received only 5 per cent increases when inflation was running at 8 per cent. The union argued that PRP should be added on top of the normal negotiated increase. British Airports Authority has a site-specific bonus scheme. In 1991 staff at Heathrow were told they would receive no bonus despite a 10 per cent overall profit rise, because Heathrow had failed to meet its agreed targets as a result of slow revenue growth and rising costs. The unions threatened action because 55 per cent of overall profits came from Heathrow and arguably the failure to meet targets was not attributable to the workforce. The bonus ranged from 0 – 4 per cent of pay and the issue was resolved.

A final case illustrates what can go wrong. The Inland Revenue Staff Federation used consultants Coopers and Lybrand Deloitte to review the Inland Revenue PRP scheme after it had encountered widespread staff resistance. Alarmingly, they said too much emphasis was placed on quantitative rather than qualitative targets, such as the number of tax returns dealt with rather than the quality of the work done on them. Management applied the scheme inconsistently and were often not operating the scheme properly because of pressure on their own time. Meanwhile, senior management was putting further pressure on middle-level managers to minimise the number of their staff who were judged to have performed sufficiently well to justify a performance-related bonus, as a means of saving staff costs. This meant that some people got bonuses while others performing at apparently the same target levels did not. The union members voted to abandon the scheme, but as a compromise a joint union/management team was set up to review its operation. More recently, a union-sponsored survey of the workforce found that only 12 per cent felt the scheme in any way increased their motivation, many were unhappy about the distortions it caused and few could see any impact on the quality or quantity of their work (Richardson and Marsden 1991).

There is no clear evidence that Employee Share Ownership Programmes (ESOPs) have had an impact on industrial relations. There is however quite extensive research on attitudes towards ESOPs and the impact of ESOPs on attitudes; this latter research has implications for industrial relations, if it can be shown that ESOPs improve relations. The available evidence suggests that they do not. Dunn, Richardson and Dewe (1991) report a longitudinal study at a manufacturing plant where an all-employee share ownership scheme was introduced. Those who eventually took up the share options were fewer in number than those who had originally expressed interest and were typically those already committed to the company. Attitudes of those who did not take up shares tended to deteriorate over time. Another study by Nichols and O'Connell Davidson (1991) of a plant in a privatised company found that share ownership had no impact on attitudes to 'us and them', nor on motivation, and these views seemed to be endorsed as much by managers as by workers.

Taken together, the evidence suggests that the unions, while retaining their opposition to payment systems that fragment collective arrangements and hand discretion to management, have been pragmatic in their response to PRP initiatives. It further suggests that PRP has not in itself resulted in any weakening in trade union power or representation and that where it is poorly applied or where the industrial relations climate is not based on high trust, it may provide unions with a powerful issue over which to negotiate.

The responses of managers

Only when we turn to the views of managers do we find a more positive picture. Survey data generally reveals that managers are satisfied with their schemes. The survey conducted by Bevan and Thompson (1992) found that 75 per cent of organisations operating a formal performance management system claimed to evaluate its impact. The most popular measures cited were labour turnover, productivity, profitability and salary costs. However, the cases explored by Wood (1991), Metcalf and Thompson (1990), Kinnie and Lowe (1990) and Fletcher and Williams (1992) all reveal that managers have not undertaken any systematic evaluation of performance management and, more especially, PRP. Summarising the findings of their case studies of performance management, Fletcher and Williams note that 'For the most part, systematic monitoring does not take place' (p 78).

One important reason for the absence of systematic evaluation is that performance management and PRP are often introduced alongside other changes and it is impossible to disentangle the effects of the various changes. A more pragmatic reason might be that subjective evaluations of a scheme to which managers have expressed commitment is more important, and possibly less embarrassing, than hard data. A third and more plausible one is that the benefits were not defined in terms of tangible cost reduction or performance improvement and were seen as likely to accrue over a long time-scale. The ambiguity in the evaluation process leaves managers free to interpret as they wish any evidence that may exist.

Despite the lack of systematic evaluation, the managers interviewed for the case studies cited a number of benefits of PRP. In order of popularity, these were:

- improvements in the commitment and capability of staff;
- improved job satisfaction and sense of achievement among staff;
- an effective complement to other HRM initiatives, including harmonisation of conditions of employment between manual and clerical staff and greater flexibility;
- improved communication and greater awareness among staff of business concerns and objectives, which includes greater awareness of quality and costs and timing;
- greater devolvement of responsibility to first-line supervisors and

managers, particularly with respect to clarifying their own role and goals and that of their subordinates;
* easier identification of poor performers;
* more feedback, recognition and clarification of objectives.

Despite the absence of positive evidence, there is a clear belief among managers that PRP brings benefits. For example, a 1990 CBI company survey of Employee Share Ownership Schemes (ESOPs) revealed that 82 per cent of managers believe employee share schemes motivate the workforce either definitely or to some extent; 79 per cent believe they make workers more profit-conscious; 78 per cent believe they assist staff recruitment and retention; and 49 per cent believe they facilitate better communication. Given the evidence of rather more limited impact, it would appear that the introduction of ESOPs for employees is based rather more on sentiment and tax incentives for the company than on any rational analysis of their impact.

In summary, while managers generally believe that the impact of PRP has been positive, more dispassionate analysis has generally failed to support them. There is little evidence that PRP schemes have, in themselves, increased productivity, increased employee commitment to the organisation or weakened the role of trade unions. Much of the reason for the limited impact appears, in so far as it is possible to judge, to result from poor application of the schemes by management. Once again, the quality of application of HRM is called into question.

THE ROLE OF STRATEGY

The evidence from surveys of developments in selection, training and performance-related pay points to lots of activity and innovation within UK Personnel Departments. However, the general impact on performance of the range of HRM innovations, in so far as can be judged from the limited available evidence (see, for example, Edwards 1987; Storey 1992) is at best patchy. There are several possible explanations for this. First, the evidence may be wrong. Second, it may be based on the wrong sample of organisations. Third, it may focus on too short a time-scale. However, if we accept for a moment that the evidence is broadly correct, we must look for explanations of limited impact. One that recurs is the lack of strategic focus. Techniques are introduced without any coherent long-term strategic context. They therefore become fads that appear attractive for a while before falling by the wayside. The recent history of personnel management is littered with these and HRM risks the same fate. It is for this reason that a number of writers have focused on the importance of strategy as a distinctive feature of HRM.

Hendry and Pettigrew (1990) have explored the operation of HRM strategy in a number of cases. They provide a useful analytic framework within which to explore influences on strategy and its likely effectiveness. However, to gauge the extent to which the importance of a strategic perspective has been recognised we can look to the Price Waterhouse Cranfield comparative study which surveys a major sample of the head offices of large organisations in both the public and private sectors, and allows us to place UK developments in an international, comparative perspective. The survey has been conducted in successive years, although the results over the first two years show some inconsistency, often as a result of tightening some of the questions. The sample in the first survey consisted of nearly 2500 UK organisations. The second survey had a rather lower response. Similar surveys were conducted in France, Spain, Sweden and West Germany in the first survey and five further countries participated in the second round. The first survey, on which we will concentrate, was conducted in the winter of 1989 – 90.

The results reveal a positive picture of the extent to which strategic HRM exists in the UK. In the first survey, 63 per cent of UK organisations had the top personnel/HRM person on the board, although in the second survey and based on a more realistic question, this had fallen to 47 per cent. In fact, this figure was even higher in the other countries with the exception of West Germany where it was only 19 per cent. Forty-nine per cent of UK organisations claimed to have a written mission statement with a further 10 per cent saying it existed but was unwritten. (This compares with 65 per cent in the Bevan and Thompson survey.) In the first survey, 83 per cent of UK organisations had a corporate strategy, unwritten in 19 per cent of cases, and 73 per cent had a personnel/HRM strategy, unwritten in 30 per cent of cases. These figures were similar in the second survey. Seventy-two per cent of those organisations with a personnel/HRM strategy claimed it was translated into a work programme. The proportion with a written HR strategy was higher than average across the countries and the proportion with a programme of implementation was the highest of all the countries. In the second expanded survey, the UK was about average across the ten countries.

The level in the organisation at which personnel/HR policy was fixed seemed to vary widely from place to place, but one consistent trend in all countries and across all issues was that line managers were becoming more involved. This finding is open to a number of interpretations, ranging from a deliberate move by HR managers to involve their line counterparts to a view that HR managers were dealing ineffectively with important issues, leading to a requirement for line intervention. Finally, 46 per cent of respondents in the first survey claimed their personnel/HR departments were systematically evaluated, mainly through feedback from line management and by performance against budget, but also by numbers trained and recruited.

These are extraordinary figures. The first survey in particular gives the impression of a highly strategic, well integrated, carefully evaluated function. In contrast, the evidence from the more detailed analysis of particular policy areas highlighted in earlier sections of this chapter reveals a high level of opportunistic activity, little evidence of integrated, planned policy and an almost total absence of systematic evaluation. Either the Cranfield responses represent wishful thinking, or a series of independent, often more detailed studies have arrived at some wrong conclusions. The weight of evidence suggests that the former is the more likely. It seems probable that in many organisations there is an embryonic strategy and planning process for HRM, just as there will probably be a cursory process of evaluation when annual budgets are determined and readily available data is provided. But this is far from the systematic use of an integrated strategy, carefully translated into policy and practice and subsequently monitored and reviewed, which the advocates of a strategic approach generally have in mind.

In this context it is worth returning to the recent surveys of policy and practice sponsored by the Institute of Personnel Management. Bevan and Thompson (1991) report that

> for many employers a key purpose of performance management is to facilitate the integration of various human resource activities, mesh them more closely with the business objectives of the organization and thereby improve overall performance. (p 38)

However, they go on to note that

> Most organizations are carrying out some of the activities associated with this approach, but few appear to be integrating all of them successfully. (p 39)

More specifically, they are concerned that the approach is being dominated by a concern to introduce performance-related pay at the expense of development of competence among staff. The significance of this is that a PRP-focused approach can much less easily integrate the wider range of human resource policy and practice into a coherent strategy.

Fletcher and Williams (1992) in their detailed case studies of performance management found that

> many of those claiming to operate performance management do not have in place procedures which meet the wide-ranging definition offered in the IMS report. (p 77)

Furthermore, they found little evidence of strategic thinking. As they note

> what was most striking about the origination of formal performance management systems was their often reactive nature. There were only isolated examples of organizations setting out in a proactive way to establish structures for the management of the business and the integration of these with procedures for managing the performance of staff. This suggests an absence, in most organizations, of an over-arching strategic rationale for the introduction of performance management (p 77).

These types of finding stand in stark contrast to the more optimistic picture emerging from the surveys.

Other evidence reminds us of the scale of the problem still confronting British industry. As a recent CBI report (CBI 1991) noted, productivity levels in UK manufacturing are still 30 per cent lower than in Germany, 35 per cent lower than in Japan and about 45 per cent lower than in the USA. Even within the UK, the encouraging rise in productivity during part of the 1980s was disproportionately concentrated in foreign-owned companies. It would appear that they, together with a handful of major international UK companies, make the running in the field of HRM and they are far from typical of industry as a whole.

What, then, are we to make of the results of the Price Waterhouse Cranfield survey? At a general level, and focusing only on the UK, the answer is probably not very much. But if we can assume consistent bias across countries, then there are interesting comparative insights to be gained. In this respect we can conclude that the HRM function is as well developed in the UK as elsewhere, with the possible exception of Sweden, but is probably less well integrated into business strategy than in most other countries included in the survey (Brewster, Holt and Larsen 1992). We can also conclude that similar questions are being asked of the role of HRM professionals in each country. But it would be dangerous to conclude that there is an effective strategic approach to HRM in each country.

In practice, organisations are forced to think ahead and to plan over a time horizon; and this process invariably extends to HRM issues. It might well entail analysis of labour costs, manpower and succession plans and possibly the impact of employment legislation. Where major organisational change is under way, including the opening or closing of sites, HRM issues are likely to become more prominent. To this extent there will be forward thinking. In many cases it will be given the label of strategy. For some analysts (see, for example, Mintzberg 1990), this emergent process, if it is reasonably consistent, is as much as we should realistically seek from the strategy process. This is rather different from the more normative view of a powerful, systematic, rational and fully integrated process of planning and implementation. The survey may be capturing elements of the more informal process. In many cases organisations can get by with this. However, the analysis of specific policy areas, combined with the evidence of the persisting decline of the low productivity indigenous British manufacturing base, raises serious doubts about whether it is sufficient.

REFERENCES

ACAS (1989) *Developments in Payments Systems.* Occasional Paper 45, ACAS, London

Adams, K (1991) 'Externalization vs specialization: what is happening to personnel?', *Human Resource Management Journal*, Vol 1,4, pp 40–54

Bevan, S and Fryatt, J (1988) *Employee Selection in the UK*, IMS, Falmer, Sussex

Bevan, S and Thompson, M (1991) 'Performance management at the crossroads', *Personnel Management*, November, 36–9

Bevan, S and Thompson M (1992) 'An Overview of Policy and Practice' in *Performance Management*, IPM, London

Brewster, C, Holt and Larsen, H (1992) 'Human Resource Management in Europe: Evidence from Ten Countries', *International Journal of Human Resource Management*, Vol 3,3, pp 409–34

Buchanan, D and McCalman, J (1989) *High Performance Work Systems: The Digital Experience*, Routledge, London

CBI (1991) *Competing with the World's Best*, CBI, London

Dunn, S (1990) 'Root metaphor in the old and new industrial relations', *British Journal of Industrial Relations*, Vol 28,1, pp 1–31

Dunn, S, Richardson, R and Dewe, P (1991) 'The impact of employee share ownership on worker attitudes: a longitudinal case study', *Human Resource Management Journal*, Vol 1,3, pp 1–17

Edwards, P K (1987) *Managing the Factory*, Blackwell, Oxford

Feltham, R (1988) 'Justifying investment', *Personnel Management*, August, pp 17–18

Finegold, D (1991) 'The implications of training in Britain for the analysis of Britain's skills problem: a comment on Paul Ryan's 'How much do employers spend on training?', *Human Resource Management Journal*, Vol 2,1, pp 110–15

Fletcher, C and Williams, R (1992) 'Organizational experience' in *Performance Management*, IPM, London

Giles, E (1989) '*Is Xerox's Human Resource Management Worth Copying?*. Paper presented to British Academy of Management Annual Conference, Manchester, September

Gregg, P, Machin, S and Szymanski, S (1993) 'The disappearing relationship between directors' pay and corporate performance', *British Journal of Industrial Relations*, Vol 31, 1, pp 1–10

Guest, D (1987) 'Human resource management and industrial relations', *Journal of Management Studies*, 24, 503–21

Guest, D (1989) 'Human resource management: its implications for industrial relations and trade unions,' in Storey, J (ed), *New Perspectives on Human Resource Management*, Routledge, London

Handy, C (1987) *The Making of Managers*, NEDO, London

Hendry, C and Pettigrew, A (1990) 'Human resource management: an agenda for research', *International Journal of Human Resource Management*, Vol 1.1, pp 17–43

Ingram, P (1991) 'Changes in working practices in British manufacturing industry in the 1980s: a study of employee concessions made during wage negotiations', *British Journal of Industrial Relations*, Vol 29,1, pp 1–13

Keep, E (1989) 'Corporate Training Strategies; The Vital component' in Storey, J (ed), *New Perspectives on Human Resource Management*, Routledge, London

Kinnie, N and Lowe, D (1990) 'Performance-related pay on the shop floor', *Personnel Management*, November, 45–9

Legge, K (1989) 'Human resource management: a critical analysis.' in Storey, J (ed), *New Perspectives on Human Resource Management*, Routledge, London

Lewis, C (1991) *Employee Selection* (2nd ed), Stanley Thorne, Cheltenham

Mabey, B (1989) 'The majority of large companies use occupational tests', *Guidance and Assessment Review*, Vol 5,3, pp 1–4

Mangham, I and Silver, M (1986) *Management Training; Context and Practice*, University of Bath, ESRC/DTI

Marchington, M, Goodman, J, Wilkinson, A and Ackers, P (1992) *New*

Developments in Employee Involvement, Employment Department, Research Series 2, London

Marsden, D and Thompson, M (1990) 'Flexibility agreements and their significance in the increase in productivity in British manufacturing since 1980', *Work, Employment and Society*, Vol 4, pp 83–104

Merseyside Chamber of Industry and Commerce (1991) *Quarterly Economic Survey*, Liverpool

Metcalf, D (1989) 'Water notes dry up: the impact of the Donovan reform proposals and Thatcherism at work on labour productivity in British manufacturing industry', *British Journal of Industrial Relations*, Vol 27.1, pp 1–28

Metcalf, H and Thompson, M (1990) *Pay Pressures in the Private Sector: Managerial Strategies*, Institute of Manpower Studies, Brighton

Miles, R and Snow, C (1984) 'Designing strategic human resource systems', *Organizational Dynamics*, Summer, pp 36–52

Millward, N, Stevens, M, Smart, D and Hawes, W (1992) *Workplace Industrial Relations in Transition*, Dartmouth, Aldershot

Mintzberg, H (1990) 'The design school: reconsidering the basic premises of strategic management', *Strategic Management Journal*, Vol 11,3, pp 271–96

Nicols, T and O'Connell Davidson, J (1991) 'It is still "us" and "them"', *Financial Times*, 7 March 1991

Nolan, P and Marginson, P (1990) 'Skating on thin ice? David Metcalf on trade unions and productivity', *British Journal of Industrial Relations*, Vol 28.2, pp 227–47.

Oliver, N and Wilkinson, B (1988) *The Japanization of British Industry*, Blackwell, Oxford

Pickard, J (1990) 'When pay gets personal', *Personnel Management*, July, 41–5

Porter, M (1985) *Competitive Advantage*, Free Press, New York

Prais, S and Wagner, K (1988) 'Productivity and management: the training of foremen in Britain and Germany', *National Institute Economic Review*, February, 35–47

Purcell, J Marginson, P Edwards, P and Sisson, K (1986) 'The industrial relations practices of multi-plant foreign-owned firms', *Industrial Relations Journal*, Vol 18, pp 130–7

Ramsay, H (1991) 'Reinventing the wheel? a review of the development and performance of employee involvement', *Human Resource Management Journal*, Summer, Vol 2.1, pp 1–22

Richardson, R and Marsden, D (1991) 'Motivation and Performance Related Pay in the Public Sector: A Case Study of the Inland Revenue', LSE CEP Discussion Paper 75, London

Rigg (1990) *Training in Britain*, PSI, London

Robertson, I and Makin, P (1986) 'Management selection in Britain: a survey and a critique', *Journal of Occupational Psychology*, Vol 59,1, pp 45–57

Ryan, P (1991) 'How much do employers spend on training? An assessment of the Training in Britain estimates', *Human Resource Management Journal*, Vol 1,4, pp 55–76

Sako, M (1990) '*Enterprise Training in a Comparative Perspective: West Germany, Japan and Britain*', LSE Dept. of Industrial Relations (mimeo), London

Shackleton, V and Newell, S (1991) 'Management selection: a comparative study of methods used in top British and French companies', *Journal of Occupational Psychology*, Vol 64,1, pp 23–36

Smith, M and George, D (1992) 'Selection Methods' in Cooper, C and Robertson, I (eds) *International Review of Industrial and Organizational Psychology, vol 7*, Wiley, Chichester

Steedman, H and Wagner, K (1987) 'A second look at productivity, machinery and skills in Britain and Germany', *National Institute Economic Review*, November, pp 121–32

Steedman, H and Wagner, K (1989) 'Productivity, machinery and skills: clothing manufacturing in Britain and Germany', *National Institute Economic Review*, May, pp 133–50

Storey, J (1987) *Development in the Management of Human Resources: An Interim Report*, Warwick Papers in Industrial Relations, no 17, Warwick University IRRU, Coventry

Storey, J (1992) *Developments in the Management of Human Resources*, Blackwell, Oxford

Training Agency (1989) *Training in Britain*, Training Agency, Sheffield

Training Statistics, 1991 HMSO, London

Trevor, M (1988) *Toshiba's New British Company*, PSI, London

Wickens, P (1987) *The Road to Nissan*, Macmillan, London

Williams, R (1991) *Psychological Testing and Management Selection Practices in Local Government*, Local Government Management Board, Herts

Wood, S (1991) *Final Report to the Steering Committee of the IPM/NEDO Study of Incentive Schemes*, LSE, London

INDEX

237

Works Constitution Act (1972)
(Germany) 157
works councils *see* communication,
employee
World Competitiveness Report (1990)
56

World Congress of International
Industrial Relations Labour
Office (1986) 157

young, individual, freedom-minded
employees (YIFFIES) 123